PRAISE FOR LETTING GO(D)

"In *Letting Go(d)*, Aaron Simnowitz shines an incredible light on the harrowing experience so many people have within Christianity: the exasperating, endless, impossible task of changing one's innate sexual orientation in an effort to obey God. Aaron writes with courage, conviction, honesty, and humor. He candidly brings you into his deeply human experience as a gay man in an evangelical world. His earnest love for Jesus throughout his journey is obvious. The candor with which he tells his story pulled me into his anguish, and his sense of humor kept me afloat with comic relief. So many share a similar story and come away bitter and resentful. It's hard to fault them for it. Aaron, however, uses his experience to become more full of grace, wisdom, humor, optimism, understanding, and compassion for himself and others...even the ones who deeply hurt him. I'm grateful he didn't simply move on, but gifted us with his deeply personal journey to glean wisdom from. I hope that anyone wrestling with the issue of homosexuality within the church will take the time to read this important book and let it inform their heart and mind."

— **Heather Hamilton**, Author, *Returning to Eden: A Field Guide for the Spiritual Journey*

"This text provides an outlet for so many us who have experienced sexual orientation change efforts. As a survivor myself, I became engulfed in this story—finding my own wrapped up in Aaron's. This book will be relatable to so many in the LGBTQIA+ community."

— **Seth Showalter** is a Licensed Clinical Social Worker who works as a therapist and occasional host of *Mental Health Uncovered Podcast*

"Aaron Simnowitz's *Letting Go(d)* is a poignant and powerful memoir sharing Simnowitz's unique journey to reconcile his gay identity with his Christian faith. Combining a sarcastic wit, raw authenticity, and profound hope, this book takes readers deep into the struggles that many LGBTQ+ people face and demonstrates the importance of affirming families, friends, and faith communities along the journey to reconcile faith and sexuality. This book provides a cathartic release and a healing balm for LGBTQ+ people of faith and profound insight for those seeking to better understand our stories."

— **Brandan Robertson**, Public Theologian and Author,
Filled to Be Emptied: The Path of Liberation for Privileged People

"Aaron Simnowitz reminds us how unique and personable all of our relationships are with God. As a Life Coach who helps other gay men free themselves from Church-shame, I always remind my clients that it's not my job to bring you to church or to pull you out of it; it's my job to help you to love yourself deeply, as and because of who you are. It's my job to help you to find God. Aaron's journey beautifully shows us that every path is different, but at the end of the day, we are all searching for God. His story leaves us wanting more and reminds readers that the quest for God is a never-ending journey, and that in reality, it's in the quest itself that we find God. Through Aaron's reflections of his own ups and downs, we are invited to get to know the God of love through vulnerability, strength, and perseverance."

— **Eric Feltes**, Life Coach and Speaker

"*Letting Go(d)* pulls no punches and spares no details as Aaron recounts the harrowing story of his life, his God, and his sexuality. He invites us into some of the most intimate parts of his life with full transparency. The church has historically failed the LGBTQI+ community. But Aaron lets us in on the deep and fearful structures and struggles that this community has faced for far too long. With grit and gumption, but also sorrow and a tragic truthfulness, his readers get a front row seat as to what it looks like when you are told not to be who you were born to be as a matter of faith, church, and God. Only his story doesn't end there. We see him move through so much with bravery and courage. He is honest about what he has lost, yet celebrates all the freedom he has gained. It is rare that we get such an up close and personal look at a story such as Aaron's. This is a must read for anyone who has ever had an opinion about the Queer community as far as Christianity is concerned. This book is an undeserved gift. A magnum opus!"

— **Maria Francesca French**, author of *Safer than the Known Way*

AARON SIMNOWITZ

Letting Go

HOW I FAILED GAY CONVERSION THERAPY AND LEARNED TO LOVE MYSELF

ALL RIGHTS RESERVED. No part of this book may be used or reproduced, stored in a retrieval system, or transmitted in any form or by any means, electronic, mechanical, photocopying, recording, scanning, or otherwise, without written permission from the publisher except in the case of brief quotations embodied in critical articles and reviews. Permission for wider usage of this material can be obtained through Quoir by emailing permission@quoir.com.

Copyright © 2022 by Aaron Simnowitz
First Edition

Email from Craig Gross to the author used with permission.

Scriptures taken from the Holy Bible, New International Version®, NIV®. Copyright © 1973, 1978, 1984, 2011 by Biblica, Inc.™ Used by permission of Zondervan. All rights reserved worldwide. www.zondervan.com. The "NIV" and "New International Version" are trademarks registered in the United States Patent and Trademark Office by Biblica, Inc.™

The events in this book are portrayed to the best of the author's memory. While all the stories within this book are true, some names, identifying details, and locations have been changed to protect the privacy of the people involved.

Cover design by Rafael Polendo (polendo.net)
Interior Layout by Matthew J. Distefano

ISBN 978-1-957007-49-6

This volume is printed on acid free paper and meets ANSI Z39.48 standards. Printed in the United States of America

Published by Quoir
Chico, California
www.quoir.com

CONTENTS

PREFACE	VII
INTRODUCTION	XI
1. GUYS AND DOLLS	1
2. JUST ONE OF THE GUYS	9
3. SHE'S THE MAN	13
4. THE RULES OF ATTRACTION	19
5. BUBBLE BOY	29
6. THE GODFATHER	37
7. ALWAYS BE MY MAYBE	45
8. FATAL ATTRACTION	51
9. GONE GIRL	61
10. LIAR LIAR	71
11. BRING IT ON	81
12. BOY ERASED	93
13. PRAY AWAY	103
14. AWAKENINGS	111
15. TITANIC	117
16. THE TRUTH ABOUT CHARLIE	121
17. THE PURSUIT OF HAPPYNESS	133
18. THE BLIND SIDE	139

19.	RELIGULOUS	149
20.	A GOOD YEAR	155
21.	ISN'T IT ROMANTIC	161
22.	50 SHADES OF GREY	169
23.	THE SPECTACULAR NOW	177
ACKNOWLEDGMENTS		185
END NOTES		187
REFERENCES		191

PREFACE

Just imagine walking into a movie theater, popcorn and root beer in hand, and watching only the second half of a movie. Let's take *The Lion King*, for example. Once you find your seat, away from people kicking your chair from behind and chomping on their nachos, you attempt to put the pieces and characters together after missing the first 40 minutes. Some questions you may have could be:

What is Hakuna Matata?
Are Mufasa and Simba the same lion?
Why is the weird monkey screaming, "HE'S ALIVE, HE'S ALIVE?"
Who died exactly?

    Confusing as it all is to make sense of the story, what you *would* know if you were a tween girl or a sexually repressed boy in the '90s is that Simba's voice sounds exactly to that of Jonathan Taylor Thomas—a young hottie of the decade, but I digress. Watching a movie in its entirety gives you the big picture and vast knowledge of the story, as opposed to trying to figure out half of the movie as an investigator—examining the clues scene by scene from the dialogue you just walked in on.
    Can the same be said about humans? Are people's lives just one long movie of thematic scenes that is comprised of different chapters that has shaped them into the person they are today? You cannot completely understand a person without having some insight to their entire backstory; however, this is how we start many friendships and relationships. Typically, we make assumptions about others based merely on what we see right in front of us in the moment, but maybe we've missed the most important scenes of their personal movie because we were stuck in Los Angeles traffic on the way to the theater or held up at the ticket counter with a new trainee who does not know how to use the computer. Missing how their story begins and the events thereafter make us ignorant to the most important stuff, like knowing

Simba was destined to be king, but his Uncle Scar became so jealous that he killed his brother King Mufasa, Simba's dad and hero, to claim the throne for himself. Scar manipulated Simba in believing that he killed his own father and shamed him into leaving Pride Rock, never to return. Simba carried that guilt around his neck as thick as his mane for years, never wanting to talk about the past and the alleged role he had in his father's death. Yes, that is what is missed in those first 40 minutes! That's *huge*!

I just spent the last five hours barhopping in Minneapolis asking people exactly this: what is your story? As a casting producer for reality TV, my hope and ultimate goal is to find people with an attractive personality and an exciting story that defines who they are. I want to go beyond the mundane details of where they grew up, where they went to school, whom they married, and how many children they have. The answers to these questions are crucial to their story and powerfully relevant, but I want to get deeper. Let's get deep enough to discover if this person's story has the power to influence and inspire others' lives. The beautiful blonde bartender may be a student paying her way through college, but does anyone know that she had leukemia when she was ten years old and wasn't supposed to be alive today? What about that frat guy in the corner who is getting wasted with his buddies? He may be having fun today, but no one knows with simply a glance that as a child he was bounced around from foster home to foster home, the tragic result of his parents having been killed in a car accident when he was five years old.

Events that occur around the life of any person shape who they are and who they become. There is no doubt in my mind that the bartender or frat guy would have a different outlook on life as adults had they not suffered through the traumatic events that altered their childhood. These events are massive scenes in the film of their lives and a significant part of *how* their story is told.

I want to tell my story, the one that is unique yet relatable. My hope is not to bore you with another story of a person struggling with the very controversial conflict of religion and homosexuality. The sole purpose of this book is for you to gain a deeper understanding of what happens in the mind and soul of a person when the conflict of religion and homosexuality has dominated their life. Keep in mind, however, that my words could never fully convey the painful emotional stretching of being pulled in two opposing directions or witness the gross ignorance conveyed by so many who have never experienced walking in my shoes.

I have been consumed with so many agonizing thoughts and questions of how to defend a faith where homosexuality isn't accepted yet come to terms with my own truth of being attracted to other men. This journey of finding answers to these questions led me to conclusions I would have never envisioned and beliefs I would have never fathomed. Where did I go wrong? Or did I do something right?

Striving to please everyone will lead to inevitable failure. Whether I suppress my homosexuality by submitting to God's alleged heterosexual intentions for romantic relationships *OR* embrace my homosexuality by giving myself the freedom to love another man, I will have upset someone. As you read this book, I ask that no matter what you believe, whether you are religious or atheist, pro-gay or anti-gay, that you silence what you deem right or wrong and take an open-minded, non-biased journey with me as I tell this story. My story.

INTRODUCTION

AS A YOUNG BOY, I had a fascination with actors I watched on television. Antonio Sabato, Jr., from *General Hospital* and Luke Perry from *Beverly Hills, 90210* had me doing double takes the instant their shirts would be violently ripped off in the throes of passion with a female co-star or exiting the shower soaking wet with only a small towel covering what I ultimately wanted to see the most. What did his penis look like? And why, as a young boy, did I care? The masculine body intrigued me for reasons I did not understand but what I did know is that those feelings were raw and authentic, overwhelming my curiosity. Years later, thanks to the 2003 movie *Testosterone* and an episode of HBO's *Oz,* I was able to see both Antonio and Luke's manhood in all its glory, respectively, finally revealing what kept me so curious as that innocent 13-year-old boy. I was not disappointed. I never questioned what it could be about older, attractive men that captivated me as a child, but the fascination never weakened; on the contrary, it only amplified.

There was another man on my TV screen who exceeded the rest, keeping me glued to my couch every Tuesday at 8:00 PM EST, and that was none other than Tony Miceli. *Who's The Boss* was the Connecticut based sitcom starring Judith Light as Angela Bower. Her Brooklyn-bred housekeeper, Tony Miceli, was played by Tony Danza. I was a slightly prepubescent 13-year-old in the decade of Alyssa Milano's *Teen Beat* craze, but I was at a hormonal deficit when it came to Alyssa, who played the daughter, Samantha Miceli.

I adored the dad, Tony Danza. It could have been his funny and extroverted Brooklyn-Italian personality. Maybe it was his thick brunette head of hair that fell softly over his forehead when butting heads with Angela. It could have been the masculinity he possessed, regardless of the cooking, cleaning, and laundry he was required to do as the housekeeper. Maybe, just maybe, it was his impeccably defined shirtless body I stared at frequently throughout many episodes of the show's run. Whatever drew me to Tony Danza, I was hooked on that man without any context or explanation. The obsessive fanboy within me tracked down an address to the ABC

Studio and sent a letter to Tony, confessing my adoration of him and requesting an autographed picture. About a month later, I received a questionably large yellow envelope in the mail with no clue of its contents. I carefully opened it to pull out a glossy 8 x 11 headshot of Tony Danza with a scribbled note and signature in blue sharpie from the man I obsessed over:

> "To Aaron, all my best, Love Tony Danza."

Had Phoebe Buffay's version of "Tiny Dancer" existed in the early '90s, I would have sung it relentlessly, *Hold me close, young Tony Danza*. I was geeked out at receiving such an extraordinary gift from my idol. *He knows where I live!* Please do not tell me that his assistant or the Tony Danza fan club sent me that autograph photo; my heart couldn't take the disappointment. I hung that picture on my bedroom wall and felt special every time I walked by it as Tony smiled back at me.

Over 20 years later, I will find myself in Memphis, Tennessee, at a Christian-based organization called Love in Action, a program with the intent to remove homosexual attraction through therapy, counseling, and "praying the gay away." Many people I've met along the way have been surprised that these camps exist, and that gay people attend—whether at the command of their parents or of their own volition—to become straight. Oh, but they do. My experience in the Love in Action program was a less exaggerated version of what happened in the movie comedy, *But I'm a Cheerleader*, but for a fictitious satire, it was not too far off from the reality.

In the movie, Megan, played brilliantly by Natasha Lyonne, is a high school cheerleader ambushed by her parents, best friend, and boyfriend who believe she has lesbian tendencies. They conduct an intervention to have her sent to a gay conversion Christian program called True Directions. Megan's fellow camp buddy and object of her lust, a moody girl named Graham, fed up with the program's quest to de-lesbianize her, frustratingly tells Megan, *"This is bullshit Megan, it doesn't work! You are who you are. The only trick is not getting caught."*

I will spend nearly fifteen years of my life trying to "not get caught" to save myself from a one-way ticket to eternal damnation. Among many countless attempts to become heterosexual, I voluntarily attended the Love in Action program in Memphis, TN. I pursued heterosexuality as if it was life or death, and quite literally, I thought it was. One must wonder, what does it look like to attempt to become heterosexual when everything innately within you is homosexual? Well, I started with some denial, added a little bit of pretending, a smidge of deceit, a pinch of lying to myself, and a big fat scoop of insanity. I devoured the dish, but my stomach could not handle the lies and sickness clouded my judgment. I continued to administer these poisonous solutions to an illness I desperately believed needed a cure.

Sounds fun, right?

Ralph Waldo Emerson once wrote, "Life is about the journey, not the destination." It's not terribly exciting to only hear the end of a movie and not know how the story unfolded. In the *Wizard of Oz*, Dorothy came back to Kansas. In *Home Alone*, Kevin was reunited with his family just in time for Christmas. In *While You Were Sleeping*, Lucy chose the *other* brother. But wait, what is the *story*? How did it all happen? The juicy details lie in how the protagonist got there, and the same can be said about me. My epiphanies were not an overnight tale. It took years of navigating my issues with other males, my emotional dependencies, and my sexual addiction, and untangling their relationships to my Christian faith vs. my sexuality. I tell my story and how I came out, not only from the perspective of a closeted homosexual but also from the perspective of a devout Christian seeking a life of peace, logic, and self-discovery.

If sharing my experience helps educate or guide even one person, one parent, one pastor, or anyone struggling with the confusion and complexity centered on this controversial topic of religious faith vs. homosexuality, then this was all worth it. I write this story with raw honesty, deepest sincerity, humble authenticity, and sarcastic humor. Get ready for this crazy journey.

"Whether it's the bullying coming from behind the pulpit or played out daily on school playgrounds, my hope is that by showing my scars it might inspire compassion instead of condemnation in those holding the stones."

—Bryan Christopher, author of *Hiding from Myself*

Chapter One

GUYS AND DOLLS

Lawn-Guyland.
 That's how you say it, *Lawn*-Guyland.
 Trying to explain Long Island to people who did not grow up there is a chore.
 No, it's not one of the five boroughs.
 Yes, Queens and Brooklyn are *on* Long Island, but they are not *part* of Long Island.
 Yes, I know how to say Amagansett, Nissequoge, and Wyandanch without a second thought.
 Long Island is a special place because, above all else, it's my home.
 The privilege of living next to the biggest city in the world was not lost on me when people I met outside of New York glamorized the lights of Times Square, the commotion on 7th Avenue, and the Christmas tree at Rockefeller Center. But "the city" is not my home. Neither is the Hamptons, home of the vacationing wealthy and *The Barefoot Contessa*, Ina Garten. Home to me is the LIRR train to Ronkonkoma filled with drunk Islander fans, the secret sauce at Branchinelli's Pizzeria in Smithtown, and the rubbernecking traffic on the Long Island Expressway congested at Exit 58 in Hauppauge.
 Long Island summers were hot, humid and mosquito infested. Nearly every day from June to August, you would find my sisters and myself in Emily's pool next door. We only would retreat from the pool when we heard the *ding-a-ling* bells from Maryann in her ice cream truck. I would chase her down, with my sisters and Emily trailing behind, in my soaking wet bathing suit, spending my unused lunch money on Strawberry Shortcake ice cream bars.
 The winters were my personal favorite. Bundled up under so much cotton, nylon, and polyester; my face barely peeked through the layers of coats, hoods, and knit hats that covered 95 percent of my body. The aroma of the Entenmann's factory, only a few miles away, would consume the air and made me crave their famous

crumb cake. The snow fell gently from the sky, inch after inch, until the soft white powder thoroughly covered the dull green grass. My dad took us kids to a nearby hill to go sledding when not building snowmen in the front yard or getting pelted with snowballs from the neighborhood teenage boys. The icy cold filled days usually ended with drinking a cup of hot chocolate with marshmallows, the sniffles, and Mom rubbing Vick's VapoRub on my chest to ease the slightest bit of congestion.

There was nothing quite like a Long Island autumn. The beauty of the orange, yellow, and red leaves that scattered across the yard is still one of my favorite sights to see. However, the beauty was short-lived when I would have to rake all those leaves into large plastic garbage bags to be placed on the curb awaiting pickup.

No matter the weather or season, *every* Sunday was church day. A mandatory excursion I met with groans and procrastination to stall the weekly religious outing. When we finally made it out the door amid my mom's annoyance at our lack of urgency, my older sister Rebecca and I would fight dibs for the front seat. Rebecca usually would get her way, so I begrudgingly found my way to the backseat next to my little sister, Sarah, in our ugly 1980 Chevy Malibu brown station wagon. Mom pulled out of our driveway in Bay Shore and made our way to Faith Tabernacle Church in West Babylon, NY. My older brother Adam came to church with us when he was home from college while my dad stayed home.

Born-Again Christianity was not the dominating religion of Long Island as the Catholics and Jews took the reigns.[1] But when loud Long Islanders praise Jesus, you'll hear them from Mineola to Montauk! Faith Tabernacle was what one would call an overly charismatic church. It was not weird nor strange to have people jumping up and down with their hands lifted to Jesus, dancing around the aisles, and "speaking in tongues." When someone spoke in tongues, it meant they were praying in another language that only God could understand, but to eight-year-old me, it was gibberish.

The sound of tambourines chimed throughout the red-carpeted building as churchgoers brought these instruments to exuberantly slap against their thigh or hand during the energetic worship. I would slide out of the row from my mom and walk to the front altar, so I could jump and dance to God along with the worship band without the constrictions of chairs and people around me.

Pastor James Graziano, a high-spirited preacher with a James Brown quaff of hair and a wonderful sense of 70's fashion, delivered his sermons with conviction, determination, and enthusiasm. My favorite part of service was toward the end when Pastor Graziano had altar calls. I would be in awe of watching the congregants get "slain in the spirit." Pastor Graziano would firmly put his hand on their head and pray over them with an army of ushers ready to catch their fall as other ushers were on standby to put a white sheet over the women in skirts to protect their privacy. I would stare in amazement.

Were they sleeping? Are they visiting heaven? I often wondered what it felt like to be slain in the spirit.

During the week, when most normal boys played with G.I. Joe action figures or played baseball, I would pop in a worship cassette in the tape player and set up the dining room chairs to replicate a church pew. After a few moments of praise, I would collapse to the floor indicating I was "slain in the spirit" right in the middle of the dining room. My parents and siblings walked right over me without a second glance. This was just another Tuesday night for me. I would lay on the cold hard floor for a few minutes, get up, worship again so I could get "slain" one more time. Ah, the wonder and awe of what was going through my naive mind was only the beginning of my faith.

Despite the Christianity, I wouldn't say my parents were extremely strict. I still played video games, rode my bike around the neighborhood, and watched way too much TV. However, television shows such as *The Smurfs* and *The Simpsons* were strictly prohibited due to either witchcraft elements or extreme adult content, although I would watch the primetime soap opera *Dallas* with my dad every Friday evening. Even as a young boy, I had an affinity for Bobby Ewing, drawn to him for reasons I never understood at that young age.

Halloween was never celebrated at home because it's allegedly the "devil's holiday." My mother handed out tracts—short informational pamphlets explaining the gospel message—to the sugar-laced hopefuls on those haunted evenings. Once, in a desperate attempt to feel like a normal kid, I begged her to hand out candy with the tracts because I was embarrassed that we were the weird Jesus family. Surprisingly she fulfilled my request one year, and next to the stack of tracts appeared a massive bowl of Trident gum. *Gum?* Well, beggars couldn't be choosers, right?! Mom was a true woman of God. Bible verses were displayed unashamedly on posters and plaques across the house. Bookshelves overflowed with Bibles of all different kinds. She was a prayer warrior and a lover of Jesus. She had such an intimate connection with God, and this was inexplicably evident in how she raised her kids, fought for her marriage, and lived out her life. It was never strange to hear the voice of my mom's prayers and praise echoing from the laundry room as she threw in another load of dirty clothes. It never fazed me when she turned on Sandi Patty's music and started worshipping in the middle of the dining room. She possessed true, authentic love and passion for the Creator and for people. My mom instilled in me a foundation for faith in God at a very early age.

There is a common ideology within the Christian faith that it's not a religion but a relationship with God. I took this very seriously. God was not an imaginary friend whom I would talk to while playing house or tea party. I believed that God was an actual spiritual being who was personally interested and invested in my life. No, I never saw God visually, but I had all the faith in the world that He was always with me, hovering like an invisible cloud that followed me everywhere. Throughout my life as a Christian, I would talk audibly to God as if he were a person sitting right next to me. He was right beside me in the passenger seat of my car. He was next to me in the classroom at school. He watched me as I slept all night long. He even watched *General Hospital* with me. Can't a higher power enjoy a good soap opera?

My mom found it necessary to keep us grounded in the gospel and adopt the Christian worldview, which meant public school would not be the best environment. Not long into my second-grade year at the local public elementary school, my parents removed us and placed us in Smithtown Christian School in Smithtown, NY. Man, I hated wearing a uniform to my new private school. Smithtown Christian School, also known as "SCS," didn't have that much of a strict dress code by private school standards, but as someone who usually wore shorts and a t-shirt to public school, wearing dress slacks and a button-down shirt made me feel overdressed as if I was attending an elementary wedding every day.

Second grade at SCS did not have the strongest of starts. My peers didn't take too well to the new kid, and "girl" became my instant nickname thanks to a wretched boy named Porter.

"Aaron, you're such a girl", he taunted every day.

This encouraged the other boys to participate in teasing me as well. Looking back, I see that this was the origin of my insecurities with other boys during my elementary years and beyond.

As the years went by at SCS, the teasing dissipated, yet I still did not want to play with the other boys at recess. The girls played "SPUD," which I found much more enjoyable than kicking around the soccer ball with the boys. SPUD is a deconstructed version of dodgeball and involved picking categories, throwing the ball up in the air, and the loser going through a "spanking machine." The girls never seemed to mind me joining their game, and I didn't care that I was the only boy in their midst. Even at that young age, a small part of me felt a bit of an outcast amongst the boys, but I never dwelled upon it too much.

Every day after school, I would play with my sister Sarah and Emily, the girl next door. Emily was an adoptive sister to me of sorts. She had a rocky family life, so she retreated to my family most likely to find some solace, peace, and belonging. Emily became part of our family and even our extended family. From family parties, holidays, and excursions, all the aunts, uncles, and cousins expected Emily to be there because she was just that—she was part of the family.

In the hotter months, we would spend hours in Emily's pool. However, it was never as simple as throwing on our bathing suits, grabbing a towel, and crawling through the broken fence that connected our yards. We had to *earn* pool time. Emily's father made us work for it, having us remove weeds that grew on our shared wired fence from the front yard all the way to the back yard. It was child labor at its worst. He would regularly come over to monitor and check our work, slurring words of a dictator explaining why we had to work in return for pool privileges.

Communicating with Emily's father was my first introduction to someone who loved his liquor. The smell of alcohol was grossly evident from the moment he approached me, even before opening his mouth. I was terrified of him. His voice only boomed louder the more alcohol he consumed. Once he agreed our de-weeding was sufficient, we had the green light to play in the pool—which we did until our fingers were a wrinkled mess.

If it rained or was after dark, Emily, Sarah, and I would play with Barbie Dolls. Emily had an incredible collection of Barbies and Barbie clothes. She often lugged all her Barbie paraphernalia to our house, and we gathered all the clothes in the middle, taking turns to pick an item of Barbie fashion we would play with that evening. My favorite outfit was an 80's inspired dress with a black and white striped, spandex top attached to a poofy, bright yellow skirt. I called it the "bumblebee dress." However, I was not as interested in the clothes as much as I loved playing with Barbie's hair and styling it in different ways. I learned how to French braid on my own because of this—something that came in handy in the later years.

There were times I would play with Barbies by myself. I did feel slightly ashamed. As a boy playing with "girl toys," it bothered me tremendously, but I enjoyed it regardless. I never knew how my parents felt about me playing with the dolls, but they never stopped me or disgraced me in any way. However, playing with Barbies was my first dirty little secret that I didn't want anyone at school to uncover. What would the other kids think? This was only the beginning of secrets that I would keep in fear of embarrassment and humiliation.

My longing for males started to peak during those years. As I already stated, I was very fond of Bobby Ewing and Tony Danza. My sister Rebecca got me hooked on *General Hospital* while I was only 13 years old. Initially, I teased her for watching a stupid soap opera, so I didn't pay much attention until a character by the name of Jagger graced the screen. Played by a young Antonio Sabato, Jr., often shirtless and sweaty, Jagger exacerbated my intrigue. My interest in Jagger was innocent, but I was drawn to him for reasons I then could not explain.

When I look back on it, *General Hospital* was not simply something I watched for entertainment but an escape. *General Hospital* got me through some tough times in my life. From the bullying I endured as a child to the confusion of my sexuality into adulthood, I found an outlet that brought me to the fictional world of Port Charles, and I temporarily forgot about the troubles that loomed over me for that one hour. Throughout all disasters, difficulties, and sorrow, *General Hospital* helped me endure it and still does today as a faithful viewer for 30 years.

General Hospital and Barbies kept me mostly occupied, but I also had Psalty. Psalty the Singing Songbook was the main character from the Kids' Praise! series of Christian children's musical albums. In a ridiculous, and sometimes scary, blue-faced makeup and extravagant costume made to look like a huge songbook, Psalty mentored and encouraged kids to sing their praises to God. The Psalty musical—*Psalty*

5: The Camping Adventure—that my mom bought me on VHS had my undivided attention in my adolescence. In the musical, a group of church kids go on a camping trip with Psalty, who guides them from the campground to the top of the mountain. It may be one of the campiest (no pun intended) Christian musicals ever to be released. On the way up the trail, they sing, dance, and learn much-needed lessons on how to trust God in times of trouble and uncertainty.

I wanted so desperately to be one of the kids in the musical, so much in fact that I pretended, at least three to four times a week, that I *was* one of those kids. I cleared out the living room, pushed the coffee table back so I could create my own imaginary hiking trail and put on my backpack, ready to "hike up the mountain." From the second I pressed play on the VCR, I was instantly transported into Psalty's Camping Adventure with the rest of the kids. I sang along, joined in with the choreography, and even gave myself speaking lines—the lines that my favorite boy said.

Yes, I had a favorite boy. I called him "vengeance boy" for my own reference. He was an ensemble cast member, so he didn't have a character name like some of the other kids. However, during the Bible alphabet song, he quoted the "V" verse. *"Vengeance is mine, saith the Lord, Romans 12:19,"* he said with a slight rasp in his voice. I didn't know why I had such a fascination toward this boy. Every time I played the video, I picked him out during the songs and dance numbers and stared at him in awe.

He should have more lines, I always thought. *Why doesn't he have a solo?*

I would have been a good agent for him concerning all future Christian kid musicals he wanted to star in. I would never be able to put my finger on my slight obsession with "vengeance boy," but I'm convinced, unbeknownst to me, my sexual attraction toward other males started to unravel. (As I was writing this chapter, curiosity took over and I did some research to see what "vengeance boy" was up to 34 years later. No, that's not creepy at all, right? Thanks to investigative skills I learned from television casting, I discovered a Facebook page of this now adult boy, who is a pastor and worship leader in Southern California, married with kids. And, might I add, extremely handsome! Even at 13 years old, I knew how to pick them.)

Growing up in a Christian home and attending a private Christian school kept me extremely sheltered. I was not aware of anything sexual relating to my own body or mindset. From 6th through 8th grade, my male peers were discovering their sexual identities, fighting over girls, and stressing about who to ask to the summer camp banquet, but those desires were utterly lost on me. I vividly remember one morning in Mrs. Franco's 6th grade class when Jason, the class "stud," walked excitedly into the classroom and boasted to the entire class that he made out with an 8th grader.

"I just made out with Janet!" he shouted.

The other boys cheered, surrounding him with high-fives and patting him on the back in horny approval. I sat in my seat, not reacting to his outburst.

A brief surge of jealousy overcame me as I watched the other boys swarm around Jason, envying how cool he was. I wanted to be cool, although I had no intense desire to kiss a girl. What also swept through my mind, to a degree, was: *How did someone make out? What does it feel like? How long do you kiss?* I was ignorant, as one probably should be in 6th grade. I had no sexual urging for either gender. I was too busy playing with Barbies and dancing in my living room to Christian musicals. Kissing girls was not on my to-do list.

Sometimes I wondered if I did have a subconscious discernment of sexuality back in those junior high years and if my desire to "be" Jason really translated to me wanting to be the person making out with him. What about my obsession with "vengeance boy" and Antonio Sabato, Jr.? Why did they capture my attention long enough for me to notice the captivation? I shrugged off the longing I had for males and did not put too much emphasis on having no desire to kiss a girl. I figured my time would come when I would be interested in girls, or so I thought.

Chapter Two

JUST ONE OF THE GUYS

An unfortunate consequence of attending school at SCS meant that my mom no longer attended Faith Tabernacle, a church I loved. SCS was under the umbrella of the Smithtown Gospel Tabernacle (SGT), and the massive building housed both the church and the school, so my mom decided to transfer churches. I did not like the services and thought they were dreadfully boring in comparison. There were no energetic congregants jumping up and down, ardently beating a tambourine against their thighs. No one got "slain" in the spirit, and the pastor was not engaging to me as Pastor Graziano.

Despite the mundane Sunday morning services, I loved attending the youth group on Wednesday nights once I entered 7th grade. SGT youth group had a very different vibe and energy from the main church. One would think it was a completely separate entity. The youth pastor welcomed the high-spirited energy, laughter, and liveliness that lacked from the dull sanctuary across the courtyard.

My time in the youth group was life-altering. Everything I am, was formed by the experiences and people I met there and grew up with. I am a product of great mentorship from many of the leaders that guided me over those six years. The Christian faith dominated my life. I wanted to surround myself with Christian influences and form close-knit godly friendships because that's what a good Christian boy does. It was bred in me that I must read my Bible daily, spend quiet time with the Lord, and try my best to lead a life that pleased Jesus, my parents, and my church.

Every Wednesday after school, some friends and I would grab pizza and hang out on campus, eagerly waiting for 7:30 PM when the youth group service would begin. Despite the genesis of insecurities in those years, I had a handful of friends in youth group. I was always on a mission, as insecure as I was, to find a place to belong, and I generally found that in youth group.

The school auditorium was packed to the brim on those highly anticipated Wednesday evenings, full of teenagers and the best of early 90's fashion you could ever imagine, from acid-washed jeans to overalls with only one strap clasped to neon windbreakers. Christian music artists like Michael W. Smith, Petra, and DC Talk blasted from the speakers as everyone gathered. It was the night of the week I looked forward to more than anything. However, with so many teens in one place, it was natural for the youth group to distribute into their smaller cliques. Quickly, I found out who the "cool" kids were and who they were not (spoiler...I was *not* a cool kid).

Youth Group events were not exclusive to Wednesday nights. There were countless opportunities to go on various activities and trips. Every January and August, we would have our annual winter retreat and summer camp respectively, but my favorite were the mission trips. I signed up for every single trip, never questioning how my parents would finance my expensive youth group hobby traveling across the states and even the globe to spread the Good News of Jesus. Our primary purpose of these trips was to evangelize to the locals and tell them about having a relationship with God. We utilized skits, choreography, and dance to portray our message. Yes, I danced. Throw on Crystal Lewis' "I Now Live" or DC Talk's "In the Light," and I'll show my moves!

Talking to people about God after our performances frightened me. Rejection was not only possible but likely when it came to saving the souls of random strangers on the street. The irony was that I loved everything about the trips except the evangelizing, the core purpose. I loved the travel, I loved making new friends and strengthening existing bonds, and I loved performing the skits and dances, but I loathed asking strangers if I could pray the sinner's prayer with them. The social aspect of the trips is what I enjoyed the most.

Although I did have some male friends in the youth group, I still very much gravitated toward the girls as if they were my safe space—I didn't have to pretend around the girls. I was naturally comfortable and not intimidated, the opposite of how I felt around boys— even with the several male friends I had. I became the resident French braider of the youth group. During these trips, all the girls came to me to get their hair braided. (Remember all the Barbies?). Braiding hair gave me lots of attention, and I loved it because I felt important and wanted. On any given day during a youth group trip, I would have 4 or 5 girls waiting, practically in a line, for me to French braid their hair. The attention was addicting, but the thing is, it's not the girls' attention I truly desired.

The unrelenting craving for male attention controlled me viciously. Even well into my early high school years, I hadn't yet pin-pointed why I had this immense desire to be around particular boys. I wanted to be noticed by them; I desperately wanted their recognition and friendship. Also, to make matters worse, insecurity consumed me, and I was a very sensitive little boy. The slightest hint of rejection would find me in a corner crying my eyes out if I felt left out, made fun of, or embarrassed...which all these things happened more often than I care to admit when attempting to fit in.

Most of my attention went to Craig, a boy two years older than me. Craig was the quintessential popular hot guy. Athletically inclined, well-liked, admired by all the girls, and overall, a very friendly person. Every girl wanted to date him, and every guy wanted to be him. He was *that* guy. This overwhelming need to be close to him was powerful but I never knew exactly why it was so prevalent. What I did know is that I wanted to be one of the cool kids. Maybe I could be cool, too, if I was friends with Craig.

When I was in 9th grade, there was a youth group mission trip to Mexico that I signed up for – also the first time I would travel outside the states. This mission trip to Mexico City was beyond exciting to me, not only because it would be the first time on a plane but also, because Craig was going. *I was thrilled!* Not surprisingly, I was more focused on interacting with Craig than the purpose of the trip—ministering to the people in the streets through dance, skits, and clown performances. Whether it meant sitting at the same lunch table or trying to sleep in the same room, I went out of my way to get Craig's attention. He was always friendly, but mostly kept in his own circle of friends—friends his age. I wanted more from him than just a passing "hello" in the hallway—I wanted to be his best friend.

When I got desperate for his attention, I would plop myself down in a corner within his eyesight and appear sad, hoping he would notice and come over to talk, put his arm around my shoulder, and comfort me. *Perfectly normal, right?* My pathetic attempts never worked. Youth leaders and other kids would check in on me, and I would tell them nothing was wrong, hoping they would leave me alone so only Craig could see me in my fake distress.

Naivety and being a late sexual bloomer did not allow me to recognize that I was probably dealing with a heavy schoolboy crush here, but I could not define it yet, even as a high school freshman. I still had no concept of romantic or sexual feelings toward one gender or another—as if I was asexual. My insecurities played a significant part. I had a dire yearning to be popular and noticed, and I starved for male peer attention. Craig was my target but how do I get him to notice me? Well, one night in Mexico, I concocted up an idea that I would tell Craig that I had a bad dream about him. *Yea, this seems like a brilliant idea.* However, no dream occurred. I made the whole thing up so I had a reason to talk to him, to tell Craig about the dream, thinking that maybe this would bring us closer together. Clearly, I was batshit crazy.

Trembling, I approached Craig and asked him to go somewhere we could speak privately. My growth spurt had yet to kick in as I looked up at him, awestruck yet intimidated. In this made-up dream, I had envisioned that danger awaited Craig and I needed to warn him. I translated my infatuation into a message from God, and believed it was my duty to report what God had told me. Craig had to be prepared and protected, right?! *Maybe he will let me put my hands on him and pray for him!* Craig responded cordially, assuring me that he was in no danger and that God was protecting him. And that was it. Talk over. The whole conversation was over in less than two minutes. *Jeez, Craig, not even a hug?*

This pursuit of becoming best friends with Craig was a constant lesson in futility. That summer, at camp, when all the boys ran with vigor to claim their cabins and beds, I beelined it to the cabin that Craig would be in which consisted of the 11th and 12th grade boys when I should have been with my age group two cabins over. During bedtime, all the guys would be in and out of the showers, in their underwear and shirtless, goofing around while getting ready for bed. I sat in my bunk, staring quietly at all of them. Suddenly it wasn't just Craig that piqued this inexpressible yearning to be close; it was every guy in that cabin that looked halfway decent without a shirt on. *What is wrong with me?*

Beyond wanting their friendship, I wanted to be athletic like them, popular like them, and attractive like them but I knew there was something else—something more intimate. Sexual thoughts had yet to cross my mind, so I didn't know what I wanted from them or why. Craig and I never formed that bond I craved with him in those years, and once he went to college he was out of sight, out of mind. There was always a new boy, or older male youth leader, year after year that I pursued. I clung to them, desiring connection, and always felt let down because none of them gave me what I wanted, except frustration and deeper insecurities.

But whatever happened to Craig? It's quite funny how life turns out sometimes. In a serendipitous turn of events, Craig and I have become close friends as adults—and even more than that, he's like a brother. Over the years, his family, including his sisters Michele and Robyn, have become a 2nd family to me—attending their family events, going on vacations, and spending Christmas together every year. Man, how I deeply cherish these relationships and I'm overcome with gratitude. Yes, Craig is still ridiculously handsome, however, I'm taller than him now, so it all evened out. Imagine if someone told 14-year-old Aaron that someday he would be on a Bahamas cruise with Craig and a routinely welcomed friend at his house—he would have wet his pants!

Chapter Three

SHE'S THE MAN

One of the most traumatizing events in my teenage years was when I went back to public school in 9th grade. It was, for the lack of a more conservative expression, fucking terrible. Due to rising Christian school tuition, my parents pulled me and my sisters out of SCS and back into the public school system. I vaguely remember not caring one way or another whether if I stayed at SCS or not, but had I known what public school would bring, I would have begged my parents to keep me at SCS. If they knew too, they would have.

My entrance to public school was quite untraditional. Brentwood School District was so large that it had four middle schools and two high schools—Sonderling and Ross—both on the same campus. The high schools housed the 10th–12th graders and the middle schools were for 6th–8th grade. So, what about the 9th graders? Well, let me introduce the hell that was the Brentwood Freshman Center, a school completely separate on its own campus. I never faced anything more petrifying in my life, especially not knowing any other kids. All my friends were at SCS and youth group, and I didn't know the neighborhood kids at all. My first public school bus ride would be a precursor of what to expect as the new kid.

The bus was overcrowded by the time it arrived at my stop, and I had no choice but to stand in the aisle—a safety hazard that was ignored. As if being the new kid wasn't awkward enough, now I had to stand up surrounded by chatter, looks, and whispers. I hated those bus rides, having to endure hard kicks to my ribs and smacks to my head, over and over again. The boys were brutal, their abuse so unfathomable, that the dread of climbing those steps on to the bus every day anesthetized my will to live.

I did not know the extent of my loneliness until I was inside the Freshman Center building. Swarms of 14 and 15-year-olds in brightly colored baggy jeans with overly gelled hair and large hoop earrings gossiped at the lockers, laughed in the bathrooms, and yelled from within their different cliques in the hallway. The bullying from the bus continued in the walls of the school. As an overweight kid with long disheveled hair who took no pride in my appearance, I was often mistaken for a girl. No, I was not being called a girl as a way of teasing. Other kids, and even adults, legitimately thought I was a female. However, in most cases, when the boys bullied and abused me, they had to know I was a boy. Otherwise, I'd like to think they would not have assaulted an actual girl like they did me.

As I waited for the bus after school, I would be thrown against the brick wall by a group of boys who cupped my chest to feel for my "fat boy boobs." Their words hurt more than what they did physically to me. It was mortifying. Escaping to the bus did not provide relief as I would endure more physical abuse from different boys on the way home, who hit and kicked me without provocation or reason. I became desensitized. I could not fight back. I did not say a word. I let them abuse me.

I *let* them abuse me.

Masterfully, I hid my emotions from my siblings and parents, and as far as I knew, they were none the wiser. I walked into the house and ran to my room, cried my eyes out, splashed water on my face, and watched my daily *General Hospital* episode to escape.

I soon realized that my often-mistaken gender would become another source of anxiety so prominent that I would develop an inferiority complex. Every time I saw kids whispering and looking at me, I instantly wondered if they were guessing if I was a male or a female. My suspicions proved correct when one of those kids detached from their circle to ask me, "Are you a *boy* or a *girl?*"

I was asked that question a few dozen times during most of my 9th grade year. It was bad enough to get asked these questions at school, but it happened in my everyday life outside of school as well. During youth group trips and events, which usually was a refuge for my emotional safety, I would be asked that same dreaded question by teens from other churches. Some did not ask at all; they just assumed I was a girl. I heard the pronouns "her" and "she" in reference to me by adults who assumed I was a female with no malicious intent.

For the most part, the youth group was my safe haven, especially during those years where I found solace and was not subjected to massive amounts of bullying. However, I recall a youth leader who once told me to "go kiss a boy," implying I may be gay. The statement stung me so hard, and I wanted to cry—I was embarrassed. He only said it that one time, and although I do not remember the context, to this day I still remember the exact moment outside the church courtyard near the parking lot and the vicious smirk that spread across his face. I have no recollection of what I said or did to receive such a hurtful insult from a church leader, someone who was supposed to encourage, mentor, protect, and uplift me.

To be on the receiving end of bullying is crippling. I already felt ugly, insecure, and worthless, and for it to be reinforced by my peers damaged my soul beyond any physical lashings. It would take many years for me to overcome the mental effects that resulted from the bullying. I knew deep down, despite not fully realizing sexuality, that the taunts and jabs at my gender cemented that I was not normal. I was not a normal boy.

Adding to all the confusion about my gender, I could not deny my curiosity about the feminine that grabbed hold of me as a young boy. I loved to watch my mom do her hair and put on her makeup and was captivated by the transformation. Sometimes I watched Rebecca do her makeup as well, but she did not like her pesky little brother staring at her as she experimented with putting on eye shadow and lip gloss. There was something about hair, makeup, and jewelry that appealed to me. At an early age, and thanks to 80's fashion, I developed a fascination for over-the-top earrings and wanted my mom to wear the most dangly and extravagant earlobe decorations. I would be over the moon if I could go into her jewelry box and pick out the pair of earrings she would wear for the day. This curiosity I had for female beauty resulted in experimenting on my own. When I had the house to myself, I would go into my mom's closet and put on the tallest high heels she had and wear them around the house right after I snuck into Rebecca's caboodle, putting on some of her eyeliner and mascara. Eventually, I phased out of this, but it's something I never told anyone. I will never know the psychology behind why wearing makeup and heels intrigued me. My curiosities were harmless and innocent, however, I was brought up to believe that girls are girls and boys are boys, and boys don't wear makeup. Shame overcame me. I sometimes flirted with the idea of becoming a hairdresser when I grew up, but it was something I didn't even consider pursuing because I believed only gay men did that—and *that* was a sin.

I found a distraction back at school—his name was Tobias. He was more than a mere distraction; he was an infatuation. From the moment Tobias walked into my health class on that first day of 9th grade, I was smitten. He was popular, athletic, and "cute" as professed by the girls. Dressed in style of the 1994 era of baggy brightly colored jeans and oversized collared polos, he looked amazingly fashionable, even though his apparent tall and thin frame screamed for some much-needed tailoring. He had big, brown, puppy dog eyes, overly moussed, sandy blonde hair, and a couple of gold chains around his neck—now that's just typical Long Island right there.

I sat in the back of class and stared at Tobias every day, finding it almost pleasurable just to look at him. He had a girlfriend that kissed him in the doorway before the bell rang at the beginning of every class before they parted ways, and I didn't like her for absolutely no reason. Did I want him kissing me instead? He swaggered to his desk, high fiving and fist pounding other guys as he made his way to his chair, and I just watched him. How he walked, talked, and interacted with everyone around him. I couldn't take my eyes off him—I desperately craved his attention. *High five me Tobias!* One day I hoped that maybe, somehow, someday, there would be some sort of interaction between us.

Health class was my first introduction to sex outside of what I tried to capture on a scrambled HBO channel on late night cable. When the teacher asked us about sex, I paid extra special attention when Tobias answered or asked questions. I enjoyed hearing him talk about sex and had these indescribable yearnings toward him that were very real and involuntary. The teacher talked about sex as if we all knew what it was and how it worked, but I didn't have a clue—even as a high school freshman. I knew sex involved nudity and kissing but had no knowledge that a penis went into a vagina. I'm telling you; my life was the epitome of sheltered. Even though I was ignorant to the mechanics of sex, I knew one thing; I wanted to see Tobias naked—I wanted to see his penis. Whatever was supposed to happen after that, I had no idea. Oddly enough, I didn't even think of this desire as "gay," but plain curiosity.

When not in class, I went out of my way to pass Tobias in the hall, maybe "accidentally" bumping into him near his locker. Any interaction at this point, big or small, would suffice. This radical feeling of obsession for Tobias mirrored exactly how I felt toward Craig simultaneously, however the pull toward Tobias was much stronger (sorry Craig). I ached for closeness to Tobias and be his friend but wanted something beyond that, something more, and I couldn't decipher it. This infatuation with Tobias lasted all four years of high school. That's a cruelly long time to obsess over someone from afar—never receiving satisfaction from reciprocity. I did finally talk to him a couple of times throughout those years thanks to my job in the front office where I would see him coming and going from the principal's office (cue *Bad Boys* theme song). However, my interactions with him were nothing significant, to my dismay.

As I walked the hallways at school, passing by dozens of couples making out in the corridors or by their locker, I often wondered when I would eventually have a girlfriend. I admitted that I had these unexplained longings for Craig and Tobias, but I never grasped the sexuality of it at the time. What I understood is that as a boy I would grow up and marry a girl. I was informed enough about relationships that I was supposed to like girls because I was a boy and that was the "normal" thing to do. Thankfully by 10th grade, I officially found out what really happens during sex. Every Friday, my chemistry teacher would answer anonymous questions we wrote down and threw in a bowl. He picked up a question from the pile that asked how sperm fertilizes an egg. The question alone made me wince in bewilderment. As he began his explanation, his first sentence was, "when the hard penis goes into the vagina..." I didn't hear anything else he said after that, a bit traumatized by this new information, letting it sink in. *A penis goes into a vagina?* One thing I knew for sure in that moment—I had NO desire to do *that* with any vagina!

As with any decade, pop culture dictated the studs and babes that one should have hanging in their school locker. Jennifer Love Hewitt, Janet Jackson, and Alyssa Milano were the top female stars in the mid-90s that sent most boys' hormones into overdrive. Oh, but not I. I was pretty sure I would marry Kimmy Gibbler from *Full House* or Andrea Zuckerman from *Beverly Hills, 90210*.

To emulate bedrooms of teenage guys I saw on TV, which consisted of plastering pictures of hot girls on their walls, I scotch taped a poster of Andrea Zuckerman on the wall behind my bed to insinuate attraction to this girl. Yes, while most boys my age were popping boners for Brenda, Kelly, and Donna, I took to the plain-Jane: Andrea. However, I did enjoy watching Dylan McKay emerge from the beach soaking wet in his tight wet suit, and when he unzipped it to reveal his bare chest and flat abs, but I digress. I was drawn to Andrea because I related to her as an outcast. She did not ooze the sex appeal of the other three leading ladies but hanging her poster in my bedroom made me feel like a normal boy, even as it confirmed how different I was. The poster showed the actress Gabrielle Carteris smiling innocently on the beach in a white ruffled blouse that just barely went off the shoulders, glasses, and a hair bow—I know, super-hot! My conservative brother did not approve of the poster of Andrea hanging on the wall of our shared bedroom. I assumed, from his perspective, the poster incited an action of lust and indulging impure thoughts. He obviously was as clueless to my sexuality as I was. Trust me, brother, the only impure thoughts I entertained during that year was not finishing a bowl of spaghetti.

Growing up in the evangelical church, I was not allowed to listen to secular music. When Whitney Houston, Naughty by Nature, and Madonna topped the music charts, my cassette tape purchases were Christian singers like Amy Grant, Keith Green, and DC Talk. DC Talk broke barriers in the contemporary Christian world. Known as a "Christian rap group," they stood out from the faith-filled norm with their funky and rap styled Christ-centered lyrics. Rap music within the Christian circle was mostly considered an ungodly genre. DC Talk made their mark attracting thousands of Christian teenagers with their secular appearance but portrayed a genuine love for Jesus Christ. One of their songs, blatant in their message, spoke about waiting for sex until marriage. The song in question, "I Don't Want It" from their 1992 *Free at Last* album, clearly and explicitly sends the message that purity until marriage is what we, as *real* believers, should strive for. To even mention the word "sex" in a song clearly redefined Christian music as we knew it.

My mom was wary of letting me buy my first DC Talk album, but I convinced her that they were as Christian as they come. After reading the lyrics to *all* the songs, she gave me her blessing to have the album. The music engaged me like it did all the other Christian teens, but there was something that DC Talk inhabited that I would not realize until years later—sex appeal. All three members—Toby McKeehan, Kevin Max Smith, and Michael Tait—were attractive young males. I found myself drawn to Kevin. I loved looking at him, and when I watched DC Talk music videos over and over, my eyes would not stray from Kevin. With a long-haired, 90's curtained cut, ocean blue eyes, and a soulful singing voice, I succumbed to a deep trance engaging with him on the video. I loved the way he danced, dressed, and looked straight into the camera as if he could see directly into my soul. These feelings for Kevin were the same I had for Craig and Tobias, and it inspired confusion on my teenage soul. I needed an answer for this big question mark relating to the mystery of my longing for them. It was not until I was around 18 years old that I finally had an answer—thanks to a movie.

The 1994 movie *Serial Mom* is a dark comedy crime film starring Kathleen Turner. A character named Scotty, played by actor Justin Whalin, was an adorable, brown-eyed teenager with thick, long brown hair that swooped over his eyebrows and a pair of dimples that could charm the habit off a nun. There is a scene in the movie of Scotty watching porn, climbing into his bed, and getting under the covers. A sound effect and a hand motion convey to the viewer he is unzipping his pants. Scotty then proceeds to masturbate furiously, his hand seemingly hitting the top of the sheet up and down, up and down. Still, as a sexual late bloomer, masturbation was not something I practiced like other eighteen-year-old boys. Still, I suddenly became aware, without a shadow of a doubt, I was sexually interested in watching Scotty pleasure himself. In such an insignificant moment from a random movie, my eyes were suddenly open to the sexual attraction I had not only for Scotty but for males in general. *Does this mean I am gay? No!!! I can't be gay!*

Being gay is a sin! My sudden epiphany didn't stop me from rewinding and watching Scotty masturbate repeatedly. I had finally acknowledged, although reluctantly, my gravitational pull toward males was indeed a hardcore, overwhelming, eye-opening sexual attraction. I scrolled through my mental Rolodex for all the males I had ever found intriguing over the years. Vengeance Boy, Tobias, Luke Perry, Tony Danza, and *Serial Mom* Scotty were not some guys I had innocent admirations for. I desired them sexually, lustfully, and sinfully. *Nooooo!* Instantly, I felt perverted, dirty, and guilt-ridden.

I was terrified and confused. As a devout evangelical Christian, there were two things that I knew for certain about gay people. They *chose* to be gay, and they were certainly going to hell. *But I didn't choose this*, I thought. However, I convinced myself that I did, in fact, choose these attractions and I needed to *unchoose* them (I'm aware, "unchoose" is not a real word but go with me here) ...but I had no idea how to do that. Most importantly, I could not tell *anyone*. Passionate prayer and reading my Bible would help me get rid of this evil I had allowed in my heart. That night after watching *Serial Mom*, prominently aware of my homosexual feelings, I cried and cried. All I needed to do was to bow down in worship to Christ and surrender my sins at the cross of Jesus. I will fix this, and Jesus will help me.

Dear Jesus, please help me.

Chapter Four

THE RULES OF ATTRACTION

I SLID MY FINGER across the page of my teen study Bible, *"This is the confidence we have in approaching God: that if we ask anything according to his will, he hears us. And if we know that he hears us—whatever we ask—we know that we have what we asked of him."* 1 John 5:14-15. This verse became a promise that I put all my hope in. If I ask God to make me not attracted to other males, since homosexuality is not his will, then he would have to do what I asked him to do.

In those pivotal sexual awakening years following my *Serial Mom* revelation, I privately battled with this sexual attraction to men and didn't tell anyone. This "problem" was colossally bigger than God just being mad at me. I believed wholeheartedly this was a heaven or hell issue—if I indulged, then my only afterlife option is hell, living the rest of my life *weeping and gnashing of teeth* as it says in Matthew 13. I had not physically acted on any impulse but lived fully ashamed of my lustful thoughts. I prayed and cried daily for these feelings to go away.

> *Jesus, please make me like girls.*
> *I want to be obedient to your word.*
> *Make me more like you, Jesus.*
> *Forgive me of my sin of homosexuality.*

Despite the conflicting feelings I had for other men because of my Christian faith, life continued as normally as it could after high school. I worked at the local grocery store (shout out to Waldbaums!) while taking some liberal arts classes at Suffolk County Community College. Any free time I had was filled up with the youth group and my two closest friends—Ruth and Serena.

Ruth and I met at Smithtown Christian School and Serena was a member of the Smithtown youth group whom I met when she was dating one of my best friends at the time. We became our own little version of *Three's Company*, becoming mostly inseparable. We often hung out in Ruth's basement bedroom to watch movies, gossip, eat cheese doodles, and have sleepovers. I could imagine any other 19-year-old boy and his hormones would dream for this fantasy scenario hanging with two attractive girls on a bed in a basement, but the only things I was guilty of doing with Ruth and Serena was painting nails, dyeing hair, and watching *Romy and Michele's High School Reunion* non-stop.

There was something uniquely special about the time I spent together with Ruth and Serena. You know those times when you laugh so hard you can't breathe, and tears fill up your eyes? That was us. There was an intimacy that bonded us as friends, producing a strength of friendship that could not be broken. What made this friendship with Ruth and Serena so powerful and extraordinary for me is that I finally found my circle. After years of forcing myself to fit into a particular youth group clique, I finally had my own. The friendship between the three of us had its highs and lows as we laughed and cried together over the years, but what we shared was unmatched. Ruth and Serena were the first two people I ever told that I "struggled" with homosexuality. Neither of them judged me, disowned me, or made me feel different or diseased, which was comforting considering this was exactly how I saw myself. Our friendship was smooth, effortless, and relatively drama-free. They loved me unconditionally, and they didn't care about my "problem."

My sexuality started to become the focal point of my life once I defined it and tried to fight it off. College, work, friends, and family all took a backseat to my priorities as I learned how to navigate this sexual attraction to men. I thought about it every day and became anxious every time I noticed an attractive guy. I would have an impure thought about him, and my chest would feel like it was closing in on me.

Youth Group was only intended for teens up to 12th grade, so after graduation, I became a youth leader, yet harboring a deep dark secret that would most likely, or so I assumed, get me kicked out. The youth group was my everything, my world, and I could not risk anyone finding out that I was attracted to guys. I fully immersed myself in youth worker life. I continued to go on every mission trip, every summer camp, every winter retreat, and showed up at the auditorium early every Wednesday night and stayed late to run the snack table. By definition, a youth leader led the youth. I never really saw myself as a spiritual leader, but it came naturally to me as I befriended the new incoming teens year after year.

Regardless of my new status as a youth leader, I had no idea how to deal with my daily attraction to other guys. My integrity became significantly important to me, and I didn't want to have these attractions while being in Christian leadership. I did not want to be a fraud, but more so, I did not want to get caught. Unfortunately, my curiosity would win the battle against my integrity, and I would find myself an outlet to indulge my urgings.

America Online, or AOL, was the early pioneer of the internet that provided people with web browsing, instant messaging, and email. Oh, and chat rooms. At first, I joined a *General Hospital* chat room to talk with other fans about the show, but all my questions around sexuality ultimately led me to the gay chats.

Initially, the gay chat rooms were innocent—a bunch of faceless username handles chatting with each other in the groups from all over the country, but the intense desire to connect more tangibly with other men left me longing for it the more I didn't have it. Since the global chat rooms weren't doing it for me, I cautiously explored the local Long Island gay chat room. I was so scared of getting caught despite being completely anonymous. What if someone I knew was in there?

I started to converse with the other guys in the local chat frequently, despite my fear of public embarrassment if someone found out about me. Their profiles ranged from mild to wild, and as someone clueless of gay sex at this point in my life (or sex at all), I didn't know what half of the words, terms, and acronyms meant.

What is BDSM? What the heck does ASL mean? And what's with trying to find a guy to give them a facial—couldn't they just make an appointment with an esthetician?

The fear that I would come across someone I knew in those chat rooms was soon to be justified. I struck up a conversation with a guy who was as fearful of someone finding him out as well. After chatting with him for several days, we both found out that we attended the same school and not public school—Smithtown Christian School! *Wow! Someone like me who is a Christian and has these feelings?* I felt comforted in my distress. Eventually, after weeks of chatting, we became comfortable enough to disclose our identities; however, fear of consequence or how closely I knew this person loomed. When he confessed his real name to me, I exhaled in relief. I knew of him, and he knew of me, but we never engaged with one another during our SCS years, mostly because he was several years older than me. We knew mutual people, but I kept his secret and he kept mine. He and I regularly chatted about our mutual homosexual struggle as Christian kids but never met in person. I wanted to meet with him, but he succumbed to his guilt and told me he was no longer frequenting the chat room, and sadly, we lost contact. I ached for my chats with him because he could relate to navigating these sinful gay feelings. As short as our virtual time together was, it helped me champion through the struggle a little bit more.

I will often say throughout my journey that I *struggled* with homosexuality. Since the Christian religion recognizes it as a sin, the term "struggle" is a fitting word to define the fight within because it's something you *don't* want. Merriam-Webster defines struggle as making "strenuous or violent efforts in the face of difficulties or opposition." My sexuality was indeed a strenuous fight, a fight to the death, even though I was losing the fight every single day.

My curiosity for male-on-male intimacy increased daily, and since Showtime late night was not cutting it with their lack of male nudity, I discovered the world of gay pornography. The family computer sat in the corner of our dining room in a small nook right before the kitchen entrance. Living with four other people meant privacy did not exist. My internet usage intensified late at night as the rest of the family retired to their bedrooms. Once my parents' bedroom door closed for the evening, like clockwork, I beelined to the computer and clicked my way to dial-up Darren, a much older man from Massapequa, Long Island. Our conversations were usually sexually charged, and our communication increasingly piqued my interest in gay sex. The idea of meeting Darren face-to-face frightened me too much to act on it, so to scratch the itch, I began to peruse the internet for gay porn. At first, the movies were more educational than arousing. The grunting, cursing, and orgasming amongst sweaty male bodies terrified and intrigued me. Unlike late night Showtime, there were no bed sheets or a women's naked body perfectly arranged to block the visual of the male genitalia—with gay porn absolutely nothing was left to the imagination.

I made a habit of saving short video clips and placed them in a folder within a folder within another folder somewhere in the depths of the computer's hard drive, assuming I hid them well enough that no one could ever find them.

Nope.

Of all people, my mom found them. She was loving and concerned in her approach, but I was filled with embarrassment and shame. When she came into my room to talk, I had no idea what was coming; she caught me completely off-guard. The moment she said, "I found something on the computer," my stomach sank. I knew instantly I was in deep shit.

In attempt to do damage control, I made up a pitiful lie about how the movie clips were spam that I accidentally opened. She asked to pray for me, and the issue was dropped until it happened again only a few weeks later because I obviously didn't learn my lesson the first go-round. This time, mom came into my room and expressed her disgust and disappointment. The fear in her eyes told me this was not about the porn in and of itself as it was about it being *gay* porn. No Christian parent wants to face the gruesome truth that their child may be homosexual. They would have to admit their child would go to hell. Again, I denied it, saying the porn was not mine, and that it was some sort of spam. We never spoke about it again, but this time the fear of getting caught a third time stuck and dissuaded me from downloading any more video clips on the family computer. *What the hell was I thinking?*

Life outside the internet and AOL chat rooms was bleak. I sluggishly made my way through college, changing my major several times while working my way up the grocery store ladder from cashier to customer service to bookkeeper, a job I quite enjoyed. When not hanging with Ruth and Serena, my time remained active in the youth group, mentoring the lives of Long Island teens while chatting with men in the gay AOL chat rooms, mostly with Darren. After chatting with Darren for several weeks, he told me he wanted to meet in person. This notion thrilled me as much as it frightened me. Darren, thirty-one years old and living alone, portrayed himself as a kind and friendly man but took advantage of my naivety. I fell hard for his grooming—something I recognized in retrospect. Chatting with Darren was effortless and exciting despite grappling with the guilt of indulging the homosexuality. Darren assured me that he would take care of me, knowing it would be my first time.

We chatted on the phone briefly to discuss the details, which was the first time we spoke verbally. His gentle masculine voice only intrigued me more to see him face-to-face. Darren suggested we meet at a 7-Eleven instead of asking me to his house, which I'm sure was for his own comfort as much as mine.

My hands gripped the steering wheel tightly as I drove down Sunrise Highway, but an irresistible curiosity surpassed any thought that would dissuade me from turning my car around. I never saw a picture of him, nor did he see mine. This was not the current days of gay hook up culture where meeting a fling without a pic would be unheard of.

What am I doing? I thought as I drove, heart racing and body trembling. The fear of hell and spiritual punishment for indulging in this sin did not take me out of the equation as much as I thought it would.

I arrived at the 7-Eleven and pulled up in a parking spot. What if he doesn't show up? *Well, at least I can go get a Slurpee.* Not too long after I arrived, a very attractive man with a Yankees baseball cap pulled up next to me, rolled down his window, and asked, "Aaron?"

Instantly, I was relieved. He looked exactly how he described himself, and my relief rested upon how extremely handsome he appeared. He asked me if I would still like to go to his house, barely finishing the last syllable before *yes* came out of my mouth. Whether it was sheer nerves that shuddered through my veins, an inquisitive lust, or fear of the unknown, I followed Darren down the street to his house eagerly and nervously. He offered me some water as I sat down on his living room couch, my heart pounding out of my chest. The questions I pondered only perpetuated more anguish.

What the hell am I doing in this strange man's house?
What is going to happen?
Am I going to lose my virginity?
Can a man lose his virginity to another man?
What if he poisoned the water he gave me?
Is that door over there to his basement where he will stash my body?
Will I get to see his penis?

The sinful nature of the situation only exacerbated my concerns, but my curiosities and sexual yearnings urged me otherwise. Excitement and apprehension took turns canceling each other out as we sat on the couch and engaged in mundane conversation about life. I brought up that it was wrong for me to have sexual encounters with other men because it was against God and the Bible. With no obvious consideration to my little sermon, he made the first move and started fondling me. At that moment, I no longer thought about guilt or God. Suffice it to say, I experienced oral sex and seeing a man's extremely large erect penis in person for the first time at nineteen years old.

I met Darren consistently after that evening. We became "hookup buddies," so driving to Massapequa once or twice a week became routine. I craved him relentlessly, waiting for him to pop up on AOL instant messenger, hoping he would be available for me to come over. Without cell phones, instant messenger was our only way to make plans as I was not comfortable giving him my household landline. He never turned down my offer to come over. It was as if he waited for me as eagerly as I waited for him. Our meetings were simple, easy, and relaxing, and no matter how sinful I believed our relationship was, I enjoyed being with him.

During one of our "hang outs," he warned me before we "got down to business" that he expected his cable guy at some point during the day but assured me that they most likely would not arrive until later. As fate would have it, while his pants were down and erection fully in my mouth, a loud knock on the door startled me enough where I almost bit off his tip. He panicked a bit, led me to a bedroom, and apologetically asked me to wait in the closet. *The closet?*

I reluctantly walked into the small closet as Darren left the room to let the cable guy in. I heard them converse, going in and out of the bedroom while I peeked through the slats that covered the closet door. After fifteen minutes or so passed by, he rescued me from the closet, apologizing profusely. I was slightly annoyed and ready to go home until he flashed his perfect smile and placed my hand on his crotch that was somehow still decently firm despite the disturbance. It did not take much for me to ignore being stuffed in a closet like a pile of dirty clothes, and so we proceeded to finish where we left off.

As much as I enjoyed my meetings with Darren, I became brave enough to meet up with other guys for variety. The sexual encounters with all these guys were mostly limited to oral sex. I never wanted to kiss any of them because I swore to myself, and to God, that my first kiss was to be with a girl. I firmly believed this whole "hooking up with guys" thing was a phase that would eventually fade away, and I would be with a woman for the rest of my life. I wanted my virgin lips to remain "pure" for this hypothetical girl.

My plans to save my first game of tonsil hockey for a girl were derailed when I met Shawn. Shawn intrigued me in a much more different way than Darren. Encounters with Darren were straightforward and predictably routine, but Shawn opened me up to another realm of gay sex I never experienced. Shawn and I exchanged pictures before meeting, and to be honest, he was not as attractive as Darren. Still, his luminous emerald eyes and curly mop of hair intrigued me enough to meet in person. The more I met with guys from the chatrooms, the easier it was for me to let my guard down and enter their house without so much a thought that an ax murderer could be on the other side of their front door.

As Shawn opened the door to my soft knock, I was relieved to find that he was cuter than his digital pictures had led me to believe. We sat on his couch, and as our small talk gradually came to an obvious ending, things started to get intimate, with Shawn making the first move by removing his pants. He leaned in for a kiss, but I jumped back as if his lips had been marked with the kiss of death. I told him not to kiss me as I was saving my first kiss to be with a girl. Shawn looked at me like I had three heads and the word "delusional" tattooed across my forehead. Here I was, holding his erect penis in my hand yet telling him I am saving my first kiss to be with a girl. Although I had been serious about him respecting my request, I did not fight Shawn off when he ignored my plea and stuck his tongue in my mouth anyway.

Well, there goes that.

The moment was everything I hoped for, besides that whole girl part. My body seized and then relaxed as we continued to kiss, delighted that he disregarded my wishes because, man oh man, how I did love kissing him.

I continued to see Shawn several more times, but it never turned into anything serious, mostly because I wouldn't let it. There was another guy, Fred, that I also met up with occasionally at his home in nearby Central Islip who desired more from me beyond the casual hookup. Fred and I didn't only have sex. We talked and bonded, becoming friends—something I truly admired about our relationship. After a month or so of meeting, he asked to be my boyfriend.

His boyfriend??

Well, that was out of the question. It was one thing that I had already booked my reservation in hell by indulging in these secret sexual encounters with guys, but to be linked romantically was not something that could ever happen, nor was it something I wanted. I admitted to spending the better part of the last year having sex with guys, but I vowed that I would marry a girl, have kids, a white picket fence, and the whole shebang. I told Fred that I could not be his boyfriend and cut ties with him quickly, which was a shame because even though I enjoyed my "no strings" hookups with Darren and Shawn, I developed a very special and intimate relationship with Fred. I missed him terribly after I cut him out of my life. But my religion dictated whom I could love, and he, unfortunately, became the first casualty of the war between my sexuality and Christianity.

Every day I found myself feeling like Michelle in the *Full House* episode when Uncle Jesse asked her to not touch his music equipment. Remember that episode? Michelle is left alone in the room, struggling with the forces of good and evil. "Good"

Michelle, in an angelic white dress and floral crown, tells human Michelle good girls always follow the rules. "Bad" Michelle, dressed in black leather and a skull cap, tempts human Michelle, telling her breaking the rules is fine if you don't get caught. In an adorable moment that you can only get away with in a 90's sitcom, "good" Michelle and "bad" Michelle get into a shouting match with each other, confusing human Michelle, who didn't know which side she should listen to. In a moment of impulsiveness, human Michelle gives in to "bad" Michelle, plays with Uncle Jesse's equipment, gets caught, punished, and by the end of the 30 minutes, she and Uncle Jesse are friends again, and all's right with the world.

Unfortunately, my predicament was not wrapped up in thirty minutes while leaning on Uncle Jesse for comfort, but I will happily let John Stamos console me any time he wants. The spiritual side of me that passionately loved Jesus and wanted to obey him told me to "stay away from the gay chat rooms. It's sinful and wrong!" The devilish side told me, "Go ahead, meet guys, have fun, be yourself." Ultimately, I gave into "bad Aaron" often and occupied my free time with meeting various guys, all the while an active youth leader in the youth group. Let it be known that *all* my encounters were with guys of legal age who did not attend the church.

I often thought about how the youth group kids, especially the boys, would have reacted if they knew I hooked up with guys while giving them advice to keep pure and stay on track spiritually with God.

"Are you not a Christian anymore?"
"You aren't attracted to me, are you?"
"I don't understand."
"Two guys doing it is gross."

Hypocrisy made a home in my heart, and this poison that ate away my soul made me physically sick at times. I felt ashamed, guilty, and dirty. However, no matter how disgusted with myself I became, the emotions didn't prevent me from making those trips to Massapequa.

In early 2000, I dropped out of college and got a second job along with the grocery store working as a bank teller. My life lacked direction and dealing with my sexuality consumed much more of my focus than figuring out what I wanted to be "when I grew up," despite already hitting the very grown-up age of twenty-one. My life, as much as I enjoyed so many aspects of it, needed a change. The weight of my secret became too much for me to carry. The guilt, the shame, the lying, the fear of getting caught; it was unbearable. I no longer wanted to live a stressful double life, and I wanted to attain some healing and breakthrough. My frantic prayers for these homosexual feelings to go away were not getting answered, so I figured I needed to dig deeper and do something a bit radical to show God that I was serious about my relationship with him, and my healing.

Chapter Five

BUBBLE BOY

As I approached the baggage claim, my eyes locked on the strapping blue-eyed blonde Nordic stud holding a piece of paper with my name on it. Kristoffer introduced himself, his sexy Norwegian accent attracting me more to him than I wanted it to. We made small talk at the carousel waiting for my luggage to make its rounds, eventually hitting the road heading north on the 405 freeway to the San Fernando Valley of Los Angeles.

I hopped in the passenger side of Kristoffer's car, still coming to terms with the decision that I made a month earlier to leave my life on Long Island behind and come to California to join YWAM, known as *Youth with a Mission*, a Christian missionary organization. I knew of YWAM through my church, as many of my friends were affiliated with it.

The mission of YWAM is simple: *"To know God and make him known."*[1] The mission's purpose is to bring the gospel of Jesus to people who do not have a relationship with him. The organization started back in 1960 to get youth involved in mission work and now has expanded to 180 countries with more than 1,100 base locations. Anyone interested in joining YWAM must attend a DTS (Discipleship Training School). The structure of a DTS is a three-month "lecture phase" where students sit in lectures taught by seasoned YWAMers (the official term for all students and veterans) and guest speakers on different topics to prepare the class for the two-month "outreach phase" where students go to another country to do mission work, putting all the learning into practice.

For me, though, YWAM was an escape from the homosexual struggle, as if same-sex attraction was geographical, right?! I vowed that aspect of my life would be forgotten and hoped to meet and marry a cute girl from YWAM. God was going to heal me. *I knew it!*

We arrived at the Lake View Terrace YWAM campus close to 10:00 PM. Kristoffer escorted me to the men's dorm, which resembled a large trailer of sorts. My flight arrived later than all the others, so I missed the ice-breaking events where everyone already had the opportunity to meet each other. As I entered the trailer, with Kristoffer carrying my luggage behind me, I instantly got ambushed by a bunch of shirtless dudes in their boxer shorts excitedly introducing themselves to me. I thought to myself—*this isn't starting out well for de-programming myself of gay attractions, and which of these hotties is my roommate?*

Within the first few weeks I became acclimated to living on the YWAM base, involving myself into the curriculum and making treasured friendships. Despite attempting to actively halt my attraction toward the guys, my DTS experience overall was probably one of the greatest times of my life. The YWAM base became home to me. I adored all the people I met and the experience of getting to know God better through the friendships I made.

I missed life on Long Island, but I did not miss sneaking around and meeting up with anonymous guys nor the shame that accompanied those meetings. This YWAM bubble kept me pure...at least physically. My homosexual thoughts pervaded my consciousness day and night. Two guys had my attention: Devon, an athletic and stunningly beautiful tall drink of Irish water with piercing grey eyes that complemented his sexy Dublin brogue, and Nate, the "metrosexual," with bright blue eyes and blonde-tipped hair that he finessed to the perfect style every day. They both possessed a confident charm and erotic appeal, that had me at X-rated thoughts. With prayers and suppression, I did my best to keep my imagination of these guys to a PG rating as I interacted with them daily.

As I was growing up, I heard 2 Corinthians 10:5 referenced countless times when referring to lust. *"We demolish arguments and every pretension that sets itself up against the knowledge of God, and we take captive every thought to make it obedient to Christ."* Essentially, taking a thought captive is to destroy the thought in your mind before it enters your heart. It took very intentional focus and hard work, and when I failed, I retreated to the chapel in the back of campus so I could pray, be alone, and confess my sins to God.

Regardless of my wandering eye toward the attractive guys around the YWAM campus, my intentions to rid myself of homosexuality were honest and real. I loved God *so* much and desperately needed to make him proud of me through my obedience. James 5:16 reads, *"Therefore confess your sins to each other and pray for each other so that you may be healed. The prayer of a righteous person is powerful and effective."* My belief in the Bible was the core foundation as a follower of Christ, so if the Bible said I needed to confess to be healed, then gosh darn it, I was going to do it! Besides, the burden became too heavy to carry on my own, and I needed to tell someone—to share my burden as per Galatians 6:2, *"Carry each other's burdens, and in this way, you will fulfill the law of Christ."*

I decided to confess to Kirk, the head leader of the DTS. The reality to tell Kirk shook my nerves something fierce. I expected the worst yet hoped for the best. Was he going to kick me out of DTS? Would he transfer me out of the guys' dorm and give me my own trailer? Would he perform an exorcism and bind the devil out of me? So many thoughts ran through my head, and I figured that if I told him real fast, like ripping off a Band-Aid, the agony of confessing wouldn't be too much to bear.

We met privately and chatted on surface topics until he finally asked why I intentionally pursued a meeting with him. I sputtered fragments, fighting to get the words out that I had same-sex attractions. When I finally did, I braced myself for his response. To my surprise, he responded in love, acceptance, and grace. I should have known better than to be nervous, because Kirk embodied a character rooted in kindness. Relieved, I felt the heaviness of this sinful burden that spiritually asphyxiated me lift instantly.

The thoughts inside me danced around in an excited freedom. *Well, this is it, God. I confessed! Bring on those female attractions now! Will I be a boob or an ass guy?* God had to be true to his word, right? Although I'm sure God didn't need to be reminded of his promises, it couldn't hurt to speed up the process. However, Kirk was not quite done with our conversation. Nothing could have prepared me for what was about to come out of his mouth. As he spoke about the power of confession and how it breaks strongholds in our lives, I could never have anticipated where he was going with this train of thought after I had confessed not even two minutes ago. What else is left to do? Then he said,

"Aaron, I want you to confess this to the entire DTS."

Huh?? What?? Come again?

Extremely shocked and put on the spot, I was unable to speak. Kirk continued with why he believed a public confession would be a good idea, but my mind went blank, and all I heard was noise clamoring from his mouth, like the teacher from the *Peanuts* cartoon.

"Whah waa whaa wa wwaa wha wha—"

This guy is crazy; I am not telling anyone else, I silently proclaimed. I then told Kirk that I would think about it, but internally I had already made my decision. Confessing to the entire DTS class was not only unnecessary but not going to happen. Despite the impossible challenge that Kirk left me with, I walked away from that meeting in high spirits, believing all this was finally over and that my homosexual attractions would dissolve since I had confessed. Nobody else needed to know.

About a week after my meeting with Kirk, the DTS school gathered one Tuesday evening in our meeting hall for what was called "Family Time." Family Time was an opportunity for the DTS students to tell their testimony or life story and pretty much anything they wanted to share about their past.

The day was October 10, 2000. All DTS staff and students crammed into our meeting space in a huge circle. There were 40 students in the DTS so that smaller groups of friends naturally formed here and there. One of my peers, John, held the mic in hand, trembling as he began to speak. John, a blond-haired, blue-eyed, athletic guy from Japan, and I never really bonded or even talked that much up to this night. Now that I had become familiar with the global culture of YWAM, to meet a white person who could speak, read, and write Japanese did not surprise me.

Tension filled the room as his voice trembled with his opening words. There was so much leading up to his confession; it became apparent he could have been stalling. I leaned in a little closer; the more he spoke, the more I related to what he said. I had an inkling of what he was about to confess the second he said, "This is something I have only told two other people."

In my case, this was my same truth, as I had only told Ruth and Serena. After a few more stumbling sentences about embarrassment, secrecy, and shame, he finally said it:

"I struggle with homosexuality."

Doctors say when a human goes into shock, they suffer from a weak pulse, nausea, clammy skin, and confusion, among other things. In that one moment, I suffered from all those symptoms, almost unaware of where I was. I lost my grip on reality and convinced myself it was impossible that I heard what I heard. Stunned and practically in a catatonic state, I stared at John as he continued to speak for what seemed to be an eternity but was not much more than sixty seconds.

When I snapped out of it and reality set in again, Kirk took the microphone and asked for only the guys to surround and lay hands on John in prayer. As all the guys flocked around this defeated and confused kid, I did the opposite and ran out of the room. With seemingly no control over my emotions, I dashed outside of the meeting room, collapsed to my knees, and cried.

My sorrow had nothing to do with John directly, but I was confused, and I cried aloud to God, *"I don't understand God. I'm the only one who struggles with this. I'm the only one. I'm the only one."*

After nearly a year of walking through this struggle alone I took it as my own personal cross to bear. I don't know how to explain it even to this day, but I found it unlikely and impossible that other guys shared in this struggle. My tears dripped down, smacking the cold concrete while shame immobilized my body. My knees buried painfully into the cement ground, ripping off layers of skin, but the emotional pain hurt much more harshly. I never felt so broken.

What do I do now?

Once I composed myself, I hesitantly went back into the meeting hall where the guys were still surrounding John in prayer. I stood in the far back, pacing back and forth, my heart beating out of my chest. At that moment, I had an overwhelming need to confess as well. A spontaneous force that I could not control had me walking up to the front and taking the microphone from Kirk.

The room became quiet as I sat down in the front; everyone looking at me, waiting for me to speak. I uttered into the microphone, through fear, trepidation, and unmanageable quivering, similar words that John used when he confessed. "I also struggle with homosexuality". No sooner had the words vibrated from the speakers that my arm felt weak. I dropped the microphone and wept in front of my entire DTS class.

In a few short seconds, someone came over to me and clenched me tightly, the strongest yet most comforting hug I ever received in my entire life. It was John. I drenched his shirt with my tears as the rest of the students and staff gathered around us, praying against the devil and his control over my life. In that moment, an unmistakable bond formed between John and me as we embraced and sobbed in each other's shoulders. As the prayer died down, we began to worship Jesus together as a unified family, ending the night singing, "Did You Hear the Mountains Tremble," a popular worship song by the band Delirious?.

That was an evening I will remember for the rest of my life. I felt free. I believed I received a special touch from God that night, and it only gave me more hope that I conquered my homosexual sin. My secret was exposed. Confession took place, and now God could start healing away the gayness within me.

That night brought my passion and love for Jesus to another level. I was on a spiritual high. I tested my attractions and purposely stared at Devon, the hot Irish dude, curious to see if my hormones responded. Did I still think he was hot? Yes, the natural desire to rip off his clothes and have my way with him still existed, but my faith rested believing that healing would be slow and gradual.

After the three-month lecture phase ended, we had to choose between South Africa, China, Nepal, and India for where we would do our global outreach. I chose South Africa and anxiously awaited to see which of the other guys chose that country as well. I predicted there would be some sexual anxiety if any of the guys I was attracted to were also going to South Africa—but hey, if hot Irish Devon wanted to strip down at night because of the African heat, why would I stop him? I really wanted John to be on my team because we developed a close connection with each other since the night of our confession—but to no avail; he chose China. Hot Irish guy Devon decided on Nepal, which admittedly bummed me out. However, Nate, the cute metrosexual, was going to South Africa. At least I had one piece of eye candy for the next two months!

Experiencing South Africa amazed me, and the ministry we accomplished fulfilled me spiritually. During the two months there, I had many opportunities to speak at churches and tent revivals full of people about how God healed me of homosexuality. It was quite the mindfuck to profess all this homosexual healing was taking place in my life and then go back to the hostel and wait for Nate to take his shirt off so I could stare.

Despite that my attraction to men were still very much present, I ignored it for the sake of preaching my story, hoping that other people who struggled with this sin could be set free. I shared my story of transformation, using the biblical book of Esther as an example, paralleling my life to hers. God used Esther to save her Jewish people from death, and God will use me to save my people, the ones struggling with same-sex attractions, so they can submit their lives over to God and live a life of heterosexuality. It felt damn good to share my story, knowing God had his hand on my life, and he used my testimony to reach out to people, whether they struggled with homosexuality or not. I was an instrument of God, and I felt empowered to have a purpose, a voice, and freedom like I was *king of the world*—minus a sinking ship and Kate Winslet. Soon enough, it would be time to leave South Africa and return to Los Angeles.

I kept in touch with John while he was in China thanks to internet cafés, the only opportunity in early 2000s to read and send emails. John planned to attend Biola University immediately after he returned from China. I never heard of Biola, a private Christian University in Southern California, until that time. I wanted to stay close to John, mainly because of our shared struggle of homosexuality. We related to each other, supported each other, and had someone to talk to who understood the complexities of homosexuality and how it conflicted with Christianity. Above any other reason, my friendship with John was the motivating factor to stay in Los Angeles and not return to New York.

After being separated from each other for two months, all four teams gathered again for one more week after returning from our respective countries, catching up, swapping stories, and giving testimonies of what God had done. The last night of that week, there would be a graduation ceremony that would summarize the last five months of our time at DTS. Friends, family, and financial supporters would be able to experience our trip through slideshows and personal stories by team members. I approached my staff leader volunteering to speak at the graduation.

The pride in my alleged redemption from homosexuality consumed me, and I wanted to share it with the world. I believed with every fiber of my being and soul that I was healed on YWAM confession night despite the unwavering physical attraction I still had for Devon, Nate, and other guys during those months in YWAM, and I could not shake this imaginary certainty that my attraction to men had depleted from my system.

When I called my mom to let her know I landed safely back in the states, she exuberantly broke the news that she was coming to Los Angeles for the graduation. She had booked a trip to Sedona, Arizona, to visit my Uncle Chris, her brother, who recently moved out west from Long Island. Coincidentally, she would be there during the week of my graduation, so she and my Aunt Jackie would make the seven-hour drive.

What do you mean you are coming to my graduation?

I wanted to tell her not to come without diminishing her excitement. I had not seen her in five months and while I wanted so badly to hug her, I could not bear the discomfort of having her in the audience to hear my homosexuality freedom testimony. I knew deep down my mom would be proud and beam with joy to hear it, but I could not get past the potential awkwardness that only I was creating. She already knew that I had an issue with this "sin" since discovering the porn on the computer. However, that fact did not ease my stress, mainly because we never talked about it since. I planned to speak to her briefly before the ceremony to prepare her for when I took the stage and microphone.

On graduation night, I only had a few minutes before starting time to debrief my mom quickly of my testimony when she arrived. I gave her the CliffsNotes version of what God had done in my life at YWAM. She looked deeply into my eyes with pure love, the only way my mom knows how, hugged me tight, and said, "Aaron, I always knew you struggled with this."

Gee, Mom, thanks.

All the frantic worry that I created due to my mom's presence at my graduation proved unnecessary. I proudly walked that stage and told my story of how God healed me from homosexuality and of my newfound mission to minister to gay people. I shared my vow to show them the love of Jesus and that hope and freedom within their sexuality was possible. With the conclusion of the ceremony, my DTS came to an end.

After a quick three-week trip back to Long Island to prepare more fundraising letters and visit family and friends, I packed up my Hyundai to drive back to Los Angeles to attend a secondary YWAM school called School of Ministry Development (SOMD). I had lost contact with Darren by this point, and amazingly, I had no temptation in those three weeks to return to the AOL gay chats. I took it as another sign, or so I thought, that God had begun his work to heal me of all homosexual tendencies.

If I had to be honest, the hankering to attend the SOMD rested on the fact that I had no other options. If I chose to stay on Long Island, I knew I would get caught up in the same monotonous routine I was in before DTS. I missed my family and friends terribly, but there was nowhere I wanted to be more than the YWAM base, my new safe place, and stay close to John, who was about forty-five minutes away at Biola University—or two hours depending on Los Angeles traffic (The struggle was real).

Going back to college was always the eventual plan, but I figured I would go to Hofstra or Dowling in New York and stay close to home. However, I loved the idea of attending a Christian college to keep me accountable in my homosexual struggle. I applied to Biola for the upcoming fall semester. Truth be told, I would not have considered Biola if John was not going there, as my emotional attachment to him formed rapidly. During any free time from SOMD, I visited John at Biola. I became friends with his friends, namely two girls named Megan and Anna, and got a feel for the university since I would hope to start there that upcoming August.

During my time in SOMD, my thoughts focused on Christ, and I stayed obedient to his Word. However, just because I ignored my attraction to other men didn't mean that they ceased to exist. They were *very* much present, which I realized when I saw Devon or Nate walking around campus. Devon played soccer nearly every day on the field and he looked damn cute in those short soccer shorts. I plopped myself on the sidelines and watched in a lustful trance, dreaming of being intimate with him. Nate's charisma melted me just as intensely as his bright blue eyes throughout the day—and much more enjoyable in the evenings when he would often walk around shirtless. I knew deep down this war against my homosexuality was a losing battle, but with that fear of hell always in the forefront of my mind, it never occurred to me to give up trying to fight against it. Even for a hot minute, I convinced myself I had a crush on a female student, Shannon.

Shannon and I became fast friends and hung out all the time, to the point where we were inseparable. I was under this self-deception that I was legitimately attracted to her so much that I fantasized marrying her—if only to feel normal. I wanted to be attracted to her so I could claim God truly healed me. I loved Shannon, and our friendship was uniquely special. I cherished every moment of laughter and time spent together during our three months at SOMD, but no matter how close we were, the sexual attraction we needed to sustain a relationship did not exist, and it bummed me out that I could not formulate sexual feelings toward her and pursue something more.

In the spring of 2001, I graduated from my second YWAM school. I headed back to Long Island for the summer before returning to attend Biola. Years later, I look back on my short nine months in YWAM and can sincerely say it was the best year of my life. The experiences I had there, and the friendships and self-awareness I developed, changed my life. My time in the YWAM bubble also filled me with so much hope that I could live life as a straight man and no longer be burdened with homosexual desires. But as with all bubbles – they eventually burst.

Chapter Six

THE GODFATHER

FINALLY, BEING FREE FROM the devil's grip of homosexuality, and radiating from the "YWAM high," I waved goodbye to Long Island and headed to Biola. I didn't hook up with other guys that summer and basked in my obedience to God.

I was healed!

To be clear, my gauge of healing was measured by how long I abstained from sexual encounters and *not* if the attraction to other men decreased. This created a flawed reality that convinced me I was not gay anymore because my behavior was not exhibiting it. But I had to live with my thoughts. My very gay thoughts. The thoughts in which I was having sex with Johnny Depp every day since I saw *Chocolat*. I mean, did you see how he licks his fingers after eating the chocolate Juliette Binoche gave him? Yea, I wanted to be those fingers.

But I digress. I remained vigilant in my defense of God's ultimate healing. I spent most of the three-day drive remembering and processing the last nine months of YWAM and anticipated the huge things that God had in store for me at college. I hoped that living in another Christian bubble, I could be supported and strengthened in my walk with God and that this would help me with my continued healing.

Above all, I could not bear the thought of separating from the only friend who truly understood my struggle—John. I gave no consideration of the pricey private university tuition. The Financial Aid Office staff quickly became my new best friends, and Citibank student loans piled up every semester. I *had* to be at Biola, and nothing would derail that plan.

I arrived at Stewart Hall to inspect my three-bed dorm room which was situated in a quad of four rooms with a shared bathroom. John and I shared the dorm with a third roommate, Louis, who rarely left the room and played video games all day. I made my rounds to introduce myself to the other guys, pinpointing who was hot enough for a peek in the bathroom when they showered.

My emotional dependency on John started to become out of control. I always had this fierce yearning to talk with him. Since we both struggled with the same sexual sin, I created this irrational need to be constantly communicating with him because I desperately needed someone to relate to. Even back when I was living at the YWAM base, we would stay up late on AOL messenger chats almost every night, talking about life, struggles, school, and more. I found peace in the validation I received from John, and it became addictive. Even after I moved onto campus and we became roommates, I would retreat unreasonably to assumptions that he was mad at me if we did not have a chance to connect, with no basis for such agonizing. I needed to know everything John was doing and who he was with. If he had any sexual temptations, I had to know so I could support him, pray for him, and keep him accountable. This deep sense of control I deemed necessary to have over him eventually consumed me to the point where I became so anxious, I could not focus on school. I did not have a name for it at the time, but this *emotional dependence* on John took an uncontrollable force over me.

The beginning of the first semester did prove to be somewhat challenging regarding John and I being roommates, which tested our friendship. First off, there were some obstacles to overcome with my mom and uncle who disapproved of John and me living together as roommates because we both struggled with homosexuality.

My Uncle Chris was a devout Christian like my mother, and he and I had a pretty close relationship. Not only was he my uncle, but he was also my godfather, which made my relationship with him a little more unique. Growing up, it was understood he had a drug dependency problem. I never fully grasped what that consisted of as a young kid but knew it was not acceptable. Eventually, Uncle Chris became a Christian, cleaned up his act, and stayed sober.

When driving through Arizona on my way to Biola, I made a pit stop at Uncle Chris's and Aunt Beth's. Before I left for Biola, I chatted with him about a significant shortage of tuition money I owed for that first semester and asked him for a loan. When I arrived, we sat down to chat, and I updated him on my life, my experience in YWAM, and my plans with Biola. He generously gave me the remainder of my tuition as a gift and not as a loan, which blessed me beyond words.

Shortly after YWAM, I sent a letter to Uncle Chris and Aunt Beth detailing my experiences there, my struggle with homosexuality, and how God healed me. I mentioned in the letter how another guy who also struggled with homosexuality inspired me to confess my secret. Uncle Chris had no idea that this guy in question happened to be my roommate John. I did not intentionally hide this information, nor saw it necessary to volunteer it. Looking back, I had nothing to hide. My friendship with John, despite what everyone may have thought, was 100% platonic. The appearance of evil would be enough for me to know that Uncle Chris would never approve of our roommate situation, knowing that I was living with a guy who struggled with the same sin. When Uncle Chris, my mother, and John's father, a missionary himself, all found out that we were living together, all hell broke loose.

John and I were both discouraged by the response over our choice to be roommates. The frustration mounted as we had to defend our friendship and convince everyone we were not sexually involved. On the contrary, we were keeping each other accountable in our temptations to act out in any way that could defile ourselves and bring shame to the name of God. The goal was to tell each other if we were tempted to hook up with a guy or watch gay porn, so we could pray for each other. Sometimes the accountability was as simple as "checking in" and asking each other "How are you doing?" in the event we weren't initiating our own confessions. Our motives were pure. The overreaction baffled us, and no matter what we said, it seemed evident that no one believed our story. Even the presence of our third roommate Louis did not seem to diminish what everyone assumed: John and I were lovers and were "living together" in our dorm room.

I took a deep breath before answering the phone to Uncle Chris's incoming call. The ringing threw me into a slight panic, and dread propelled the heartbeat pumping forcibly in my chest. As expected, Uncle Chris denounced us living together. Yet, I did my best to maintain my composure, explicitly telling him that my friendship with John did not cross any lines of sexual nature or impropriety, and that we were friends upholding God's truth and keeping each other accountable.

Uncle Chris retorted, "Aaron, I'm a recovering drug addict. I wouldn't live with another drug addict; you are asking for trouble."

Was he implying that John and I will become lovers? His ignorant comment felt like a knife to my stomach. Uncle Chris then said, in not so many words, that he regretted giving me tuition money believing now he paid for me to live with my boyfriend. These words hurt. I thought I was doing the right thing, living with someone who had the same spiritual goals of homosexual healing, purity, and furthering their relationship to Christ; yet, in return, I received grief and condemnation. John and I lamented together but did not back down to these false accusations and continued to keep our living situation as it was. Besides, it would've been a colossal pain in the ass to change rooms, and who would be the one to move? We did not consider it. Meanwhile, Louis was still playing video games, unaware of the drama that had been unfolding around him for over a week.

Uncle Chris may have been wrong about the potential sexual nature of the relationship between John and me. Still, his words of us asking for trouble living together reverberated loudly once I found myself in the depths of an emotionally dependent relationship that I would have never admitted being problematic.

Only a few weeks into the semester, the avoidance of real-world temptations would soon come to blows. I had not hooked up with a guy in over a year since being in YWAM. The reality that homosexual healing did not progress as much as I wanted depressed me. My addiction to AOL local gay chat rooms resurfaced and the secret rendezvous of my former ways returned, and I went with it, not putting up too much resistance. However, finding guys to meet turned out to be especially tricky while a student at Biola. Getting caught was not an option, so I kept all homosexuality activity outside the Christian campus. It never occurred to me to seek out fellow Biola guys to hook up with—not that I would know how to find them as I am sure they were hiding deep in the closet as I was.

Even though I argued and defended my relationship with John as accountability partners, I never confessed to him any of my "extracurricular activities." However, a double standard insisted that he keep me informed of his sexual temptations so that I could help him defeat his homosexual demons. I was aware of the hypocrisy taking place, but my emotional dependence on John surpassed any semblance of rational thought.

John is the first of many guys on whom I would have developed emotional dependency. It's a crippling mentality, a disease that left me broken, frustrated, and awash in self-loathing too many times to count.

Psychology Today defines emotional dependency as "a neediness that is marked by an over-reliance on others. His or her emotional and physical needs are dependent on the people closest. It's a pervasive and excessive need to be taken care of that leads to submissive and clinging behavior as well as fears of separation. This pattern begins by early adulthood and is present in a variety of contexts. The dependent and submissive behaviors are designed to elicit caregiving and arise from a self-perception of being unable to function adequately without the help of others."[1]

Margaret Paul, Ph.D., a best-selling author, and relationship expert, pinpoints the signs of an emotionally dependent relationship very clearly:

- Have you made your partner/friend responsible for your happiness, worth, and safety?

- Do you feel anxious or panicked when you are not with your partner/friend, or when he or she doesn't call when you expected?

- Do you have a list of expectations that your partner has to meet for you to feel loved and safe?

- Do you feel that you can't live without this person?

- Do you feel empty and alone inside unless your partner/friend is with you, giving you the attention and approval that you are not giving to yourself?

- Do you feel jealous and possessive of your partner/friend?[2]

When it came to John, *Check! Check! Check!* All the way down the list.

For the better part of that first semester, John and I were inseparable and did nearly everything together. We shared the same friends. Our joined-at-the-hip relationship would be difficult to break. We also were in the same major, so we shared classes. In a sense, we were boyfriends—just without the sex.

This dependency drained me to exhaustion so much that I could not stay focused on class, homework, and my on-campus job. I could not get through a minute without thinking about John, and the obsession became emotionally damaging to my spirit. Anytime I sensed that John had become distant or withdrew from me, an overwhelming sense of rejection pulsed through my body. The possessiveness was the worst part of this "disease". God forbid he wanted to eat lunch with another friend or go to lacrosse practice. I hated that he was on the lacrosse team. I couldn't tolerate John forming friendships with all the hot guys on the team—as if he was cheating on me. I had no clue as to whether John could sense any of this, but I believed he was utterly ignorant of my dependence on him.

During that first semester, my mom mentioned she was planning another trip to see Uncle Chris and Aunt Beth. As much as I wanted to see her, college life had me busy, and I did not think I could make the drive to Sedona over her short visit. She understood. The roommate issue was never resolved with Uncle Chris and my mother, so for all I knew, they still thought the worst—I was "living in sin" with John.

I casually mentioned to John that my mom was in Arizona visiting but expressed how I did not want to make the long drive. He insisted and volunteered to drive through the night with me so that I could surprise her in the morning. I could not say no, as I always loved surprising my mom with visits, and I knew it brought her joy to see me. We drove through the night on a Friday and arrived at my Uncle Chris and Aunt Beth's house early on a Saturday morning. I did not even call ahead to tell my Uncle Chris I was coming. I figured, let's surprise them all! What a mistake that was.

I knocked on the door, and as it opened, Uncle Chris stood on the other side, looked at John and me with a hesitancy, and with a forced cordiality, welcomed me into his home and called for my mom. As she turned the corner into the main entranceway, I screamed, *"Surprise!"*

The instant glee that spread widely across my mom's face was worth the long, overnight drive. She smiled big and approached me excitedly.

"Oh Aaron, my pride and joy. Thank you, Jesus!", she said as she hugged me tightly.

Aunt Beth greeted me kindly with a kiss as I suddenly remembered John, who kept quiet behind me. I introduced John to the family, then ran over to give my young cousins, Matthew and Jordan, massive hugs with the obligatory, "You guys are getting so big!"

Uncle Chris's coldness toward me was palpable. I did not think the Celsius scale went that low. His distance spoke volumes, and his disturbance with my unannounced visit did not go unnoticed, although he never said a word that would confirm my suspicions. As I chatted with my mom and Aunt Beth, I witnessed John roughhousing with my cousin Jordan, only four or five years old at the time. I didn't think much of it, but Uncle Chris took my cousins to the backyard to play shortly after, leaving John and me inside. *Jeez, Uncle Chris, what is your problem?*

Unfortunately, the epiphany of why Uncle Chris distanced himself from me did not pop up until after we left. I had not talked to Uncle Chris since the phone call earlier in the semester when he bluntly told me his disapproval of my friendship and living situation with John. When John offered to drive to Arizona with me, how did it not once cross my mind that arriving with John at Uncle Chris' front door, alongside with him, would not be one giant slap in the face? I ignorantly brought this guy to my uncle's house, someone he assumed, whether right or wrong, was my boyfriend—a lifestyle that he did not agree with. I strolled into that house with not one ounce of sensitivity towards the situation. Had I shown up alone, without John, I am confident Uncle Chris would have reacted much differently. I lacked wisdom and plead complete cluelessness.

John and I spent the night and went to church together the next morning with the family. I drove separately with Mom and John, expecting her to say something once she got the two of us alone. Not one to shy away from voicing her opinions and beliefs, she expressed her concern, once again, about us living together, and yet again, we stressed as much as we could that we were not lovers but on a spiritual journey together, supporting each other to pursue God and homosexual healing.

Nothing concrete was resolved between Uncle Chris and me on that visit. About a year afterwards, I went back to Long Island for my sister's wedding, and with no mention of the past, I told him about a girl named Gwen I was seeing. He beamed and encouraged me to "go for what is yours." I wanted him to be proud of me and portray that God had a healing hand on my sexuality, even though it was not necessarily true. I felt like a normal guy bragging about having an interest in a girl. It was as if I received some sort of twisted sense of accomplishment from telling a lie to make him happy.

Years later, in 2015, Uncle Chris and Aunt Beth were visiting my cousin Jordan in Los Angeles, where he had recently moved. Uncle Chris called me and asked me to join them for dinner, and I happily obliged. We made our way to the Americana in Glendale and decided on the Cheesecake Factory. Up to this point, we had never brought up anything from our past, nor had any closure. Our interactions at family get-togethers were cordial and normal. It had been approximately 14 years, and I had figured by now to let bygones be bygones. Most of the resentment I felt had diminished, but there was always a piece of me that held on to some anger about the phone call that day, but I buried it, not seeing a purpose to dig it up. Toward the end of the meal, systematically, Jordan left the table to run across the way to the

Apple Store, and only one minute later, Aunt Beth excused herself as well. It seemed obvious that there was a plan to get Uncle Chris and me alone together. When it was only us, he looked at me.

"I have something to tell you," he said.

Oh God, here we go again.

Before words even came out of his mouth, I braced myself for an anti-gay, Bible-quoting, Jesus-filled pep talk.

Can we not do this at the Cheesecake Factory, please? I silently pleaded. But no, that's not what happened.

He apologized.

He looked me straight in the eyes, without reluctance or stammering, and apologized, not specifically for the phone call, but for his overall actions and reactions to my struggle as a whole. He attempted to empathize with me, understanding that it had to be challenging to change sexual attractions. He concluded that I am loved exactly the way I am.

Wow.

I sat there somewhat in shock, processing what a monumental moment this was for me—the first time I felt affirmed and validated that this struggle with my sexuality was real and not something that could easily be willed or prayed away. My body tingled and I choked up as Uncle Chris looked at me with nothing but love in his eyes. After all these years, that one gesture of apology took hold of any hatred and hurt left in my soul and released it like a helium balloon headed toward the sky.

As we were finished, Aunt Beth and Jordan resurfaced. We said our goodbyes and went to our separate cars. My heart raced with overwhelming peace and gratitude from the moment that just took place. As I got in my car, closed the door, and let the silence consume me, I wept. A broken piece of my heart healed that day.

Chapter Seven

ALWAYS BE MY MAYBE

Biola University's stance on homosexuality, not surprisingly, was against it. Every student must sign a contract upon admission to Biola agreeing to the community standards, which states you cannot drink, do drugs, have pre-marital sex, and, of course, cannot engage in homosexual behavior. As of 2012, the community standards read, "Furthermore, students at Biola commit to refrain from practices that Scripture forbids, such as sexual relations outside of marriage, homosexual behavior, theft and dishonesty."[1]

In Biola's defense, they also had this in their guidelines:

"Due to the complexity of issues related to same-sex behavior, same-sex attraction, and sexual orientation, we are committed to engaging this conversation with courage, humility, prayerfulness, and care. We believe, in accordance with Scripture, that we are all broken. Therefore, a primary goal of Student Development at Biola is to help each student find God amid their unique history and struggles and discern how to walk with Him and others along the way."[2]

I found some solace knowing Biola would not kick me out of school because I struggled with homosexuality. However, if I chose to live this lifestyle without getting "help," then they would act, including expulsion.

Despite the impending humiliation that I could suffer if I got caught, I continued sneaking around, hooking up with guys in the neighborhood. My friendship with John began to deteriorate. My dependence on him did a 180, from clinging to him obsessively to not wanting to be around him at all. All the turmoil we went through to be roommates for the sake of accountability was in vain. I even moved out of our dorm room and secured my own room on the other side of the building, so I didn't have to look him in the eyes and face my own guilt.

My behavior dictated that I needed a plan to "save face" if I was caught, so I started meeting with my extremely attractive, dorm resident director, Landon, and begrudgingly told him about my struggle. The motivation to talk to Landon did not solely revolve around the appearance of getting help. Cultivating godly Christian friendships with straight males was said to be a vital step in the homosexual healing process. Meeting with Landon could not possibly decrease the intense gravitational pull to be sexual with other guys, so the effort proved counterproductive. As a straight, Christian, alpha male, Landon did not know how to help me and was noticeably unfamiliar with this issue. Sure, he was a listening ear, but he was hot, and I craved intimacy with him—case closed. There was no logic using him to "help" me. It's like proclaiming to eat healthier but throwing Little Debbie's in my grocery basket. The action contradicted the goal. Landon was my snack cake, and man, I wanted a taste.

Since Landon was off the table (damn straight guys), I found suitors who drove in my lane but kept all encounters off-campus, not risking gambling away my education and reputation. One of the reasons I wanted to attend Biola was to be secluded in a Christian bubble, like YWAM, in hopes the limited contact with the outside world would keep me on the straight and narrow (pun intended). Contrarily, I just became a pro at sneaking around.

Sometime during that semester, I started dating a guy named Luis, who I met through an online gay group. At first, my meetings with Luis were quickies, but he became the first guy I dated and had a relationship with that wasn't only about sex. We had fun together, going out to eat and to the movies. Luis understood I went to Biola and what that entailed, so our relationship's secrecy didn't seem to bother him at first. One evening after seeing a movie, we wanted to hang out, but my dorm room would be the only private option we had that evening. Should I really bring this guy on campus? Well, of course I did. As I stepped on Biola's grounds with him next to me, the fear and terror overwhelmed me as we walked from one side of campus to another. How awkward it would be to potentially pass a friend and be obligated to introduce him.

What would I even say? *This is Luis, he's my dirty little secret, and we are about to have sex in my dorm room.*

Being with Luis was disorienting. I loved being with him yet was ashamed to be with him. I felt riveted yet dirty. Unfortunately, the tryst with Luis was brief, as my wishy washiness in our relationship started to become unappealing for him, understandingly enough. He wanted more than what I could give him. Another opportunity to have a significant other, a potential first love, vanished because the religion I placed on a pedestal firmly denied me of living my truth.

Once Luis was out of the picture, I decided I needed a "fresh start," and I looked for a church where I could find and cultivate Christian male friendships outside of Biola. After some research, I decided on the Anaheim Vineyard Christian Fellowship in Orange County, California. What stood out to me is that the church partnered with Desert Stream Ministries with a program called Living Waters that is described as providing "a thoughtful and safe place to look at the ways we've become ensnared.

Through weekly times of worship, teaching and small group prayer, our program leaders walk with participants in their struggle so they can live in freedom and truth. We pray for God's healing to restore broken areas of life so that people can 'love well' as God intended."[3]

Many issues are listed on the website on why someone would want to attend Living Waters including, but not limited to, gender identity issues and unwanted same sex attraction:

Through the worship, teaching, prayer, and small groups of Living Waters, we learn about:

• *God's powerful love for us and how Jesus is central to our hope for wholeness• The depth of our brokenness and our profound need for Him• The power of the cross to restore our souls, sexuality, and relationships• The process of walking out our healing• Our place in the church and loving others honorably*[4]

The River is the same program as Living Waters, except its focus was geared for college-aged and young adults. *The River* program catered to people struggling with other sexual issues outside homosexuality; however, it seemed to be the primary focus. Many of the leaders were "ex-gay," and the attendance of homosexual strugglers were numerous. We gathered one night a week for worship and then would retreat into our "small groups" that consisted of five or six people of the same gender to talk about our struggles, which were mostly sexual. This would be my first experience in a gay conversion therapy setting, and even though the program never claimed it to be therapy, the intent was clear. This program would help me heal completely from homosexuality once and for all.

This was a 12-week program, and I jumped in feet first. My expectations were vast, and I believed that God would (finally) heal me of homosexuality. So, for the first few weeks, I did what was told. I showed up at the meeting every week, worshipped, prayed, read the Bible, and connected with my small group. I looked forward to the small group every week but not because I was experiencing some super spiritual sexual freedom. No, I wanted to go to the small group because of Kyle.

Kyle was a fine-looking stud, too gorgeous to exist in a church building and better suited for a *GQ* shirtless magazine spread. Standing taller than six feet, he had a thick crop of spikey, brown hair and a smile that made me want to lick his teeth. To my disappointment, he was straight. However, it did not lessen my fantasy of removing his clothes and slathering his body in oil.

Dammit Aaron, you shouldn't be thinking these things. Think of God and healing and girls!

The small group was structured where the guys would sit in a circle and take turns confessing our weekly sins. I waited in anticipation when it was Kyle's turn to unload his dirty secrets. I marveled at his tightly shirt covered chest when he spoke about his problem with lust. I stared at his kissable lips as he embarrassingly expressed his disgrace with looking at porn. I gazed lustfully at his crotch while he disclosed his guilt for masturbating frequently. The irony here is baffling and problematic as I recognized that his shame was my *pleasure*. If my healing depended on not enjoying Kyle talking about jerking himself off, I was doomed. In the meantime, get me popcorn and keep talking, Kyle; I'm still listening.

Fantasies of Kyle alone were not enough to keep me attending in *The River* program, and I dropped out four or five weeks into it. The leaders genuinely cared about each of us and authentically wanted healing for us as much as we wanted it for ourselves. I sought after Harry, one of the leaders, to talk with one-on-one because I needed a mentor who could walk alongside me to conquer this homosexual attraction. Harry was "ex-gay" and married to a woman. If I have this living example of homosexual freedom right in front of me, why wouldn't I want to walk side-by-side with someone and see how they did it? The conversation meetups with Harry were sparse, but his testimony kept me hopeful that if God can heal someone like him from homosexuality, he can do it for me, too! I believed that if God could only send me a girlfriend to marry someday like he did for Harry, I could be straight as well.

The pressure to find a significant other, or more specifically, the love of your life while at Biola, plagued the mind of most students by junior year. Obtaining that "Ring Before Spring" or "MRS." degree didn't exactly bode well for my wishes; however, I kept my ears and eyes open for any girl that captured my attention. My sexual attraction to other guys did not prohibit me from actively hoping for the girl who would "cure" me, although I never actually looked or initiated anything.

I met a girl named Gwen toward the end of my first semester, sort of. She initiated a conversation with me on Biola's email system, BUBBS (Biola University Bulletin Board System). She asked me about something on my student profile, and we continued to banter about mostly ridiculous things. We chatted back and forth, shooting the breeze on surface topics, amusing ourselves endlessly. I had no idea who she was or what she looked like, but her expressiveness and joyfulness radiated through her words to the screen. Our chat ended naturally, but she told me she had a cast on her arm due to a recent injury, so if I were to see a girl around campus sporting a bright blue arm cast, to scream her name, run over to her with my arms spread wide, and pretend we were long lost friends reuniting. That Gwen…she's a funny girl.

Early in the next semester, as I walked into Biola's cafeteria, known as "The Café" to Biolans, I saw a girl with a bright blue cast on her arm outside near the entrance. Without hesitation, I looked in her direction and screamed, "GWEN!"

Her eyes widened with the purest expression of happiness as she ran over to me as if we were actually reuniting after several years. Instantly, we were the best of friends.

The spring semester of 2002 challenged me exponentially, specifically in navigating my sexuality and relationship with God. I dropped out of *The River* program, which I thought would put a significant dent in overcoming my homosexuality. My quiet times with God were few and far between, and I battled with lusting after other males while curiously, cautiously, and enthusiastically spending as much time with

Gwen as I could. Hanging out with Gwen made my life more exciting. As the flowers of that spring bloomed so beautifully, so did my relationship with her. The purity of my friendship with Gwen contrasted with the dirty and perverted secret life I had with neighborhood men for sexual encounters. I came to love Gwen, but as nothing more than a friend, although I started to initiate beliefs in my head that she could be the ticket to a "normal" life. I never met someone so full of vibrance, beaming with happiness every second we were together. As much as I wanted to convince myself that she could be a potential girlfriend, the sexual attraction was only but a fantasy.

Regardless, our friendship progressed throughout the entire semester, as did my extra-curricular activities with other guys, but my time with Gwen gave me a sense of normalcy I craved. Gwen's animated personality permeated my heart as I recognized the gorgeous person that she was inside and out. I believed that maybe she was what I needed for that attraction towards males to decrease.

Let me start dating a girl and see what happens, I thought. *It can't hurt, right?*

I wanted to hang out with her all the time, and I did. Besides regular hangouts during the day, we often had random dates at three in the morning. We would go to the 24-hour McDonald's to get a couple of Cokes from the drive-thru and chat in my car for hours and hours about everything and nothing, until the sun came up.

I wish I knew that her romantic feelings toward me were more substantial than my friendship feelings for her. I convinced myself that my relationship with her had nothing to do with my struggle with homosexuality—they were two different issues that did not overlap. Man, never have I been so wrong. So much heartache could have been avoided had I known the extent of my ignorance and stupidity.

During one of our late-night hangouts at NORMS restaurant, snacking on tater tots and milkshakes, I said, "Gwen, I have something that I want to tell you, but I don't want it to impact our friendship."

She smiled hugely as if she was expecting me to give her a new puppy and enthusiastically said, "Okay! Go for it!"

I then went into some detail about my "past" and how I struggled with homosexuality and indulged in gay sin. Her eyes maintained that sparkle that captivated me from when I first met her.

She responded gracefully, "I love you. That doesn't change how I feel about you."

I didn't deserve such an honor from this girl because my homosexuality kept me from accepting that I had any value. I made it clear to her that homosexuality was something God would eventually heal me from. The more I spent time with Gwen, the more I believed she was "the one." I liked this girl. I believed in God's perfect plan that in time, with enough faith, healing, and counseling, my sexual attraction for her would surface.

I decided to see a Christian therapist to help me deal more professionally with my homosexuality. Biola Counseling Center offered students the availability to meet with Biola graduate students in the Psychology program for free as they trained to become licensed psychologists. I figured free counseling couldn't hurt, so I volunteered to be someone's guinea pig. So far, my attempts, including YWAM and *The River* didn't do squat. Even my meetings with Landon did not provide me with anything spectacular except a piece of eye candy to talk with. Maybe a real therapist would work, even if they were "in training."

Unfortunately, my time at the Biola Counseling Center proved futile. I went through three therapists in a month, not liking any of them. I don't know if the therapist themselves were to blame or that nothing they did or said helped alleviate any homosexual tendencies. Frustrated and angry, I discontinued my pursuit after the third therapist. Although their inexperience in therapy did seem prominent, my anger was displaced, taking it out on them when the real reason for my anger was that nothing they said or did fixed me.

The end of the semester quickly approached, and I would soon be going off on a mission trip to Nepal for the summer. Gwen and I never had a "define the relationship" conversation but organically we both could tell it was headed toward something more serious after practically being inseparable the last four months. While in Nepal, I received an email from her that sent me for a loop. She wrote she was no longer returning to Biola and decided to attend Covenant Bible College in Ecuador the next school year. I remember so vividly the emotions I felt sitting in that Nepali hostel's excruciatingly humid lobby, which was my home for the month. I was consumed with overwhelming hopelessness and distress, fearing I had lost the girl who would turn me into a normal heterosexual man. My stomach dropped as if someone punched me. I was barely able to breathe. As the tears formed, I re-read the email a few more times utterly distraught but kept hope alive and determined to make this—whatever "this" was— work with Gwen.

Chapter Eight

FATAL ATTRACTION

Very few heartaches are as great as those that come from wanting someone you cannot have. Some people will go to great lengths to go after something or someone that isn't meant to be.

I will soon experience this first-hand. While hanging out with Gwen and cultivating our friendship and my hopeful homosexual healing, I became "involved" with another Biola student. A male student. A *straight*, male student.

Oh Jesus, take the wheel.

Hooking up with guys that attended Biola never really occurred to me. Not so much because I thought that John and I were the only gay strugglers in the 5,000+ student body, but I knew they would not be easy to pinpoint. There was no Biola gay support group. Pride t-shirts did not make a splash on any of the student body. Gay apps weren't even a thing yet to see who was one hundred feet away from you on Grindr. Since I was hiding my sexual attractions and not telling anyone, there must be dozens of other guys that probably did the same.

Most of the time I assumed everyone was straight, and the guys that caught my eye would go no further than a fleeting lustful daydream. I secretly hoped that maybe one or two of them swung my way, but even if they did, I would never know since Biola had an unspoken mantra like the old military adage of, "Don't ask, don't tell."

One guy that captured my interest during my second semester was a mysterious fellow student, Stitch, a nickname he labeled himself to heighten his mystique. I saw him frequently around campus the prior semester and caught myself staring quite a few times. He emitted a potent sexuality that went *way* beyond his face and body. His allure, wardrobe, and swagger only intensified his erotic presence without any additional effort on his part. Later, I learned this was called BDE, or "Big Dick Energy." If a guy possesses an unparalleled over-confidence and justified cockiness (plenty of pun intended), he had BDE, which Stitch easily exemplified. From top to bottom, he was the perfect male specimen, a modern-day James Dean. Stitch had thick curly brown hair, stunning green eyes, and a chiseled body that proved evident when his sculpted chest and toned abs protruded through his tight shirts. His perfectly fitted jeans were worn so snug, you could tell Stitch's BDE was a fact, not just symbolic.

Stitch and I had mutual friends but had never been introduced. Girls flocked to him like moths to a flame, and judging his body language alone, he more than enjoyed the attention. A couple of my female friends had told me they hooked up with him in the past, so I never thoroughly questioned his sexual orientation, but maybe, just maybe, if he's bi-closeted or curious, I could have a chance? Day by day, I'd see him whether he walked by the student mailboxes, shirtless around the dorm, or sweating on the lacrosse field. I became increasingly aware of my overpowering raw lust for him.

I pondered how I could get Stitch's attention and knew I would have to get creative. Should I use the ole, "God told me to tell you this through a dream" tactic that I used on Craig back in the day?

Nah, I had an inclination that a scary dream from a complete stranger would not drop Stitch's pants, but I was willing to go to desperate lengths, no matter how disappointed I'd be if he rejected me. Maybe not a fake dream but how about a fake email! I clicked on Yahoo and created an email account to send an anonymous message to his Biola BUBBS account:

> Hey, I'm a guy who goes to Biola. We don't have any classes together, but I've seen you around campus, and I think you're really hot. I don't know if you've ever considered messing around with a guy, but I'd love to hear back if interested in chatting further. If not, don't worry. I'm not a crazy stalker. If I don't hear back from you, I'll never bother you again.

My expectations for a response were small. Even if he did respond, I had no promise anything would come of it. This whole scheme had "risky" written all over it. I could potentially be exposing myself for him to turn me into the Biola administration if, for any reason, he was offended, threatened, or a goody two-shoes Christian with hypersensitive homophobia. Also, I did lie in that email—crazy stalker, indeed.

My relationship with God and pursuing heterosexuality did not fit on my list of priorities at this time. After I dropped out of *The River* and my friendship with John fizzled, indulging in my lust toward Stitch was an outlet, and I did not have much guilt about it—not yet anyway. As usual, I went about my life, went to class, did homework, enjoyed spending time with Gwen, and went to work, so this operation to get Stitch naked in my room did not completely consume me. It was more of a side hobby.

I was ready to give up checking that fake yahoo email account but by the fourth day after I sent it, a response finally came through. I rubbed my eyes to make sure I was not seeing things but, there it was, an email from Stitch@biola.edu. I gasped, alone in my room, holding out on clicking the message so the moment could last a bit longer.

As predicted, Stitch was not interested in hooking up with a guy, proclaiming to be completely straight. However, he was intrigued enough to keep the conversation from ending. We exchanged emails back and forth. Our correspondence was mildly sexual in content, but I sensed caution from him since I had yet to reveal my identity. So, I finally revealed my real name to him, and we moved our conversations to BUBBS. Biola also had a chat feature on BUBBS, where students could message each other individually, like instant messaging. As our online relationship commenced, Stitch became more comfortable sexually. Our chats were about getting to know each other and asking each other graphic questions about sex, including our sexual histories, interests, and fantasies. Interestingly, Stitch did not seem grossed out by homosexuality and gay sex. In fact, he was extremely curious and asked me tons of questions. The more he was invested in our chats, the more I fell for him. My infuriating and thrilling quest for Stitch no longer was a hobby but a full-on out fanaticism, and I loved every second of the chase.

Day after day, our emails were more frequent. Waiting for a response to each email caused so much anticipation, I could barely sit still in class longing for my computer to check if he wrote me back. One day, I returned to my dorm to see my phone blinking, indicating there was a voicemail, and I speculated that it was most likely my dad asking me how my car was holding up or a classmate needing a time for our study session. To my surprise, it was a quick message from Stitch, who must have gotten my number from the college switchboard, saying hello and that we would chat soon. How could such a brief message send my body into massive convulsions? *Now, this guy is calling me?* Hearing him say my name made me quiver, which confirmed our relationship was so much more real than mere computerized words on a screen.

We hadn't yet made a specific plan, but I figured we would eventually bump into one another around campus. Ironically, as much as I saw Stitch walking around campus before our email communication, I never saw him afterward. I believed, at the time, it was God's doing, supernaturally manipulating his route to class, so I would stay focused on Jesus, my healing, and not gratifying the lustful, sinful desires of my flesh. Well, God, here's the kicker—it was way too late for that.

I yearned for Stitch, but the joy I received from being with Gwen overshadowed any guilt. I had convinced myself that Gwen would be my future, so if anything could happen with Stitch, now was the time to "get it out of my system." I could ask God for forgiveness later. Sadly, I was blind to how this infatuation with Stitch could affect Gwen and, worse, how it contradicted everything I wanted in comparison to a Christ-centered, romantic relationship with a girl.

With such a small campus, running into Stitch was inevitable, and every morning I woke up wondering if today would be the day. I often mused how I would react and feel, looking at him face to face, his eyes looking into mine. It had only been four days since we first started communicating, yet it felt much longer, as if we had been best friends for years even though he was a stranger. I'd never been in the same room with him, let alone close enough to smell his scent that I dreamt was spice and musk.

One afternoon as I routinely headed out of my dorm room and made my way to the mailboxes, I saw Stitch walking out of The Café about 40 to 50 feet away from me. If he kept walking straight, he would not see me; however, if he turned left, he would head in my direction. I froze while a million thoughts collided with one another. I was unsure if I was ready to talk to him yet admired his beauty as he approached.

Please walk straight, I'm not ready.
No, wait, make a left; shit, I forgot to Listerine!
Ok, he's turning left; he's gonna see me. Oh, God, he sees me! He's smiling!
Damn, he's so hot. I really want to give him a blowjob.
Oh God, he's walking over. Ok, ok. Calm down, Aaron, calm down.

My heart rate increased to deathly beats as Stitch greeted me enthusiastically like we had known each other for years. He gave me a hug short enough for onlookers not to be suspicious but long enough for me to revel in the closeness of his manly physique. This moment terrified me as much as it thrilled me. I feared it would be awkward and intimidating. Still, I should have known that Stitch's charisma and personality would melt any uneasiness from finally meeting face to face. He pulled away from the hug and looked me right in the eyes with an unwavering confidence.

"Hey, what's going on!?" he beamed.

I smiled, staring at his beautiful green eyes living behind studious eyeglasses that amplified his handsomeness.

"I'm good, just heading to get my mail and get some lunch," I uttered nervously while dropping my voice down a couple of octaves.

I'm convinced the sunny SoCal day made his teeth look even more white than they were. I was oblivious to anyone walking around us. It was as if it was just him and I in the middle of this very busy part of campus.

If he noticed my anxiousness, he was not deterred. I was literally staring my sin in the face, yet after feeling his hard body close to mine after the initial hug, I didn't care.

"Awesome man, well I have to jet off to lacrosse practice, I'll talk to you soon." He smiled and winked seductively as we both knew there was more beneath the surface of this conversation.

"Yea, talk soon," I smiled back.

I was about to burst, like a cork shooting out of a champagne bottle. I could barely contain myself and knew it was soon time to walk past the lacrosse field where Stitch would be sweaty and shirtless.

The worry that he may not want to continue our friendship after we met in person subsided when he called my room later that day and initiated a hang out that same evening. *Ok then, I didn't scare him off. Phewww!*

Since I lived alone in my dorm room, the opportunity presented itself for us to have privacy. Despite the graphic sexual nature of our emails, Stitch never agreed to or even hinted at doing anything sexual with me. I respected his wishes and would not initiate anything he was not comfortable with. However, when discussing what we would do when he came over, he told me he was he interested in watching gay porn. *He wants to watch WHAT??*

He said "From there we'll just see how the evening unfolds"

Stitch knocked on my door, and I anxiously let him in. He sat on my bed in track pants, presumably not aware of the weakness it caused me to notice his prominent bulge. Although this was the first time that we were talking one-on-one, an air of calmness soothed my unsteady nerves. Spiritual whispers of conviction pressed against my ears, fighting for my purity. But they gradually faded as I abandon my plight to be "homosexually healed" in that moment.

After some small talk, Stitch flung himself off my bed and took a seat next to me at my computer as I outsmarted Biola's internet censors and pulled up some gay porn. Most people form bonds of friendship chit-chatting over a hot cup of coffee, slapping high-fives at sporting events or laughing through an Adam Sandler film. Stitch and I took a different approach in breaking the ice—gay porn. I enjoyed watching Stitch watch the porn. It felt euphoric. My eyes took turns glancing at his face and crotch more than the computer screen. Was he getting aroused? What is he thinking? After a few dirty movies and some conversation, he left, and I felt unsatisfied—mainly because I wanted to rip off his clothes and lick him from head to toe. He said he enjoyed the evening and wanted to hang again.

I waited for the moment that something physical would happen between us, but Stitch had all the control. The unspoken boundaries were clear, and I never dared to test the waters by crossing a line without his permission, but God only knows how much I wanted to put my hand on his crotch during our "movie" night. *Let me just touch it!* But if something were to happen, Stitch had to make the first move. I loved being close to him, and my yearning for something more was immeasurable. *He's such a fuckin' tease!* I didn't care, though. My desire for Stitch was out of control. I was fully aware that I had become numb to my pursuit for healing, falling deeper and deeper into homosexual sin.

I'm sorry, God. I'm so sorry

Despite the guilt, I sadistically enjoyed having Stitch as my dirty secret. I did not tell a soul, not even my closest friend at the time, Megan, who probably would have understood since she hooked up with Stitch frequently. I knew he hooked up with girls often, which at first did not bother me. However, the more time we spent together, the more the pangs of jealousy twisted my stomach. I had this delusion that he was all mine, and when I would see Stitch hypnotizing girls with his charm around campus, I would grit my teeth in a silent rage.

Strangely, during all this, I had a desire to go on a mission trip. "Strange" because my relationship with God had seen better days, and I was not in a spiritual mindset to go somewhere to spread the love of Christ and preach the Word. I loved going on mission trips with my youth group back in the day, so it's not that this stirring came out of the blue. Quite possibly, the decision to go on a mission trip could have been some act of penitence to ease the guilt of Stitch. Biola University had a missionary department known as the SMU (Student Missionary Union). I walked into the SMU to read about the trip options available for that upcoming summer. Nepal jumped out at me as I remembered the slide show of the Nepal team from YWAM, hoping to go there someday. Without any consideration to any other destination, I signed up, applied, and waited for a response.

A couple of days later, I walked into the SMU to meet with the Nepal team leaders, and I saw Stitch taking a nap on the couch. It was not weird to see students randomly taking naps all over campus, whether outside on a bench, in the student union, or on the soccer field when the Los Angeles sun warmed the grass. Even in the stillness of the SMU offices, to see someone taking a snooze with a textbook over their face would not give me any reason to wince. *But Stitch?* What was *he* doing there?

As I looked down at him, at his jean-covered bulge, and then back to his face, he woke up quickly as if he knew he was being watched. He was pleasantly surprised to see me, and I asked him what he was doing there. In a shocking turn of events, he told me that he was interested in going on a mission trip to Nepal.

Say What?!? Holy Plot Twist Batman!

I was in complete and utter disbelief. Astonished, I told him I was going to Nepal as well, and he flashed that smile that hindered my ability to induce body movement. He expressed excitement that we were going on the trip together but in my mind, I saw this as a problem. The conflict of my immorality and Christianity were now overlapping, and although I was pleasantly surprised that he was also going to Nepal, my integrity faintly knocked on my heart's door. *This will end badly,* I thought to myself.

Stitch and I never talked about "normal" stuff. There was never a conversation about how our days went, or if he won the lacrosse game on Saturday, or how terrible the lasagna was in The Café. Our conversations and hangouts all revolved around a sexual nature, so there would be no way either of us would have known that we were both interested in going on a mission trip. This was a complete and unadulterated coincidence. As the saying goes, "You can't make this shit up."

So now what?

My dirty little secret is getting on a plane with me and going 8,000 miles away to a third world country and on a *mission trip*. From a Christian standpoint, neither of us had any business representing Jesus Christ and Biola University on a mission trip since we were deep in perverted sin. I wondered how this turn of events would affect the relationship we had. Fortunately, everything was business as usual, and he even came to my dorm for another gay porn viewing. We never talked about going to Nepal during our hangouts, but I knew it was looming and a small amount of guilt slithered into my conscience, which I squashed every time he walked into my room. Stitch's luminous green eyes and bulge in those track pants thwarted any possibility that I would put an end to our sexual camaraderie.

Even though I had no plans to cease my relationship with Stitch, I had to face several of my worlds colliding: my love for God vs. Stitch and homosexuality vs. Gwen. I could keep them exclusive for now, but I did not know how long it would last, if at all. This could all implode at any minute.

The Nepal team consisted of only six people, including myself and Stitch. Our team bonded quickly and easily during meetings and fundraising events. These group meetups were the first time I hung out with Stitch outside the context of sex and porn, realizing that he was an actual person and not only an object of my sexual gratification. I watched him interact with the other team members and saw different sides to him besides the charm, swag, and flirt I already knew he possessed. He was funny, kind, and an all-around good guy. These discoveries only complicated my feelings for him, and I wanted him to be more than a "porn buddy." Still, I knew that he did not reciprocate my longings to be more intimate and wanting something so desperately that I could not have took a toll on my heart and spirit.

My excitement for Nepal hinged on Stitch's accompaniment. I knew this was a red flag from the beginning. Still, I ignored any thought, idea, or conviction that nudged my heart that what I had been doing with Stitch and deceiving the rest of the Nepal team was spiritually and emotionally unhealthy. Mission trips were important to me, and I loved doing the work of the Lord, traveling to foreign countries, and helping those in need. However, what I envisioned for Nepal turned into a Nepalese fantasy of me and Stitch sharing a bed in the hot and sticky humid weather of the South Asian summer, waking up to sweat glistening on his bare chest and his morning wood poking underneath the damp sheet only inches away from my thigh—not that I gave it much thought.

One evening, I was sitting in my dorm room staring at the computer, innocently surfing the web and checking email. Per usual, I hopped on BUBBS to check if Stitch was online, hoping to have another one of our sexual conversations and to invite him over to my room to hang out. As luck would have it, he was available, and we started having our routine sexual discussion. That evening's chat, in particular, had been much more sexually charged than in the past because for the first time, the conversation resulted in us discussing taking our encounters a step further. Stitch, the self-admitted exhibitionist, suggested that he come to my room and masturbate while I watched.

Umm…ok!

He signed off and made his way to my dorm room. He would be there in a matter of minutes. Freaking out, I started to pace the floor, and within an instant, an intense blow to my gut brought me to my knees in a dire crisis of faith. A staggering and solemn vehemence of Christian guilt weighed on my shoulders and heart. *I'm going on a mission trip with this guy, what am I doing?* The sacrilege of this impending homosexual encounter with someone I was about to minister with crushed my conscience.

Still on my knees, I called out, *"God, I can't do this, I want to do this, but I can't, help me!"*

Knock. Knock. Knock.

I opened the door, and Stitch walked in dressed in those track pants I love. The outline of his large penis was visible.

He sat down somewhat eagerly and asked, *"Ok, what now?"*

I stared at him while my rapidly beating heart convulsed inside of my chest, and he looked at me with those seductive eyes. I gazed at his perfect athletic body that I wanted to touch, yet my moral awareness took a firm grip on my mind. This is a moment I had been waiting for—the culmination of our relationship from the beginning was about to climax—literally. He waited for me to give him some direction, and I was unsure why he expected me to guide him to the next step. Had he taken control, the night would have ended differently. It felt like an eternity as we waited for someone to say or do something but somehow, I softly uttered the words:

"Stitch, I can't do this…we are going on a mission trip together."

Wow!! Really, Aaron!? Did you just say that!?!

The lustfulness that spread across his face transformed into an expression of confusion and disbelief. I'd like to think he understood where I was coming from, considering our school's Christian culture, but he was quite shocked and visibly disappointed. I blue-balled him! I never conveyed any kind of remorse or guilt about our relationship to him until this point, so my sudden termination of the encounter completely caught him off guard. Did I crush his ego? Did I humiliate him? He somberly left my room, and I feared that our friendship would never be the same. I hoped and prayed that we would still be friends, and he would not hold it against me that I threw him out of my room—erection and all.

As much as I regretted that nothing happened between Stitch and me that night, our friendship continued. However, the sexual relationship ended and that was a bummer. I wanted a redo! A few days later, I attempted to apologize for not going through with the evening and asked him to come back to my room and finish what we started, but he was not "feeling it" and declined. Who could blame him? What would stop me from having another spiritual breakdown and throwing him out again? The connection we had during our "porn" hangouts was a huge loss for me because I thrived off our intimacy and feeling close to him.

The conflict of my desires resonated heavily. I missed being with Stitch yet still enjoyed time with Gwen but was frustrated that I could not be attracted to her the way that I was to him. I continued to have anonymous sexual encounters outside of Stitch. The guilt and shame of indulging in these homosexual lusts and encounters routinely confused me.

But I like Gwen!! Right?

The only person I needed to convince was myself. Sure, I "liked" Gwen, as I liked talking and spending time with her, but "liked" her as in, sexually attracted and desired a romance? No. I believed this lie that I would eventually want to romanticize her, but this false hope would only breed desolation and grief. I questioned why I was still attracted to men if Gwen was the one to reverse that homosexual attraction.

My heart ached. I wanted these homosexual attractions to magically disappear and held on to hope that with Jesus's help, mercy, and promises of the Bible, that they could and would someday. I also wanted Stitch back in my room in his bulging track pants. I wanted to sit close to him while watching dirty gay videos. Confusion and heartache were my default emotion every moment of every day, but I did a damn good job hiding it all with a smile.

About a week before we took off for Nepal, Stitch told me he could not go due to family obligations. I no longer wanted to go without him. I didn't care about the mission work. Sadly, my devastation for Stitch's void surpassed any desire or purpose for the ministry. However, my ticket was purchased, and the funds were raised in my name, and I had no concrete reason to tell my leaders why I didn't want to go. Everyone on the team was disappointed that Stitch couldn't come because we bonded so much as a group the past month in preparation for the trip, but they didn't know him like I did. My heart and mind were not in the right place, and it transpired during that month in Nepal. There were moments I enjoyed. Experiencing my first third-world country was life-changing and, surprisingly, a restaurant in Kathmandu provided one of the best bowls of spaghetti I ever had in my life. I wanted to snap out of my funk and regretfully found myself sulking at times, wanting to leave, miserable that Stitch wasn't there.

My friendship with Stitch sustained throughout the rest of college. We even became roommates over the next year and a half until graduation. We were close *platonic* friends. Believe it or not, nothing sexual ever happened between us even after becoming roommates but I was still very much attracted to him, and always wondered "what if", and still do. One evening while we were roommates, we had a deep conversation, reminiscing on how we initially met, and Stitch poignantly said to me that "God protected our friendship". Maybe he was saying if our relationship crossed the line back then, it could have prevented us from establishing the friendship that we formed, which was much more fulfilling than any potential sexual involvement.

Stitch is one of the very few friends from college that I still am close with, a friendship that began in an unorthodox fashion, yet one I deeply treasure. He will always have a hypnotizing effect on me, and I'll never be opposed to hanging out with him again, especially if he's wearing those crotch-bulging track pants he knows I love.

Chapter Nine

GONE GIRL

I CAN BE ATTRACTED to guys and still date Gwen, right? I often pondered. As a Bible believing Christian struggling with homosexuality, is this what I'm supposed to do to stay obedient to God and not be alone for the rest of my life? Force a relationship with the opposite sex? Pretend I am sexually attracted to these girls? Ignore my desire to be seduced by Ewan McGregor with him wearing nothing but a kilt as he whispers raunchy poetry in my ear in his seductive Scottish accent all night long? Man, it's getting hot in here. What was I talking about? Oh yea, how much I like girls...

Throughout our respective summers in Nepal and Ecuador, Gwen and I stayed close. Our long-distance relationship excited *and* confused me for obvious reasons.

I was in deeper denial than Rachel believing she wasn't on a break from Ross. Despite the denial, Gwen and I talked about the future, marriage, and sharing a life together. The relationship was in full bloom, yet so were my homosexual desires. It felt strange even to call her my girlfriend. We never even kissed, nor would I be able to because of the distance. Furthermore, I did not even think about kissing her, no matter how much I truly missed her. I *did* think about kissing most of the guys on the Biola baseball team, but that's another story.

After returning that fall semester, I reconnected with Harry from the Desert Stream ministries at Anaheim Vineyard to have another attempt at *The River* program. I figured these homosexual feelings still existed because I did not complete the program the first time. So that was the plan: attend *The River* again, finish it, officially become straight, and fall truly in love with Gwen. I went through the motions of doing the program all over again, but it was pretty much the same shit but different people from the previous year. I went to all the group sessions, participated in the curriculum, and met with my leaders. I continually prayed and read my Bible, but I did not feel changed as I hoped or as God had promised. I developed a massive crush on one of the other guys, Colton, who struggled with homosexuality. We became friendly, but I wanted more. I wanted him to be my boyfriend. The whole scenario was contradictory to the healing I was attempting to receive. There I was: struggling with same-sex desires with a girlfriend in Ecuador while in a program to become straight while desiring to take Colton in the back alley of the church and have my way with him.

I mean, that's pretty screwed up, right? Clearly, I didn't need a gay conversion group, I needed an insane asylum.

On graduation night of *The River* program, we each had to develop a presentation to represent what we learned and received from the program. One kid, the most flamboyant of the bunch, displayed his freedom of homosexuality with an interpretive dance. I watched how he exaggeratedly flung his limbs from one end of the room to another with a worship song playing in the background, silently amused that *this* is how he was showing off his gay healing.

I really shouldn't throw shade as my presentation was just as whimsical choosing to perform an expressive sign language to a Rebecca St. James song based on Psalm 139. I know, so masc, bro. Why I didn't think of buying and showing off a gas guzzling muscle car and Cuban cigars, while proclaiming a newfound manly love for Bruce Willis, I'll never know.

I kept my eye on Colton throughout graduation evening, wandering to thoughts of sharing a life and making out with him for hours. I figured if I'm not healed, then he probably wasn't either. We chatted a few times after the program ended, and I would often see him at church on occasion. We hung out in group settings with other church friends, but a close friendship between us never happened. I still yearned for that closeness to another male, and the longing never went away. All this confusion meant I had to press into God even more because I was doing something wrong. Evidently, I was a failure.

Although I was constantly tormented mentally dealing with my sexuality, the semester was going great. I didn't engage in random hookups, I loved my classes, and my relationship with Gwen was progressing (even though we were long distance). My friendships were many, but most were with girls. I lacked male friendships, which did not matter to me much, but for homosexual healing purposes, I knew I had to have those "strong Christian male friendships" to help in the healing process which was advised from leadership in *The River*. I was always on the lookout for a guy to befriend and emulate who could support, strengthen, and keep me accountable. He also had to be attractive, which was just my personal rule. You got eight-pack abs, thick curly hair, and a smirk that will weaken me to my knees in front of your crotch? Great, you have just qualified to help me become straight.

Enter Curt. I'm pretty sure everyone at Biola knew Curt. He had no problem making his presence known. Curt exhibited this loud, deep, booming voice that would probably annoy most people if it wasn't for his relenting friendliness and spirited personality. He greeted everyone boisterously as he walked by. Curt knew he was larger-than-life and didn't seem to give a shit what people thought of him.

You guessed it, Curt was a cute dude—swimmer extraordinaire and eyes that sparkled like the Maldives ocean water. His personality, although at times a bit overbearing, still fueled my attraction to him. He would often hang around outside my dorm for what seemed like no reason at all, talking to people as they walked past him. One day, Curt stopped me as I scurried by him, and engaged in small talk. Part of me wanted to chat because he was cute, but he also came off as intimidating with his deep baritone voice and extroverted nature—I didn't think I would click with him. After a few days of getting trapped in a conversation with him every time I tried to enter my dorm, it became apparent that Curt wanted to pursue a friendship with me, especially when he gave me his email and dorm room number in case I ever wanted to hang out, and I reciprocated. It was a friendly gesture, but I doubted either one of us would initiate.

Welp, I was wrong. Curt full-on pursued me. I started to feel a bit more comfortable with him the more we hung out, and he was not as obnoxious as I initially thought but a decently kind human being who passionately loved Jesus.

One day as we were chatting in my dorm, he caught me off guard and bluntly asked, "Aaron, do you have any guys in your life, like guys you can just chat with and tell crap to?"

Why is he asking me this? Why was he taking such an active interest in my life?

Curt saw something in me that made him want to reach out, and I didn't question it, but welcomed it. I accepted his offer to be friends without much hesitation. And truth be told, he passed my hot guy test to be my heterosexual savior.

The more I got to know Curt, the more I trusted him as a safe place to let my guard down. I imagined that he must be the guy God brought into my life to save me from myself, so I had to tell him about my homosexual struggle. I expected and feared rejection, not knowing how he would handle it, but hopeful he would not be fazed by my confession. Not only did Curt care less but admitted to having other friends who also struggled with being gay. I was relieved. From that moment on, Curt became one of the closest male friends that I ever had. There are no words to convey the impact that he had on my life throughout the rest of my years at Biola. Our friendship was effortless, pure, and fun. I recognized my attraction to him but did not excessively lust after him like I did with Stitch or become emotionally dependent on him like John. However, I'm sure to no one's surprise, my relationship with Curt did not alleviate any homosexual attractions nor give me a desire to pinup scantily clad posters of Pamela Anderson on my dorm room wall.

Curt was by my side during one of the scariest times in my life – when I got my second HIV test. I got my first HIV test at some seedy clinic in the San Fernando Valley while attending YWAM. The building was not in a great part of town and pretty run down. If I didn't have HIV before walking in, I was sure to contract that and every other virus just walking through the parking lot. During one of my meetings with Landon, he urged me to get tested at the Biola Health Center, but I couldn't afford $90 as a broke college kid. Even though Biola had its rules and regulations on homosexual activity, anything that occurred in the Biola Health Center was confidential. Generously Landon paid for my HIV test, a gesture that surpassed my expectations of him. I told Curt about the test, and he volunteered to be by my side every step of the way. This is why I was so intensely drawn to Curt, and it went way beyond his physical attractiveness. He showed me my worth and validated me as a person and not as some broken guy who needed to change his sexuality to be a whole person. Curt saw me as human, not as a project.

The day of the test, I walked in on him kneeling in prayer in the Biola Health Center waiting room. Literally on his knees, praying for me. This sight took my breath away. He didn't know I was there which made the moment so much more special. He stood by my side as the nurse drew the blood, holding my hand, emotionally and physically supporting me in a time I did not want to be alone. I was petrified of the probability I could be HIV positive due to hooking up with most of the gay men in Orange County the year prior. Curt comforted me and eased my nerves. He rejoiced and celebrated with me when I received my negative results. My love and gratitude for him is abundant—I will never forget him.

Although I treasured my friendship with Curt, his presence in my life did not make me straight as I had hoped. I believed that if I created and cultivated healthy relationships with straight Christian males, my attractions would gradually start to change. The belief was that once I started emulating and feeding off their masculine energy, it would somehow seep into my pores, through my bloodstream, up to my frontal lobe and boot out the nastiness that made me prefer being stranded on a deserted island with a naked Jude Law over...well, any woman.

Things with Gwen still moved along as much as they could with her living in Ecuador; however, I was not hooking up with guys, so I figured that my homosexual healing was progressing. Gwen and I still talked as much as opportunity allowed, but the distance made conversation through email our primary form of communication. When possible, we talked on the phone, and hearing her joyful voice filled me with so much excitement and, simultaneously, agony. I missed her so much, but in the best friend kind of way. The guilt I felt for not being more interested romantically weighed heavily, but I still wanted to pursue her. I needed to become straight, and for some reason, beyond my realm of understanding, I convinced myself that if I married Gwen, I would achieve my goal. I even mailed my mother a picture of Gwen and me so that she could pray for us as a couple. It's embarrassing and foolish that my obliviousness of non-existent sexual feelings for Gwen did not concern me as much as they should have.

By May of 2003, I had completed my second year at Biola. Only one more year to graduation! That summer, I did not return to Long Island as usual but stayed on campus because I got a job waiting tables at the restaurant chain, BJ's Brewhouse, in Cerritos. Working at BJ's was my only interaction with the secular world. My life was saturated with all things Christian—college, friends, and church—so getting this job allowed me to venture into life outside the Biola bubble. BJ's also tested how I would deal with non-Christians and homosexuality. I tried to avoid personal conversations with the staff. God forbid anyone find out that I was attracted to guys. I needed to present a respectable life of faith, display holiness, and, if asked, express that homosexuality was not God's plan for my life. My purpose was to be a "light in the darkness" to my coworkers. If they found out that I was attracted to guys, my witness would be ruined. I would make God look bad.

No one really questioned my sexuality, at least directly, except a fellow waiter named Hunter, an all-American, tall and attractive jock-type who I naturally found extremely hot. Daily he would graphically and grotesquely make raunchy comments about all female customers and staff. Whether we were filling up sodas at the beverage station or at the computer putting in orders, it was not uncommon for Hunter to say something utterly obscene about a woman's body or what he wanted to do to her. I rarely remarked on his vulgarities, but if I did, it wasn't much more than shaking my head with a forced smile, saying, *"Shut up, Hunter,"* rolling my eyes, and walking away. His pornographic commentary about every female disinterested me, probably *because* he talked about women. However, in a sick and twisted way, the dirtier he was, the more I lusted after him. I liked being around him and often checked the schedule to see if we were working together and would even switch shifts and stations with coworkers so I could interact with him as much as possible. It was clear that he was more than comfortable with sexuality in general, and we often physically teased each other with purple nurples and ass slaps. My attraction toward him, the way he subtly flirted with me, and his salacious stories of who and where he wanted to put his dick intrigued me more than I wanted them to.

During a shift one afternoon, Hunter approached me and asked, "Hey, do you like guys or girls?"

The question stunned me. It was the first time anyone had directly asked. With a mix of fear due to his potential reaction and my spiritual state in trying to conquer my gay attractions and keep a good Christian witness, I answered him softly and unconvincingly, as if I was asking a question rather than answering one.

"Girrrls?"

I noticed Hunter looked disappointed and confused simultaneously, whether he didn't believe me or preferred a different answer.

He then asked, "So, do you ever experiment with guys?"

Why is he asking me this? I was a bit perplexed yet extremely curious. But to keep in line with how God would want me to respond, I answered, "No, I don't experiment with guys."

"Ah, damn," he said quietly, frustrated. He walked away and I stood there in shock. *Did I just turn down sex with this hot guy? What is wrong with me?*

Although never confirmed, this dude was probably bisexual or just super horny and will stick his penis in any hole. If he was indirectly asking me to be those holes, I turned him down flat. However, at that moment, the reason behind his questioning did not register, and I was more focused on being obedient to God than investigating his motives.

All my future interactions with Hunter contradicted the lie I had told him about my sexuality. From that point on, I allowed myself to be even more flirty with him, and he welcomed it. Our handsy interactions only intensified, whether it was him grabbing my ass when I got ice, me tapping his crotch while he carried a tray full of drinks, or even pinching his nipples so I could touch his toned chest, I enjoyed every opportunity to put my hands on him in some way, and he never seemed to mind. The interactions with Hunter stirred up a lot of emotion, but more so elevated hormones. Seizing an opportunity to hook up with Hunter should have been a no brainer, but I avoided it because he was someone I saw in my everyday life. He was not a stranger from down the street that I never had to see again. I wasn't quite sure how I would handle that. Frustration overwhelmed me as I had another extreme attraction to a guy that I could not control, while still planning to marry Gwen someday.

After avoiding many temptations during those months, my craving for sexual connection with another male was fueled dramatically because of the flirtatious, albeit unfulfilling, sexual interactions with Hunter. Hunter quit working at the restaurant so even if I changed my mind about investigating his sexual advances, he was no longer an option and we lost touch. Having a boyfriend would be more meaningful, but I didn't want that. I wanted to be healed, but if I were to actively disobey God, the meaningless hookups would have to suffice until the homosexual attraction eventually disappeared. Yes, I actually believed God would eventually heal me of homosexuality while still pursuing sex with other guys—It's quite baffling.

The struggle with my conflicting sexuality was an infliction deep into my core. I always felt dirty, even during weeks and months when I remained celibate. Despite avoiding the physical aspect, I could never escape my thoughts, which dominated me night and day. I would soon start pursuing random hookups again, with no regard to my relationship with Gwen.

I felt guilty, not so much because of Gwen but because I retreated into hooking up when I was celibate for so long. Even so, I felt compelled to tell her my setback. I sat at my computer, calm and confident that she would support and comfort me in my distress. By this time, she was back from Ecuador, living in Northern California. As we chatted on instant messenger, I told her I hooked up with a guy, expecting consolation and prayers. My tone was as nonchalant as if I was confessing to a friend that I had broken their bicycle, but no, I was telling a girl I wanted to marry that I had sex with a dude. The pain I was about to inflict on her never occurred to me because, from my perspective, it was "not that big of a deal," and she would understand it's just part of the struggle. I compartmentalized my relationship with Gwen and my homosexuality separately, believing they had nothing to do with each other. My stupidity was embarrassing and inexcusable. Gwen was in love with me, and I did not know the true extent. I was such a fool.

Gwen's reaction didn't seem extraordinary, as much as one could interpret through a computer screen. The next day, Gwen sent me an email saying that she wanted to end our relationship and that it was best that we did not speak anymore. I could not believe what I was reading.

What? I was livid. *What the hell happened???*

I was the victim! Satan tempted me! I had no grasp on why she was upset enough to toss our entire relationship out the window. I quickly hit the reply button to discuss why she acted so hastily; however, my email bounced back. Yeah, she blocked me.

What the actual fuck, Gwen??

I refused to let her have the last word, so I signed on to my other email account to send a reply, but as my luck would have it, my computer froze. My 2002 Gateway computer failed me at the most inopportune time, but I was familiar with how often it would freeze, and I would have to do a reboot. This was an inconvenient time for my computer to give out on me, as one could imagine. My emotions were already at an indescribable level of confusion and anger. Adding a frozen computer to the scenario when needing to send an important email could be disastrous, and it was.

In a fit of pure rage and frustration, I jumped up and smashed my keyboard on the computer screen until it broke into a million pieces, cursing Gwen out verbally with every hit and throw. Realizing that the computer would not survive my wrath, I furiously carried the tower, monitor, and scanner to the dumpster. I continued to release my anger on the equipment though, throwing them down on the concrete right there in the campus parking lot.

I have never experienced that kind of rage before or since. If anyone approached me, they would have seen an Aaron that would have terrified them. I was volatile, devastated, and heartbroken. After smashing the equipment to unrecognizable pieces and chucking them in the dumpster, I grabbed the scanner. Like a scene from a movie, right on cue, several pictures of Gwen and me flew out of the scanner and found their way face up onto the concrete. A few weeks prior, I scanned pictures of us to keep on my computer screen, forgetting the hard copies remained under the scanner lid all that time. Seeing those pictures only exacerbated my fury. In tears, I ripped them all up while saying unpleasant things about Gwen in the process.

How could she do this to me? Pathetically, that was the question I asked. *How can **she** do this to **me**??*

I'm amazed that no one walked by during my madness near the dumpster that day, as I'm sure it was a sight to see. Emotionally drained, I walked back to my dorm room to regain my composure to call Megan, my closest friend and confidante, to tell her the series of events that unfolded. I expected Megan would validate my anger and be as mad at Gwen on my behalf.

To my chagrin, Megan said, "Hey Aaron, this is all your fault."
"What?? What did I do wrong?!" I shouted back.
"You obviously do not know how females feel things, do you?" Megan asked. I had no idea what she was talking about.

Megan explained why Gwen was hurt. Gwen had believed that she would marry me someday, and I betrayed her for having sex with some strange guy when she hadn't even kissed me yet. Her words went in one ear and out the other. I could not allow them to sink in because I had this cloud of ignorance and selfishness that hovered over me. Megan continued, showing me that I was involved with two different "Gwens"—Gwen the girlfriend/future spouse and Gwen, the buddy/accountability partner. The latter should not exist. Finally, Megan's words were making sense and sinking in. I started to uncover the realization that Gwen deeply loved me. She loved me beyond the friendship level as I viewed her - as a boyfriend and her future husband.

After a week of processing my whole relationship with Gwen, she sent an email and wanted to talk things out. Still, even with Megan's revolutionary words that made me see the light, my victim mentality sustained, and I told her I did not want to talk because of how easily she threw me out of her life and blocked my email. Bitterness consumed me, and anger toward Gwen rested uncomfortably in my heart. We didn't talk for nearly two years.

When we reconnected two years later, we talked on the phone about what happened between us. I sat in my car on the phone and listened as she poured her heart out to me, telling me how much she sincerely and legitimately loved me and planned to have a future with me. I then came out of nowhere and very matter-of-factly told her that I hooked up with some guy. Hearing her cries and hurt, I finally understood how much pain I had caused her and how very wrong my actions were from the fallout. We met up at Olive Garden to continue the conversation, trying to eat our breadsticks and pasta through tears and mourning the death of our relationship. She drove eight hours from Northern to Southern California to meet face to face in hopes to put what was left of our friendship back together. The poor server at Olive Garden had no idea what to do with herself. Every time she walked by both of us had bloodshot, tear-stained faces and were slobbering all over the table. We talked for hours and hours that evening. Olive Garden management had to throw us out since we stayed well past closing. After we left, we went to Common Grounds, the on-campus coffee shop, to continue, until they threw us out as well. So much healing took place that night. She did not deserve what I did to her, and I finally took complete responsibility.

All this pain and misery could have been avoided had I been honest with *myself* about my homosexual attractions. I remember trying to convince Gwen that I did love her, but she disagreed. She said that I loved the "idea" of her. Man, that hurt because it was a concept that made sense, and she was right.

All I ever wanted was the cliché Christian life—married to a girl with 2.5 kids, a cat, and a white picket fence—so that everyone could be proud of me, especially God.

I wanted a wife and kids, but what I could not grasp, until this situation escalated, was that I *desired the desire* because a natural desire did not exist. Throughout my entire relationship with Gwen, we never had sex. We never kissed. We never even held hands. I'm sure a lot of that had to do with the bulk of our relationship being long distance, but I simply had no desire to because she was a girl. I never had sexual feelings toward any girl. End of story. I swore to myself that I would never attempt to date another woman unless I was 100 percent free from homosexual attraction. I vowed I would never put another girl through that kind of pain again. Wouldn't you know that I have not dated a girl since Gwen? Not so shocking.

Gwen will always have a piece of my heart. The girl who came running out to me in front of the Biola cafe, screaming my name, with a blue cast on her arm. She was something so very special. The past cannot be undone, but in time our wounds were mended. Gwen and I keep in contact. We had lunch a couple of months ago while I was visiting a friend up in Northern California. It warmed my heart that we could put the past behind us, have a friendship, and still enjoy life without resentment, anger, or grudges. My hat's off to Gwen; she is a class act.

My years at Biola University were coming to an end. Three years of the most amazing memories and friends one can only dream of. Yes, there were painful moments, but they were overshadowed by the most joyous and happiest of times. Graduation approached, and my future was left up for grabs. I developed a love for casting while pursuing my degree in television production. I had the opportunity to help cast actors for several Biola short films that would be produced, and that ignited my passion to pursue television casting in some form. Relieved as I was to have a career plan after graduation, I was still emotionally and spiritually a basket case.

During that last year of Biola, I sought another pastor for counseling for my struggle with homosexuality. I don't remember where I found him or even what his name was, but I needed to pursue healing wherever I could find it. At this point, I had to be only one counseling session, or one book, or one sermon away from being completely healed. I only met with him a few times as he did not seem to know how to help me beyond praying and telling me to create healthy friendships with guys and keep reading the Bible.

Ok, sure. Will do.

After graduating with the Biola University class of 2004, I stayed in La Mirada. I moved into a house with several other guys from school, a temporary situation until I figured out something more long term. That summer, I continued to work at BJ's as much as possible to make money while trying to find a job in a casting office. It was strange to be out of the Biola bubble and on my own. However, this freedom would be a true test of how I would deal with my struggle outside a stable Christian environment.

When possible, I still attended the Anaheim Vineyard as it was important to me to maintain a solid Christian foundation. Not having spiritual accountability with anyone at that time of my life, it became easier and easier to hook up with random guys. Even though I was not held to Biola's contract any longer, I could, in theory, do whatever and even pursue a boyfriend. But I did not want that. The war between my head and heart surged, and the more I wanted healing, the more I would act out and find a new guy to have sex with. My heart became so incredibly heavy, and I would often get extremely depressed.

I vividly remember one afternoon driving to BJ's for a shift. I arrived there early, so I parked my car and played some worship music to meditate, attempting to ease my shame and guilt. Shane & Shane, a hugely popular Christian worship band that I loved, released an album that year called *Carried Away* and one of their hit songs, "Be Near," started playing from my iPod. The song conveyed how much I wanted a touch from God, for him to be near me and that I needed to hear from him within my despair.

"God, please take away these homosexual feelings. I can't take it anymore. I'm so tired," I prayed.

There could not have been a more poignant song to speak to me at that very moment. I needed to feel that Jesus was near and that he had not deserted me in my time of need. As I sat in that parking lot, allowing the song's words to fill me in God's love, a tear streamed down my cheek, which turned into a whimper, then a cry, and then into a loud sob.

I finally let it all out: pent up suppression, confusion, and spiritual exhaustion, and years of built-up frustrations about same-sex attractions while desperately crying out to God, hoping he would reveal his comforting presence to me. I wept and wept. The emotional release felt good, but not much else occurred besides letting out a good cry. I hoped for a miraculous presence of God to descend on me, releasing me from these homosexual thoughts and cravings, but no, I knew they were still very present. Before I walked into the restaurant, I had to compose myself and put on my happy face for hungry customers. Letting out a good cry is soothing, and for a moment, I felt at peace. But that moment wouldn't last.

Chapter Ten

LIAR LIAR

PUBLIC SERVICE ANNOUNCEMENT: YOUR BJ's jokes are not funny and not original.

Despite the *many* customers who thought they were comedians, I loved working at the restaurant practically as a full-time employee while I searched for jobs in television casting. The sexually driven jokes around the restaurant's name got old quickly. No comment conveyed uniqueness, and if we laughed, it's because we wanted you to like us enough to splurge on a fat tip and *not* because your BJ's joke was the funniest thing since Jim Carrey. Despite the trials and tribulations I faced within my sexuality the last year, working there remained a constant. The staff were more than co-workers. In a sense, and to sound incredibly cliché, we became a family, especially since we were the opening crew.

We gossiped about co-workers at the soda fountain, talked shit about the obnoxious people at our tables while congregating at the computer station, and complained about our lack of tips when rolling silverware napkins in the break room. After our long eight hour shifts together, we often decompressed at the local TGI Fridays. Still dressed in our ranch-stained uniforms, we'd drink, eat happy hour appetizers, and continue gossiping and complaining, all in good fun.

Since waiting tables was not the intended career plan, leaving La Mirada and moving closer to the entertainment industry in Los Angeles was a priority. Luckily, a couple of my close female friends from college, Brea and Denise, had recently graduated flight attendant school—you know, putting that good ole Biola degree to use. As Los Angeles based flight attendants, they were looking for an apartment close to the airport and asked if I wanted to join them and their flight attendant friend, Mary Lynn, in the apartment hunt. We found a three-bedroom apartment in Torrance, not far from the beautiful Redondo Beach and the infamous Pacific Coast Highway. All four of us, as born-again Christians, peacefully co-existed in our living arrangements. We were not the party-type people most secular twenty-somethings could be.

Since the move to Torrance, hooking up with guys again hit me like a wrecking ball (thanks, Miley Cyrus). Discretion was in overdrive as I did not want Brea, Denise, or Mary Lynn to know about my iniquitous extracurricular activities. My promiscuity ran rampant as I met with different guys 3-4 times a week, if not more.

These countless encounters turned into a full out sex addiction. I'm no psychologist, and I have read there are different theories and studies if "sex addiction" is an actual disorder. Dr. Roberta Zanzonico stated, "While the media presents sex addiction as a recognized psychiatric entity, mental health professions debate the validity of the diagnosis."[1] A controversial disorder that has not yet made its way into DSM-5 (*Diagnostic and Statistical Manual of Mental Disorders*), sex addiction is estimated to affect between 3 percent and 6 percent of the population.[2]

Labeling myself a sex addict was a self-diagnosis, whether it was an official disorder or not. My days consisted of working, hooking up with guys, and watching *General Hospital*. The late evenings usually concluded with me crying every night to God for him to take away the gay feelings and forgive me of my sexual sin. Living with three flight attendants who were not often home gave me the ability to have guys come over freely. I strategically made sure all three of my roommates were away on work trips before making any plans, nonchalantly asking them their schedules for the upcoming week. All this sneaking around and plotting added to my already deep guilt. I was not attending church anymore since Anaheim Vineyard was no longer geographically close and I did not have any strong Christian influences that could support and help me in my struggle. My relationship with God was strained, and I felt utterly lost, drowning in regret.

The guilt and shame from the random hookups manifested in the most inconvenient of times. One time I met a guy at his house in the Hollywood Hills, and before we got naked and had a romp, I decided to give him a Bible lesson about how I believed that hooking up and being gay was sinful. Very sexy, am I right? I did this often. I can't explain why I thought these guys needed a rundown of my guilt and religious convictions. I went back to that same guy's house only a few days later, expressing my shame yet again, saying I could not do anything sexual with him. I left his residence that night proud and thankful to God I conquered temptation, only to find myself back at his place the following week going at it. The indecisiveness of my actions only created more anguish to an already fucked-up situation.

Amid my sex addiction, I was contacted to work a three-week gig as a casting assistant for an NBC game show and immediately accepted the job. The game show was called *Deal or No Deal (DOND)*, hosted by comedian Howie Mandel. The staff in the casting department worked collectively to find the best contestants for the show. *DOND* casting looked for high energy, big personalities, and people deserving of a chance to win $1 million. My duties consisted of sorting mail, processing contestant applications, and assisting the coordinators with whatever they needed. Do this Aaron, get this Aaron—typical entry level bitch work.

Over the next few days, I acclimated myself with the staff, who were an eclectic group of people. The head of the casting department, a tall, outspoken, "give no fucks," Jewish guy named Neal, was quite the character. He had this arrogant presence to him that was undeniably intimidating. When Neal walked into a room, all attention shifted to him instantly. Without a doubt, he was the guy in charge and took no shit from anyone. With all that said, Neal inhabited a twisted sense of humor and was a blast to hang out with, easily able to separate his boss persona from the real him. Behind the cocky exterior was a compassionate, generous man who cared deeply for his staff—truly one of the best people I have ever worked for in my career.

I then met head casting directors, Mary-Rachel and Brandon. Within seconds of meeting Brandon, I was instantly attracted to him. He had that frat vibe and "guys' guy" thing about him—an overall laid back and likable dude. He had a great personality and exuded genuine confidence. He emitted a sexiness that was difficult for me to ignore, and I became quietly and lustfully intrigued with him. I also met the rest of the staff, including Greg, an openly gay man, Rita and Kristin, who both would become two of my closest friends.

I avoided getting close to Greg. He was gay and clearly going to hell—I couldn't be around him. It wouldn't be "spiritually healthy" for me. Not only did my Christian beliefs alter my own truth of self, but the religion permitted me to condemn other gay people. I couldn't falter and conform to the patterns of this world.[3] I was a man on a mission: to glorify God in word and deed and not be continually tempted into the evil world of homosexuality that had trapped me long enough. I believed this with all my heart, and yet at the same time, wanted to go into a storage closet with Brandon and unzip his pants.

Deal or No Deal became an instant hit with the viewers, and my three-week gig turned into an indefinite job. As the weeks and months went by, *Deal or No Deal* became a national phenomenon. Over time, I was promoted from assistant to senior casting associate, eventually interviewing and casting my own contestants. The video submissions came in by the truckloads due to the tremendous popularity of the show. At one time, during the height of popularity, the casting team went on a bus tour, traveling to nine different cities to hold open casting calls. These events would bring up to 15,000 people. *15,000!!* As a team, we would interview *every single person* in line. We worked very hard but had fun doing it. Thousands upon thousands of people would scream and chant when they saw the huge *Deal or No Deal* tour bus drive into the venue. A mass of shrieking, excitable fans flooded to the bus, rocking it back and forth, eagerly waiting for the bus doors to open, high fiving us as we made our way out. One would think that Beyonce or The Backstreet Boys would be stepping off that bus, but no, only us *Deal or No Deal* casting folk. We received a taste of what it would feel like to be a rockstar. It was an experience, quite possibly,

I will never witness again in my lifetime. What an honor to be a part of something so extraordinary. I'm indebted to Neal for the opportunity he gave me that jumpstarted my career in television producing.

Throughout my time working in the *Deal or No Deal* office, the topic of my sexuality would be held up to scrutiny. In the first month of my employment, Neal, the brashly blunt person he was, called me out in front of a few other staffers telling me I was gay and in denial. Never being one to filter his tongue, Neal said what he wanted when he wanted, and honestly, it was a huge part of his charm. He came into my office that I shared with two other co-workers, Brianna and Liz. Neal then grilled me about my sexuality. I persistently denied I was gay, but Neal would not relent, making me feel badgered into a corner.

All I could do to glorify God was to deny! deny! deny! Brianna tried to defend me to get Neal off my back; however, Liz agreed with Neal and laughed off my denials. I worked with Liz on another project the year before and was aware of her New York-bred, "tell it like it is" attitude that was somehow missing in the Long Islander within me. The conversation ended with me reluctantly admitting that I had those feelings "in the past" but wanted to have a family with a wife and kids.

As Neal left the room, he said smugly, "You will...with a man."

Humiliated, I silently prayed to the Lord for strength. I did not know how to navigate this.

I silently prayed: *Jesus, why am I going through this!? I am trying so hard to submit to your will. This is so hard; I need you to help me endure this.*

I felt so powerless and angry. Why was God still allowing me to have these attractions, putting me in the position to defend my sexuality? Then I would feel guilty for blaming God, believing I *allowed* myself to have these sinful thoughts and not praying hard enough to make them disappear. A constant flow of shame and self-blame had my tolerance of "doing the right thing" (by God's standards) hanging by a thread.

Around this time, the Proposition 8 conversation started—another hot topic dividing the liberals from the conservatives. Prop 8, a highly controversial proposal, made its way on the statewide ballot to prohibit same-sex marriage within the state of California. If one voted "YES," they agreed to the ban on same-sex marriage, and "NO" meant they opposed the ban. This issue created a passionate outcry, not solely from my immediate office, but for all homosexuals and LGBTQ allies in the state.

Convinced that gay people should not marry because it was against God's design for humanity, I vehemently agreed with this proposition. This stance coming from me was laughable as a guy who professed these anti-gay views in the morning but had secret hookups with anonymous men in the evening. I was a Republican politician in the making. The chatter in the office about this prop flourished, and I commented contrarily to my coworkers' beliefs. Some expressed their anger and frustration toward me, asking how I would feel if I could not marry my husband.

I replied sternly that my future was with a wife, not a husband. They laughed off my comment believing full well I was gay. In a mission to prove my stance to my coworkers, myself, and God, I voted "YES" on Prop 8 at the polls, a decision I have regretted.

It bothered me when people assumed that I was gay, and I became extremely self-conscious in how coworkers and even strangers perceived me.

What is it about me? My appearance? Did my wrists bend when I walked? Do I have a gay-sounding voice? Did they notice when I stare at Brandon's crotch? Did I talk about my love for the Golden Girls too much? Damn it Aaron, get it together and start acting straight!

I tried to pay more attention to my actions and reactions to make sure they did not come off too "gay acting." I focused on strengthening my self-awareness in how I conducted conversation and mannerisms. I went through a lot to hide my sexuality, and I would find out years later I didn't do a great job. When I sat at my desk going through the contestant video submissions, I often signed into a gay hookup website on my computer to chat with guys and organize hookups for after work. Years later, I found out that when I was away from my desk, a co-worker glanced at my computer and saw the gay hookup website on display with the chat conversations I had with these men. Let me tell you, we were not chatting about how the Dodgers did the night before or discussing a good recipe for chicken piccata. This co-worker told Brianna, and then, like any office, gossip spread like wildfire, and everyone knew I was a complete hoax. I remained unaware that my "cover" had been blown, as no one ever confronted me. I condemned homosexuality while the entire staff had proof that I dabbled in the very thing I denounced. Man, I must have looked like a damn fool.

While casting the second season of *Deal or No Deal*, there was a request to have more gay men contestants pitched to the network. Whether it was to liberalize the show more or the plain fact that gay guys are fabulously entertaining, Neal assigned the staff to recruit LGBTQ people in West Hollywood, the gay neighborhood of Los Angeles.

Oh no.

You mean I must go to *that* part of town? Where rainbow flags were in abundance and men wore pink shirts, held hands, and drank iced caramel macchiatos??? Oh, *hell no*! My co-workers were thrilled to go to the gay bars and get paid for it. No one complained—except me. I had a struggle of conscience, and my spirit waged a war of good against evil in my soul. God would not approve of me subjecting myself to the evil and sin of West Hollywood. I knew if I was put in that atmosphere, the temptation of the lifestyle might appeal to me, and I did not want to give the devil an easy opportunity to defile me. Yes, this is seriously what I thought.

I assumed talking to Neal to get out of this assignment would not be an easy feat. I practiced my speech, "Hey Neal, I can't go to West Hollywood; it's Satan's playground and Jesus will be mad at me." Sounds good, right? Knowing how outspoken

Neal was, there was no telling how he would react to me saying I wouldn't do my job. However, I believed I had a good argument seeing how cavorting around West Hollywood nightlife went against my religious beliefs.

I nervously walked into Neal's office, still massively intimidated by this man despite working together for the better part of a year. I expressed my concerns to him, stating that I was trying to live my life one way, to honor God, and I couldn't subject myself to the culture of West Hollywood. To my surprise, Neal reacted with incredible kindness, but I knew he disagreed with my reasoning. He compromised and gave me the day shift in West Hollywood which would keep me away from the wild night life. I accepted the compromise happily as if I thought the gays hibernated at night and would be surrounded safely by soccer moms and pastors. Thankfully, I was paired up with Mary-Rachel, which eased my nerves since she was the talker of the group and had no problem approaching anyone.

Walking down Santa Monica Blvd., I prayed silently, asking for God's protection over my heart and mind, and for salvation of the gay souls I walked past. We spent most of our time at The Abbey, a popular gay bar, talking to and recruiting the brunch crowd. My afternoon in West Hollywood came and went, and I lived to talk about it without being accosted by a drag queen or Neil Patrick Harris ... unfortunately.

Eventually, I became more comfortable telling my coworkers about my journey and how my faith played a part in "overcoming" homosexuality. On a work trip to Boston, I sat in a cafe with Rita and Luke, a casting director who recently joined the team after Brandon left the show, which disrupted my daily sexual daydreams of him, but I digress. Rita and Luke listened and asked me questions, reserving judgment and their opinions of what they honestly thought, which I assumed to be that I was deceiving myself and in extreme denial. If that's what they thought, they would not have been wrong.

On that same trip, I was in a restaurant with Luke and Neal, and a girl walked by outside the window. I stared at her hideous dress that she must have put on in the dark. Luke assumed I was checking her out, which I let him believe.

I smiled and forced my response, "Yeah, she's hot."

This was not the first or the last time I pretended to be attracted to a female to hide my secret.

On another trip to Philadelphia, the team was out after dinner, walking the streets when we passed a gay bar. Rita and Kristin pressured me to go in with them. I refused. They did their darndest to drag me in, pulling me by my arms over the threshold of the rainbow flag laced archway, but I stood my ground, pulling away from them and yelling sternly, "No, I do *not* want to go into a gay bar!"

Their pressure infuriated me when I made it clear I did not want to go inside. I left them annoyed, headed back to my hotel room, and went online to find a guy to hook up with. As long as I was acting out my gay sexual perversions in private, I could still portray the false façade of the Christian witness I intended to be.

Despite working at *DOND* full time, I still waited tables at BJ's on the weekends, where my sexuality was not so much in question mainly because my BJ's coworkers just assumed I was gay, without me confirming or denying it. One evening, I went to BJ's off the clock with my friend Milena to have dinner with my employee discount. Milena was a good friend from college and one of the few people from Biola that I still hung out with post-graduation. We were sitting in the booth, chatting it up when one of my managers, Lisa, invited herself to sit down next to me. I introduced Milena to her, and we engaged in some small talk.

Out of the blue and catching me completely off guard, Lisa asked, "Hey Aaron, do you have a boyfriend?"

Milena knew of my homosexual struggle, and as a fellow Christian, supported me in my attempt to pursue healing. Lisa's question still pierced through my chest as if a swarm of bees stung me from the inside out. Her question mortified me, especially in front of Milena.

Why did she think I was gay? I looked at Milena in bewilderment, and then back to Lisa and said softly, "No, I do not."

Hoping this line of questioning would end, Lisa proceeded, "Well, that's too bad because you could bring him in here, and we could meet him."

What a bizarre statement, I thought. Who says that to people? I looked at her calmly but internally panicking, trying to convince myself as much as her as I said, "Lisa, I'm not gay."

The huge smile that beamed from her face in the hope she could meet my imaginary boyfriend gradually turned into a confused and embarrassed glare. There was not much else to say, and awkwardness permeated the air. She left the table. Milena and I continued the conversation we were having before Lisa interrupted, not even referencing the incident that just occurred.

Despite the Lisa incident, I tested the boundaries of my secret homosexual sin, exposing my true tendencies with another male server from BJ's. The hiding and resisting of my true self frustrated me mentally and sexually. The year before, I had avoided my coworker Hunter's advances, but this time I hoped to find a male coworker to form a secret sexual relationship.

Colin would often make sexual comments and jokes around me, and the more he did, the more I was lustfully drawn to him. He was straight as far as I knew, but I tested the waters with Colin, reciprocating his raunchy humor. We continued to tease and joke with one another and during one shift, I bluntly offered to give him a blowjob after he made an oral sex reference. "Hey man, if you need a blowjob, I can take care of that for you later bro," I said confidently, throwing in the "bro" for good masculine measure. Colin blushed and smiled, batting the longest eyelashes I've ever seen on a dude.

To my surprise, Colin did not respond with outright rejection. Instead, he laughed as he responded, "I don't think so."

Think so? So, you are saying there's a chance??

Nothing materialized with Colin, but man, the hypocrisy here was so thick, I could not see straight (pun intended). One day I was telling my manager Lisa that I wasn't gay, and in the same week, I was trying to get Colin to drop his pants for me in the back of my Honda. If Colin and Lisa ever talk about my sexuality with each other, their stories would contradict, making my claim of heterosexuality fraudulent. I never saw a psychiatrist, but there had to be a name for this type of sickness.

I would never see it coming, but soon enough, my lust for men would make its grand appearance, forgoing all the resistance of my homosexual proclivities. When the *Deal or No Deal* staff traveled to different cities to hold casting events, my coworkers gravitated toward the bars and clubs in the off hours, blowing their per diem on booze and club cover charges. The loud music, crowds, and obnoxious drunk people never appealed to me, and I still had never been drunk at this point of my life. On these evenings, I would often retreat to my hotel room, order some room service, and hopefully catch a rerun of *Full House* or *The Golden Girls*. My coworkers did not always allow me to escape to my room so easily. They wanted me to hang out, but I rarely was interested and hated the bar/club scene. I purposely made myself an outcast, knowing they wanted me to "break out of my shell" and be "who I was." Not to be a complete Debbie Downer, I sometimes relented, convincing myself to go out with them, but I would be miserable, sneak out of the club, and make my way back to my hotel room while they got sloshed.

One night in Miami, the team was at some nightclub, and I was ready to take off to my hotel room per usual when Greg, you know, the gay coworker I tried to avoid because he might put a homosexual spell on me, asked me if I wanted to get out of there. *YES!!* For some reason, I assumed he was finished for the evening and wanted to head back to the hotel.

No such luck.

Instead of getting a cab, Greg took a detour, and we walked toward another bar. Within an instant of noticing the guys on the patio drinking brightly colored cocktails and that rainbow flag I loathed hanging from the window, I knew it was a gay bar. I did not want to go in, but Greg coaxed me a little and promised me, "One drink, and we will leave." Reluctantly I agreed, at least outwardly.

Internally, I was more intrigued and curious than I let on. We headed to the bartender, and I uncomfortably took a seat on a stool. Greg asked me what I wanted to drink, and I knew he would keep pushing until I had something alcoholic in my hands, so I succumbed to Citron and Sprite. *Vodka? Aaron—you never ever drink but you order a vodka!* I'm sure ordering lemon flavored vodka didn't really help the heterosexual argument either. Since Greg was paying, I took the drink so he would leave me alone. We chatted at the bar top as we drank. I sucked up the vodka, thinking

I could get the drink down and be done with it, but before I knew it, Greg ordered another round. Already into my second drink, I felt more relaxed, but my head was spinning a bit.

After Greg and I finished the second round, he asked if I wanted to walk around the bar. I obliged. He ordered a third drink, put it in my hand, and I sipped it as we started to make our rounds. We headed downstairs to find nearly naked men dancing provocatively in every corner of the room. I was somewhere between tipsy and drunk. This was the most alcohol I had ever consumed in my life.

I knew I was in deep sin at this point, hoping God was looking the other way. The vodka has already done its job and I did not feel in control of what I was doing or saying. My inhibitions were gone, and I had to depend on Greg, but I felt safe with him, knowing instinctively that he was taking care of me. Of course, this must have been Greg's plan all along: to get a little alcohol in my system to loosen me up a bit and allow myself to explore the real me? As if entering the gay bar and drinking the alcohol excessively wasn't already preparing me for a long night of begging God's forgiveness, suddenly an incredibly hot Cuban go-go dancer, with abs for days, approached uninvited and starting lap-dancing all up in my business. I felt awkward, but my inebriated state allowed me to relish in the extreme bliss of the moment.

The dancer then took my hand and put it down his G-string, where he allowed me to grab and caress his very thick penis. I was indulging in pure sin and loving every second of it. For one fleeting moment, I thought that maybe it was OK to be gay and not care about what anyone else thought. But this euphoric moment did not last. Guilt started to creep in, and I told Greg not to tell Neal or anyone else what happened that night. Shame descended upon me for letting my guard down that evening, and I did not want anyone else knowing that I engaged in such depravity.

We had an early flight the next morning and Greg had to practically carry me out of the bar, helping me into the taxi as I could barely walk without his support. I had four vodka sprites that evening, and I was hit harder than Muhammad Ali's punching bag.

Greg dragged me to my hotel room and crashed on my bed as I drunkenly packed up my suitcase. I barely remember going to sleep, but in the middle of the night, I woke up to find Greg in bed with me. I tried to process what happened. I remembered going out the night before but not enough to wonder how Greg was in my bed. We were both fully clothed, so I assumed nothing happened but sleeping, but, oh man, it was a night I won't soon forget.

We headed to Boston the next day, and nothing was said about that night in Miami. For all I knew, the unfortunate evening of debauchery was only between Greg and me. Sobering up provided a pathway to embarrassment and guilt. I wanted to forget the evening ever happened. I disappointed God for putting myself in such a

tempting situation and should have walked away the second I realized Greg brought me to a gay bar.
Why didn't I walk away?!

Chapter Eleven

BRING IT ON

Being a disciple of Christ in Los Angeles was difficult, to say the least. I really liked both of my jobs, but they created a space that was detrimental to my healing. The temptations of homosexuality seemed to be in every corner, and I gave in more than I didn't—proving I was really good at being a failure. Behind the face of the man that was engaging potential contestants who wanted to be on a game show and impressing diners to earn a big tip was someone who was hopelessly despondent. I missed my relationship with God and craved the warmth of his grace, settling in my heart and restoring my soul. I yearned for the times in YWAM when I felt "free" and passionately in love with the Lord. I started to look for a church again, hoping to find a place where I can find belonging and accountability.

Milena told me she was attending Oasis Church located in an old theater on Wilshire Blvd. in Hollywood and suggested I check it out. I visited the website to get the vibe and scope out the staff list to see if there were any guys I could reach out to and connect with. I desired a mentor, someone who would help me with my homosexuality or, more accurately, an attractive guy who would fully devote his time to "save" me from myself.

I scrolled through the staff list and sent an email to a guy named Nathan. There was no picture, but I chose him mainly because of his position as "Connection Coordinator." He seemed like the right person. *I hope he's hot!*

Nathan wrote back enthusiastically, and after a few emails back and forth, we agreed to meet in the lobby before the following Sunday service. I arrived late and missed our meet and greet but headed into the service where worship had already started. I stood by the door and watched the band rock out to some high energy worship music. This was not a typical service but more like a full-fledged concert. The crowd jumped up and down amidst strobe lighting and fog machine effects. I started to fixate on the worship leader—a young woman, whose smile illuminated from the stage to the back of the theater. I intently stared at her. Above the sea of hands lifted in praise, her face glowed. The joy that radiated from her captivated me, and I did my best to hide my tears from the strangers around me. I once had that joy that she had, and I missed it. I wanted what she had. *Give me your joy!* I was broken, confused, and depressed. I could have watched her worship all night, wishing that the joy that flooded her would pour into me. I later learned her name was Danielle, someone who would later become significant in my life. I left after the sermon but was already eager to return the following Sunday to watch Danielle worship again.

Nathan and I made plans again to meet in the lobby the following Sunday. I walked into the Oasis theater, hopeful and expectant that my life could change that day. I proceeded to the information table and asked where I could find Nathan West. They pointed him out to me. I turned my head and saw a very familiar person.

I know him! I silently shrieked, *OMG! It's "Jan Jan, The Cheerleading Man."* The film *Bring It On* had come out seven years prior to this moment, starring Kirsten Dunst and Gabrielle Union as rival cheerleaders. Nathan played Jan, the hot straight dude who got teased for being on the cheerleading team...as if being a guy named Jan wasn't reason enough. For me, *Bring It On* was right up there with *Clueless* as one of my favorite quotable movies and now I was about to meet a cast member—and the hot guy too! I had to give myself a pep talk before the approach. *Ok Aaron, get composed, don't embarrass yourself and for God's sake do not look at his crotch.*

I went up to him and introduced myself as "Aaron from the emails." Nathan flashed his perfect smile and gave me a big hug. His exaggerated yet authentic friendly demeanor shattered the initial "star struck" feelings I had toward him. I did not confess right away that I knew who he was in fear I may scare him off. I played it *very* cool. Nathan's wife, Chyler, a celebrity in her own right, was Lexie Grey from ABC's *Grey's Anatomy*. From that moment on, Nathan took me under his wing, and his celebrity did not faze me as the weeks and months of our friendship progressed.

Nathan gave me exactly what I wanted from our friendship. As I hoped, he walked alongside me in my pursuit of homosexual healing. Nathan completely opened his heart and availability to me. We hung out whenever his schedule allowed, and I tagged along with him to all church events he oversaw so I could help him out *and* be around him. He consistently encouraged me, gave me advice, prayed with me, and provided me with the validation and affirmation I desired. No matter how much of himself he gave me, I wanted more. I wanted what I couldn't have—for him to be my boyfriend. I fell for him hard.

It did not take too long before the same emotional dependency I had with John started developing with Nathan. The need to be around him all the time became uncontainable. When he did not reply to an email I sent, I thought he was mad at me. When he did not give me the attention I wanted at church, I would take it as a rejection. The thing about emotional dependency is that it ultimately depends on irrationality and emotional instability to be fostered, both of which I had. Despite the growing dependency, Nathan's friendship saved me during that time in my life. I became immersed in church life, volunteered my time every Sunday, and discontinued random hookups. My relationship with Jesus flourished, all thanks to Nathan's guidance. I don't know if Nathan ever sensed my dependency on him, but if he did, he was a damn good sport.

Even though Nathan's spiritual support and mentorship decreased my temptations to hook up, they still were very much present. Whenever I had the urge to download Grindr (a gay hookup app), one quick text to Nathan would prohibit me from following through. "Stay the course," he encouraged. Disappointing Nathan was my greatest fear, and all I wanted was to make him proud of me, for him to applaud my strength and character when I resisted temptation. The more he saved me from making mistakes, the more my dependence on him intensified, establishing a sick reliance and addiction to him. Nathan's intentions were pure and good, but there was a part of me that enjoyed the thrill of playing victim so that Nathan would pay more attention to me. I'm not proud of my behavior, but I felt powerless to my emotions as if they were dictating my every move without my consent.

Nathan introduced me to other staff members of the church including a guy named Chris and the associate pastor, Jeff. Pastor Jeff and I bonded once he found out that I went to Biola, him being a fellow alumnus of our alma mater. He also hooked me up with many resources to help overcome my homosexuality. Granted, nothing he gave me ever worked but I admired his passion for my success. A friendship with Chris started to flourish as well. He went out of his way to befriend me and took an active interest in my life, helping me get planted in the church and finding a men's connect group. Like Nathan, Chris was unbothered by my homosexual struggle. He wanted to invest his time helping me seek the healing I desired.

Within a few months of attending Oasis, I had my little army of Christian male friendships to help me combat my gay attractions. Pastor Jeff and Chris dodged a bullet. Neither were a target for my emotional dependency. My gravitation toward Nathan was undivided.

For the first time in years, I felt hopeful. I thanked God for leading me to Oasis Church, where I would meet Nathan, Chris, and Pastor Jeff, whose advocacy for my spiritual success and sexual purity kept me grounded and close to Jesus. The glimmer of a heterosexual marriage seemed almost tangible now. A very important thing to note here is that not once did I ever feel truly "free" from homosexual attractions. No matter how close to Jesus I felt or how pure I kept my body—my brain always remained attracted to men. Yes, I wanted more than anything to be straight, and that is why I believed for it so desperately. I didn't want to go to hell. But the truth didn't seem to hold much weight—as long as I proclaimed homosexual healing—that was all that mattered.

Oasis Church reveled in the power of someone's testimony. I acquired a thrill telling people that God's healing power changed my desires from men to women. Despite that not being true, I wanted to speak it out loud to proclaim it, giving my words power that maybe, just maybe, they would be true *someday*. As Easter 2008 approached, I had been attending Oasis Church for almost a year. I did everything in my power to avoid homosexual temptations and live a pure and holy Christian lifestyle. With Chris, Nathan, and Pastor Jeff by my side, I felt never-ending adrenaline, as if homosexuality could never invade me again.

A church staff member contacted me to ask if I wanted to be featured in a video testimony to be aired in front of the entire church on Easter Sunday. Despite some initial concerns, I wanted to do it. My story would be intertwined with others' stories addressing different issues they overcame through God, whether it was a broken marriage on the verge of divorce or someone with a drug and alcohol addiction that now had been sober for years. My story of freedom from homosexuality would be as impactful. I wanted to not only believe this for myself, but I wanted other people to know that healing was possible! I always craved validation, and here was the perfect way to receive applause, a pat on the back, and a "Good job, Aaron!"

The motive was not a sole attempt to gain accolades, as I completely believed God healed me, or that I was at least in the process of healing, and I wanted the church body to know so God could be glorified. If someone out there in the congregation thought they were gay and heard my story, it could make a difference in their life, and they, too, could become straight.

A week or so before Easter Sunday, I went to the church office to film my portion of the video. I was nervous and excited. I had one looming question throughout the process: *How can I tell the church congregation that God healed me if I'm still attracted to men?*

Eh, a mere technicality.

During my first year at Oasis, I started to understand that I did not "choose" to be attracted to men. I thought my attractions were a choice for so long, which made no sense considering they came so naturally. A Christian would never choose to be attracted to the same gender, knowing the condemnation, heartache, and shame that would come with that alleged choice. This epiphany was a step in the right direction to concede that I did not have control over my desires. However, I did have control over the behavior. The plan would not change, though—to pray for a complete overhaul of my sexual tendencies. Regardless that I did not choose these attractions, God still had to reign sovereign over my life and give me new cravings for females. No one ever told me that change was not possible, so why would I not endlessly pursue healing until that change came into fruition?

When the big day came, and I watched myself on the massive three-screen projectors proclaiming God's healing of my sexuality, I was awestruck. I spoke how I was in a bondage of homosexual sin and now surrendering my sexuality to the Lord in obedience to the Bible. *This is all for you, God!* The audience erupted in applause thanking God on my behalf. Proudly, I stood out in the lobby after each service, waiting for people to come up to me in tears with big hugs, congratulate me on my faithfulness, and honor my devotion to God's plan for my life. I received all that and more and maintained a spiritual high for weeks. Also, I was elated at how proud Nathan was of me because his acceptance and praise meant more than anyone else.

My first year attending Oasis skyrocketed me to such a spiritual high and I started to make many more friends outside of Nathan, Chris, and Pastor Jeff. Chris introduced me to a friend of his, Travis, an amiable yet stunning guy with thick sandy brown hair, a built physique, and light green eyes someone could easily get lost in.

Well, hello.

Coincidentally, Travis, Chris, and Pastor Jeff all originated from the same area of New Jersey without knowing each other before moving to Los Angeles. Chris, Travis, and I ultimately became a very close threesome. Those two guys knew when to let loose and have a good time yet also inhabited an incredible love for Jesus and firmly put their faith in God and his Word.

Chris worked full-time for the church and had much less free time than Travis, who waited tables and went to college. Travis and I began to hang out one-on-one, fueling yet another emotionally dependent fire within me as I became less dependent on Nathan and more dependent on Travis. *Congrats, Travis! You are my next victim!* I became obsessed with him, enmeshed with every aspect of his life, and clung to him as much as possible. I often thought Travis would be the perfect boyfriend—if only he were not straight and actively helping me overcome homosexuality.

My friendship with Travis became focused on accountability. When I stumbled with hooking up with guys, I would confess to him and when he watched porn, he would confess to me, and we would spiritually support each other. On paper, this would translate to a solid, healthy Christ centered friendship—brothers supporting brothers upholding Proverbs 27:17 *"As iron sharpens iron, so one person sharpens another".* In reality, I lustfully delighted in when he confessed to watching porn and masturbating because I was deeply attracted to him. Nevertheless, we would pray and continue to encourage purity in each other's lives.

I lived with Travis for about a week while I transitioned from one apartment to another. He usually walked around with no shirt on, and I enjoyed the chest and abs show daily.

One day he randomly asked me, "Does it make you stumble when I walk around with no shirt on?"

I must appreciate his ego—he knew he had a good body and suspected I knew it as well. The question threw me off guard and I had to answer quickly, calmly, and bro-ey so he would not know I'm lying.

"Not at all, my brother," I spit out casually to make sure he would avoid covering up. Now only if I could convince him that it's biblical to walk around in his underwear.

Oh, and for the record, the apartment I was moving into was in Travis's complex, right underneath him because I wasn't obsessed enough. My emotions and feelings toward him were pathetically unhealthy and to this day I do not understand how he embodied the grace and patience to deal with my shenanigans. Maybe he was unaware. The emotional dependence I had on Travis far surpassed that on John and Nathan to a fanatical degree. From mind games, manipulation, dishonesty, and buying him random gifts, I did everything and anything in attempts to make myself Travis's number one priority. It was embarrassingly and shamefully bad, something I could only admit in retrospect.

Around this time Nathan and Chyler left Oasis Church and moved around quite a bit over the years. Despite the distance, he and I have kept in touch. Nathan is now the lead singer in the band, East of Eli and Chyler stars as Alex Danvers, a lesbian character on CW's *Supergirl*. I recently saw Nathan's band in San Diego, where he was performing with Chyler. Their talent is unsurpassed. The love Nathan and Chyler displayed to their audience that night touched me deeply. I could tell they had evolved from the couple I knew from Oasis Church, as I had evolved myself. Nathan and Chyler started the Create Change movement[1] and are active allies for the LGBTQ community.

As I watched the show that evening, I regretted the selfishness I possessed during my friendship with Nathan. Part of me wished I had been more emotionally mature to invest properly in our relationship. Looking back, I can see how I was too caught up in changing my sexuality and focusing on what he could do for me. However, seeing his friendly face in that moment on that San Diego stage reminded me of the selflessness and grace he bestowed upon me. Had Nathan reacted differently when I first reached out to him, my life could have turned out quite differently. If he had rejected me, I'm not sure I would have even continued attending Oasis, which would have dramatically altered my journey. Nathan saved me. He saved me from the unknown, from bad choices and decisions I potentially could have made had he not taken me in. Despite my years at Oasis Church being the crux of my sexual repression, I believe it was a safer space for me than outside the church at that time in my life, and I am indebted to Nathan eternally. When I first met Nathan West, I only thought of him as "Jan Jan, the Cheerleading Man." Now, I only see a friend—a friend I am incredibly grateful for.

My relationship with Chris and Travis progressively became much more spiritually intimate. The three of us often would get together and "do church" in Travis's living room, praying, and worshipping together for hours. It was a treasured time for me since I found what I wanted—friendships with straight guys that pursued Jesus—which will help me become straight. Because that worked so well with Curt and Nathan, am I right?

I became more involved with every aspect of the church, from volunteering to reaching out to the "lost," which were both huge passions of Chris. I suggested to Chris we do "gay ministry," and I told him about a gay sex club I used to frequent on Sycamore Avenue in Hollywood. The ministry idea was a hit, and a group of us from the church, Travis, Chris, and Pastor Jeff included, would set up shop in front of the sex club to chat with guys coming and going. Katie, a member of the church and someone I convinced myself I had a crush on, was also part of the team.

Our ministry's goal was to show these guys that they were loved, and that there was a God who could fill the void they were seeking through anonymous sex. More personally, I hoped that I could be a solid witness to some of these guys. As someone who "used to be like them," I propped myself up on a throne of gay transformation that God can and will change homosexual orientation. I was confident they would listen to me when I told them my story to show I am an example of what freedom looked like.

We stood outside, handed out water bottles, greeted the guys as they walked by, and offered prayer. We did not stop anyone from entering the club nor condemn anyone who walked out. In all honesty, we approached guys without judgment, but our presence was not received well. Most of the guys heckled us, told us to leave them alone, and assumed we hated them because we were Christians. On occasion, some of the guys stopped and talked to us and even allowed us to pray for them. If a guy who was headed into the club changed his mind after engaging with us, we saw that as a victory and praised God through our tears. I believed we were making a difference. Receiving Chris and Travis's praise because of my courage was the cherry on top.

As for Katie, I told Travis and Chris I had a crush on her and pegged her to be my future wife. She loved Jesus, cared for people, had an incredible laugh, an infectious smile, and was an all-around amazing girl. In the same vein as Gwen, I loved the *idea* of Katie. I admit attraction to her, but it was never sexual. I wanted to be around her because she was a blast to hang out with, but beyond that, true romantic feelings did not exist. However, I did my best to manufacture them. When I would receive praise from Travis and Chris because of my interest in Katie, it urged me to keep up the front. If they believed God healed me from my homosexuality, I would receive even more affirmation. The attention, especially from Travis, was addicting, and I was not going to let anything get in the way of that, especially the truth.

Another opportunity came to publicly tell the church I was healed from homosexuality. There was a trend going around within the Christian church called "Cardboard Testimonies." Lines of church attendees with a huge piece of cardboard in hand would walk up one by one to the front of their church to display a word or phrase that conveyed what they were struggling with or what their life was like before Jesus intervened. Then after a few seconds, the person would turn the cardboard around to show another phrase explaining briefly how, through Jesus, their lives were restored as the song "How He Loves" by Christian group The Dave Crowder Band played softly in the background.

For example, the front of a person's cardboard could read something to the effect of "Alcohol and drug addict for ten years," then flip it around to read, "Through God, I have been sober for two years."

The congregants would then erupt with praise, applause, and hallelujahs, exalting God for helping these individuals overcome their sin and life struggles. Oasis caught wind of the trend and wanted to participate. Danielle, the worship leader, contacted me and asked me if I wanted to share my testimony. Since I had shared publicly earlier in the year on Easter Sunday, I had no hesitation. Any opportunity I could proclaim my freedom from homosexuality and the hope it could help other gay people be free as well, I was all hands-on deck. I suggested to Danielle that the front of my cardboard would read, "Enslaved to Homosexuality," and then the back would display "God changed my desires through His love and grace."

I proudly walked onto that stage for three services in a row and showed everyone in that church that God healed me from this bondage of homosexuality. *It is possible!* Well, at least I wanted to believe this was possible. It's what I wanted Chris, Travis, Pastor Jeff, and Danielle to believe as well as the entirety of the church.

After each service, I went out into the lobby to socialize with friends but also wanted to show my face so I could receive accolades for my proclamation. A couple of strangers came up to me and wanted to talk to me about their struggles with homosexuality. Eagerly, I talked with them, telling them Jesus had the power to make them straight, as he did with me. The Kool-Aid I drank manipulated this euphoric, spiritual exhilaration and, as a result, obscured my mentality. Yes, I had radical faith that God could restore my sexuality, but I wrote checks I could not cash. There was no money in the bank. My homosexual attraction never diminished. I was a fraud, wrapped up in a fake but glittery package.

Pastor Jeff and Chris talked frequently about their dream to plant a church in northeast New Jersey, close to their hometowns. As the months passed, Chris and Jeff's dream became a reality and were making actual plans to leave Los Angeles and head back east. Travis also expressed interest in the church plant, and, naturally, now I was interested in the church plant by default because I wasn't crazy enough.

Deal or No Deal was recently canceled after nearly three years, and I was on the hunt for a new television job but wanted to be involved with Pastor Jeff and Chris in planting the New Jersey church. If I included myself in their church plant circle, maintaining these Christian male friendships would continue my healing from homosexuality. I did not have any passion for planting a church or even having a life in ministry, but I believed that holding onto these friendships would be the key to a heterosexual future. Chris, Travis, and I would often talk about adventuring to Jersey together and building the church, dreaming about finding our future wives. To them, finding their wives was a real desire and dream. For me, it was only something I said to keep the ruse going that I was "healed" from homosexuality.

I continued working on my purity during that time, abstaining from meeting up with guys and sexual hookups. I counted months of sobriety from sexual encounters, much like an alcoholic does while abstaining from taking a drink. I could go three to four months "sober" of hooking up, have a weak moment, meet up with a guy, and start my month count all over again. However, no matter how much I screwed up, those guys never condemned me or gave up on me. Their friendships were priceless, but I did not value them as much in the moment as I should have. I was so self-absorbed, insecure, and emotionally dependent, it crippled my ability to appreciate the good and pure things in my life.

As Chris and Jeff started to make their arrangements to move across country, Travis told me he first wanted to attend a ministry school for a year up in northern California, which put me in a state of panic.

My attachment to Travis was powerful, I even investigated attending the same ministry school, even though I had no desire to go. I wanted to be near him, but somehow, I had some modicum of sense not to stoop that low into my dependency. Not many weeks after he was accepted into the school, I had to come to terms that he was leaving me.

On the day of his Sunday morning departure, as we stood outside our apartment complex I felt suffocated as if someone amputated my lungs. I believed living without him nearby would be impossible. After our farewells to each other, I sat in my car, turned on the ignition, and put my foot to the pedal to drive to church. As I headed down the street with Travis's moving truck in my rearview mirror, I felt an unexpected emotion. I felt relieved. After almost a year of clinging to Travis physically, emotionally, mentally, and even spiritually, I was finally able to breathe. The invisible, yet extremely heavy cement block lifted from my chest. I realized at that moment that my life could continue without Travis.

These emotionally dependent relationships I had with John, Nathan, and Travis had one common denominator. Even though I reacted to each one differently, I was accountable to them in my quest for heterosexuality. I pursued them to fulfill the intimacy I needed from same-sex platonic friendships, which was supposed to heal my homosexuality. Every day I woke up completely dependent on their affirmation, validation, and acceptance. Saving me from homosexuality was their job, a task I placed on them, so if they were not doing their job, I became frustrated, illogical, irrational, and hyper-sensitive. None of them deserved what I put them through, whether they were aware of it or not. I did not deserve what I put myself through either. I valued those friendships, but I regret the grief and emotional exhaustion I inhabited trying to please them—drowning in my chaos only to be untrue to myself and reject who I was.

With Travis gone, my concentration focused solely on moving to Jersey with Pastor Jeff and Chris to start the church. Initially, I had no life purpose to move to Jersey. However, I came up with a passion to minister to the gays and lesbians of New Jersey, telling them my story of how Jesus set me free from a life of homosexuality. In theory, it would be a great plan if I was actually "set free," but I still entertained frequent *Grey's Anatomy* Eric Dane "McSteamy" doctor/patient role play fantasies. The hypocrisy continued to overwhelm me, but every impure thought I had for another male or desire to have a boyfriend, I shook off as another temptation that I needed Jesus to rescue me from.

Pastor Jeff and Chris seemed excited that I wanted to be a part of the church plant team. I had no plan of where I would live or how I would earn an income once there, but that was the best part of being a Christian, not having to worry or plan about stuff like that and proclaim, "God was in control." It removed all responsibility—what a life!

Shortly after Travis left, I felt a hole in my social life. Except for Chris, I did not work on maintaining old friendships or creating new ones because my dependence on Travis always took priority. I rarely made plans with other friends just in case Travis wanted to hang out, and if I did make plans, I would cancel them if he called. On occasion, I would hang out with Brea, Denise, and Mary Lynn when they were not flying or go to a movie and dinner with Milena, but those moments were far and few between. I would even hang with Rita and Kristin from *DOND* sometimes, but part of me wanted to avoid them, knowing they probably wanted to bring me to some gay club in West Hollywood.

Once again, my loneliness transpired into temptations to hook up with guys. The temptations turned to action, and I soon hooked up with several guys after many months of "sobriety." This particular fall from grace hit me harder than other times. I felt guilty, not so much because of the act, but because I knew I was not in a state where I could help lead a new church—much like how I felt going to Nepal while consumed in immorality with Stitch. In retrospect, I made my part in the church plant more prominent than it was. After the recent sexual encounters, I became a recluse for three days, shutting down from the outside world, ignoring all texts and phone calls. I had *General Hospital* and a pantry full of spaghetti, which was all I needed.

When day three rolled around, Chris and Pastor Jeff were at my apartment complex, uninvited and unexpected, looking to see if I was alive. There was no way I could hide from them, so I confessed that I "fell off the wagon," meeting up with guys online. They encouraged me, gracefully, to clean up my act, get back to work, and, most importantly, grow the hell up.

Not long after their visit, Chris came to see me to deliver bad news, but deep down, I saw this coming. He told me that it was not a good time for me to move to Jersey to help plant the church. I was utterly heartbroken and felt rejected. My grief didn't hinge so much on the inability to help with the church, but more so that I knew I would be alone in Los Angeles. Nathan and Travis were gone, and now Chris and Jeff were leaving for Jersey in a few weeks. All these Christian friendships I had formed to help me with my struggle were now crumbling before my eyes.

What does this mean for me now?

Chris's news sent me into a downward spiral, and I became apathetic, doing what I wanted and hooking up with guys like crazy. I wanted to make Chris feel guilty—a big fat "fuck you."

Look what you made me do. You cut me off from the church, and now I'm hooking up with guys again.

Unfortunately for me, Chris did not fall for my bullshit. I was aware of his love and care for me but was too angry to realize that he kept me away from moving to Jersey for my own good.

"It's just not the time," he said. "Maybe in a year."

A year??

My struggle with sexuality and the frustration that it kept ruining my life was something that I had to find a solution for, once and for all. I needed a plan beyond attending another weekly church therapy group, a Christian psychiatrist, or finding a hot guy that could be my best friend and allow his influence to make me straight—all strategies that had not worked despite my efforts. As I brainstormed, I wondered if some kind of Christian residential program could help—a place where I could live, get 24/7 counseling, be around other guys trying to become heterosexual, and shut out the rest of the world.

So, I Googled "gay conversion Christian camps." I was a bit surprised how many gay conversion therapy camps existed. Every click of the mouse sent chills down my spine as I read about each organization thoroughly, examining the potential torture and healing I could endure. Most of them were located within the bible belt of the country, except one located in New Hampshire which, at the time, was my top choice. The website scared me as much as it gave me hope that *this* could be what it takes to make me a normal, straight person.

Wow, it's really come to this, I thought.

Chapter Twelve

BOY ERASED

Behind Pastor Jeff's piercing blue eyes lived compassion and grace which mirrored how he spoke to me in his office that day. I filled him in on my late-night browsing of Christian camps that helped guys like me heal from homosexuality. The mention of that idea lit a bulb in Pastor Jeff's head. He said he would call Sy Rogers to ask his advice.

Sy Rogers, an American evangelical pastor, was one of the earliest famed personalities associated with the ex-gay movement and Exodus International, an ex-gay ministry. In all my years of attending Christian churches, conferences, and seminars, I have heard dozens upon dozens of different pastors and preachers, yet Sy Rogers was one of the best. He lived as a homosexual and then as a female for over a year, considered becoming a transgender woman in the 1980s until he encountered God. From that moment on, Sy had traveled the world, sharing his story of redemption and God's power through his struggle with sexuality and gender.

Oasis Church had Sy come as a guest speaker many times. Those Sundays, you would find me in the very front row enamored and crying as he commanded the stage. If I was a 90's teenage girl at a New Kids on The Block concert, Sy Rogers was my Joey McIntyre.

Sy spoke with such eloquence and intellect that would make even an acclaimed philosopher sound uneducated. He was extremely thorough in his thoughts and had an incredible way of communicating his ideals and beliefs with grace, beauty, and honesty. I wanted to be him. I wanted to be free.

Jeff reached out to Sy, who recommended I investigate Love in Action, a residential program in Memphis, Tennessee, for the sexually broken, but mostly for people who wanted to find freedom from homosexuality.

Love in Action has been the subject of much controversy, condemned by LGBTQ individuals and their allies who chastise parents for sending their teenagers there to be "fixed." There used to be a program explicitly designed for minors, The Refuge.

This program was the focal point of the 2018 movie *Boy Erased*. The movie, starring Nicole Kidman, Russell Crowe, and Lucas Hedges, told Garrard Conley's story, based on his memoir of his experience with gay conversion therapy while attending Love in Action.

I was distraught that it had come to this—leave my job, friends, and familiar surroundings to finally get the freedom from homosexuality I had been desperate to obtain. Despite the trepidation, I was optimistic that this program would work, and that I would eventually feel normal and someday understand what it was about Jennifer Lopez that had the power to command instant arousal for most straight dudes. Nothing else had worked up to this point, so Memphis, here I come.

After receiving my application, Jeb, a Love in Action staff member, called me to ask every personal question possible to see if I was gay enough to gain acceptance into the program. I passed with flying colors and started planning for my trip to Tennessee.

Becoming straight would come with a hefty price tag—$7,500 for six months. That was a steep dollar amount, but I imagined a lot of resources were needed for me to use "bro" in conversation and care about football.

The donations for my attendance in the program came in rapidly after I sent out financial support letters to family and Christian friends. I couldn't tell my liberal *Deal or No Deal* colleagues, who were like family, the truth about my imminent departure because had they known, they would have tried their hardest to talk me out of it. People outside of the church didn't understand my desire to be free from homosexual sin because to them, gay wasn't a sin, but something that should be embraced.

I concocted this fib that I was moving to Memphis to intern for a church, which seemed legit since they knew how heavily involved I was with Oasis Church. Once I was to arrive at Love in Action, my phone would be confiscated, and I would not be allowed to go online to check emails and Facebook due to strict rules of no contact with the outside world. Freedom and obedience to God would come with sacrifice, and it saddened me that my relationships with these people would fall victim to that sacrifice.

Within days I quit my job at BJ's, emptied my apartment, and prepared for the road trip. Chris threw me a going away party at a local pizza joint with all my college and Oasis friends to wish me farewell and good luck in the program. I held it together until my friend Milena gave me the tightest hug and wept, saying, "I will have this hole in my heart without you."

My Christian friends wanted healing for me as much as I wanted it for myself. I left the next morning with so much hope for God's complete transformation over my sexuality.

The drive to Memphis from Los Angeles became my personal two-day traveling worship service to Jesus as I blasted my praise music in expectancy of finally be healed from same-sex attraction. I also was tempted to find guys to hookup with at my hotel stays along the way, you know, so I can be with a guy one last time. Conflicting desires was my norm, but I knew this problem would be fixed once I was deep into the program.

Before I left Los Angeles, I reached out to a guy named Peterson Toscano who came up in my Google searches for Love in Action. Peterson attended the program before denouncing it and becoming a proud, outspoken gay male. He became semi-famous in the ex-gay circle, appearing on talk shows such as Tyra Banks and Montel Williams, telling his story that orientation cannot be changed, and that gay conversion therapy is emotionally and mentally damaging. I was not interested in him talking me out of attending. I just wanted the 411 on the rules and how much of my freedom would face its mortality. I read the manual backwards and forwards, but I needed to hear the experience from someone who lived it firsthand.

I wanted to be as fully prepared as possible. The LIA program enforced various rules and regulations to promote manageability and structure over their clients since anyone participating in the program must have lost those values which could be another reason resulting to their attraction of the same sex.

Our sin had a name: Same Sex Attraction. However, it became habit to minimize the struggle into the acronym, SSA. To say that I had "SSA" sounded like a dreadful disease, but in my case that is exactly what I believed, and I was looking for a cure.

Peterson did not tell me anything I didn't already know from reading the manual, but to hear from someone who was there did set me at ease. Despite his newfound stance on the topic, he did not even attempt to talk me out of going. I am sure he knew it was something I had to figure out for myself.

On Monday, March 16, 2009, I pulled into the Love in Action campus, my heart beating out of my chest. I parked my Silver Honda in the scarcely vacant parking lot with only a few scattered cars and a big white van sprawled across the lot. I took one last glance at my cell phone to read some last-minute texts, knowing it would be taken away. I powered it down, put it in my pocket, and as I headed in the front door, I was quickly met by Jeb, the admissions director, who conducted my invasive application phone interview.

Jeb had a very gentle and quiet spirit about him and was extremely friendly. No doubt, he was a former Love in Action client, which was obvious from the sequined purse that fell from his mouth—he was a flaming homo just like the rest of us. Then

I met George, the men's counselor, who put his hand out for a shake and introduced himself. Counselor George had this prevalent Memphis drawl, which added to his kindness and calming demeanor. I also met Linda, the female counselor. She was not my favorite person by any means. Linda had this obnoxious sense of entitlement and a know-it-all persona, but despite that, she had a good heart despite her tendency to come off snobby and superior.

I was ushered into an empty room. My suitcase emitted a dead echo once Jeb threw it on top of the table. As I watched Jeb unzip my suitcase and rummage through it, the small pit in my stomach that already formed metastasized into a watermelon. In the Love in Action manual, there was a strict prohibition on "False Images" which were specific items such as cologne, clothing, music, pictures, or magazines that could be considered a detriment to have in our possession. Every rule was in place to avoid "triggers" that may activate our SSA, as if having a natural attraction to men were not triggering enough. Not that it mattered. Thanks to *Brokeback Mountain*, I had stored enough mental images of Jake Gyllenhaal and Heath Ledger to have triggers for a lifetime. What I needed was a brain-erasing machine.

After my privacy was completely violated, I was asked to remove my eyebrow piercing and hand over my cell phone. Jeb asked for the keys to my car so they could continue looking for anything else that could be considered a false image. He would find nothing more than expired insurance cards and Peanut M&M wrappers. What Jeb didn't find is that I secured a Britney Spears CD that would come in handy in the coming months. It was my first day, and I was already breaking the rules.

For the first three days, I would not be allowed to talk to anyone and must live in complete silence. This was called "sanctuary." The purpose of sanctuary was to establish a concentrated focus on God and not get caught up in the concern with the approval of other clients and staff.

All residents of the program were referred to as "clients," which I always hated. I wasn't a personal training customer or asking a lawyer to represent me. The "client" label made me feel I was someone paying for a service and not a child of God who is loved unconditionally and seeking out healing.

Counselor George led the way to the meeting room to introduce me to the other clients. At that time, there were only three other people. I met Rosa, an older woman who had been at the program for almost a year, Nolan, a young southern boy obsessed with Britney Spears, and Mike, who stood tall and skinny yet aesthetically pleasing to my suppressed hormones. As the weeks and months went by, more and more clients would enter in the program weekly. Clients would leave when their time in the program came to an end with a graduation ceremony. Man, I could not wait for my very own certificate of heterosexuality.

I was not attracted to Nolan; however, he was a very funny and an exuberant individual, who had me laughing often with his wit and humor. Mike had this "hot gay nerd" endearing vibe to him that caught my eye, but I would often have to pinch myself and not let my mind wander too far off track.

In the first month, the program enforced a "no outside world contact" rule, but after one month, one would be allowed to make supervised phone calls to people on the "approved" list. The staff had a system set in place to be sure any conversations clients had on the phone were healthy and appropriate, and nobody "unhealthy" from the past could interfere with the healing process. Naturally, staff sat in while we made these phone calls, so privacy was never an option.

Another fundamental rule was called "in-phase." This meant that no matter where we went, we had to always be in groups of three.

I asked Nolan why this rule existed, and he said somewhat sarcastically, "It's easier to have a twosome than a threesome."

Wise words, my friend. Whether someone was taking out the trash, going to the bathroom, or walking to the van, we had to be in groups of at least three. Even communication between the clients was checked. One-on-one private conversations were prohibited. If anyone wanted to chat, they had to speak openly where everyone could hear, and no side conversations were allowed. If staff felt any two clients were becoming too close, they would be forced to separate, a policy I would eventually experience. We were treated as sexual deviants, and every move we made was strictly monitored.

Clients stayed in the program for different lengths of time, depending on various factors, including availability, finances, and how deeply homosexual they were. I knew that because of my love for *The Golden Girls*, Broadway shows, and shirtless international soccer teams, my work was cut out for me, so I committed to a six-month stay. The standard client stayed for three months, although they had programs for any length of time from one month to a year—for the *really* gay ones, I imagined. LIA even had one-week intensive programs for the gays that only had five days to get healed. Rapid reparative therapy!

A mixture of fear, loneliness, and excitement ravaged my soul. After all my attempts to become straight, this program was the answer to my problem. Hope had been unreliable up until this point, but my faith skyrocketed to an all-time high because I knew this program *had* to work. It was my last resort.

Living at the Love in Action house was the most surreal experience I ever had in my life. I would define it as prison yet in a suburban house on a residential Memphis street. We had two house managers, Steve and Stacy. Both Steve and Stacy had their own bedrooms upstairs while the clients had shared bedrooms downstairs, except for Rosa, and, later, Annette, who had their own bedroom, being the lone females.

Steve had a mysterious sex appeal that intrigued me from day one. He stood a few inches shorter than my 6-foot frame, a stunning mix of Korean and European ethnicity, a head of jet-black hair and a deep voice with a noticeable Canadian accent. Steve was not only a staff member, but he also used to be a client—informing us he struggled with bisexuality, among other things, but what I remember most about Steve was that he struggled with having a huge stick up his ass (which he probably enjoyed). He enforced the rules so strictly, I believed he was getting off on a power trip—maybe some revenge from his experiences as a client. Unfortunately, his attitude made him completely unlikable in a place where there was value in having someone like him who had been through the program. He could have been a person who could relate to us and understood our headspace.

Steve hardly let his guard down and exuded that "I'm not here to make friends" attitude. He had absolutely no sense of humor, appeared to be miserable 95% of the time, and overall, a dismal person to be around. Some of us clients had a running joke that he was always hibernating in his room upstairs spanking his monkey to gay porn for hours on end. In exceptionally rare moments of vulnerability and exposing a smile, I considered that in another context, Steve and I could have been friends and even had a good roll in the hay. However, for the most part, I wanted nothing to do with him.

Entirely on the complete opposite side of Steve's personality spectrum, Stacy was pure delight. Stacy was not a former client of the Love in Action program but took the house manager position to have a job that paid for room and board while attending college. Stacy enforced the rules, but she was not nearly as tyrannical as Steve. She had a vibrant and contagious personality. I think fondly of Stacy when I reminisce about my time in Love in Action. She was a shining star in a dark universe, and she sure did love Jesus. I gravitated toward Stacy much more than Steve because she inspired me to love Jesus more, whereas Steve inspired me to punch him in the face.

Coming home after counseling was not a free for all evening. Gone were the days I could come home after a long day, make a bowl of spaghetti, and watch *General Hospital*. We had a daily itinerary we had to follow. There was scheduled reading/homework time, dinner time, bathroom time, and free time. Free time didn't offer up many options, except playing cards with fellow clients. I never played cards so much in my life than in those three months. There was a television in the living room, but that was only an option on Friday nights when we would be allowed to watch a movie, so no *General Hospital*. I did enjoy movie nights even though every movie we watched had to be approved, and we even had to ask permission to make popcorn. Here I am, a thirty-one-year-old man asking permission to watch *Mary Poppins*. This was my life.

Each night a different client was scheduled to prepare dinner. I have always loved cooking, so I would cook often—even offering to take another clients' dinner chore from the ones who hated it. I knew that watching countless hours of Rachael Ray and Giada De Laurentis would finally not go to waste.

Each weekday was structured in the same way, with some minor tweaks depending on the day. On Tuesdays and Thursdays, we would be required to get up at 5:30 AM, and Steve would drive us to a nearby gym to maintain our health and fitness. We were never forced to do anything at the gym, as we could sit on the bleachers for the whole hour, but we had no option to stay home. I did not mind the gym because it distracted me from reality, and it was somewhat soothing to do something "normal" and stare at the hot sweaty guys grunting as they pushed their limits to do just one more rep.

Most days at the gym, I would play racquetball with a fellow client, Justin, and other days I would alleviate my daily stresses on the elliptical or jog around the indoor track. Those little pockets of time at the gym were priceless because I would reflect on my life and get lost in navigating my conflicting emotions. Some days I was excited to be where God wanted me to be, and other times, I would be confused, reacting to a shirtless guy in the weight room, not able to keep myself from staring at him.

How could I still be attracted to men? I'm in this program, and it should be working!
I would soon realize I was not the only one struggling with the program's efficacy.

On the way home from the gym one morning, we drove past an extremely attractive guy jogging shirtless in the neighborhood. The warm Tennessee spring heat did us all a favor in drenching his hard chest and rippling abs with sweat. I stared at the jogger as a normal reflex, then noticed that all the other guys in the van were indulging in their lusts as well. Without saying a word and with eye contact alone, we all "got" each other in that moment, and the obvious didn't need to be said. The only person not making eye contact with us or noticing the hot jogger was the girl with the "lesbian problem." Go figure.

Weekends were primarily for doing chores on Saturday and going to church on Sunday. Saturday chores consisted of us cleaning the house fully inside and outside. Sunday church was a desired outing of the week because we could see and converse with people outside of the Love in Action bubble. Before service, we had to attend a Sunday school class consisting of young adults in their twenties and thirties filled with cute southern Memphis boys. *Thank You, Jesus!* Oh, and there were donuts, a rare treat to consume besides the predictable bland food we had during the week. Besides staring at cute Sunday School guys and munching on vanilla glazed treats, I enjoyed the pastor of the church. A man so lively and filled with passion, humor, and energy which made what could have been a boring service tolerable and even something to look forward to.

Without a doubt, my absolute favorite day of the week, surpassing Sunday church and Friday movie nights, was Thursday afternoons when we would work at a food bank to hand out groceries to the less fortunate. What made this afternoon so incredibly precious was Katherine, the woman in charge of the weekly event. Katherine changed my life. I can confidently say that every person graced to meet her was touched deeply by her presence and warmth. Katherine was a mix of a nurturing loving grandmother, a wise soothing therapist, and a funny crazy comedian. I could be having the worst day or week, and she was always there with a tender hug, a word of encouragement, and a joke to laugh away my tears. My experience at LIA was better for having known her. She was a bright color in a dark space, and I will never forget her as long as I live.

Counseling sessions were the crux of the program. This was our time to dig deep into our souls and discover why we have same-sex attractions. At 9:00 AM, like clockwork, we gathered with either George or Linda. Unfortunately, Steve would sometimes conduct these meetings, which only fueled my distaste for him because he tended to sound arrogant and holier than thou. The early meetings would require us to "check-in" and talk about how the last 24 hours were for us, to confess any lustful thoughts we may have had, and discuss what shape our hearts and minds were in.

After our daily check-in, George, Linda, or Steve would bring us through different topics that contributed to our sexuality issues, including temptation, fear, and codependency, to name a few. I will never say these lessons were not useful. Most of the group counseling sessions dealt with real-life topics. Temptation, fear, and codependency transcends all religious backgrounds and sexuality. However, in our case, the goal was to see how these specific topics related to how and why we were attracted to the same gender.

We often had special projects that we had to complete as part of the "conversion therapy" curriculum. These projects ranged from craft projects to poster board presentations to essays. One project that stands out is when we had to construct a life timeline on a poster highlighting our significant moments throughout the years. We then had to present our timelines to the group, explaining each momentous occasion, good or bad, and how it affected us. The counselors would then ask us questions about those events, ultimately digging into our psyches to see if a particular event is what made us attracted to the same gender. From my bullying in school to being called a girl in my youth to the death of a family member, nothing was off the table. Sometimes it felt as if the staff were grasping at straws, investigating irrelevant information to discover why we had these homosexual tendencies such as my relationship with my siblings, how well I did in school, and the death of my cat. In retrospect, nothing we did made any sense but, at that moment, I was eating it up like Cookie Monster in a Chips Ahoy factory.

Love in Action therapy was also structured around the twelve steps of Alcoholics Anonymous (AA). Every week, in addition to other topics, we would discuss another step and how implementing that step would aid us in our homosexual recovery.

For example, the first step in AA is, "We admit we are powerless over alcohol—that our lives have become unmanageable." So, to tailor that step for myself, I replaced alcohol with "homosexuality." *I admit I am powerless over homosexuality—my life has become unmanageable.* I diligently worked on each step so I would not miss my chance to be healed. Love in Action placed a huge emphasis on Step 4: "Make a searching and fearless moral inventory of ourselves."

For moral inventories, we had to take stock of our lives and write down any incidents that were considered immoral, impure, and sinful, including our thoughts. There was no way I could write down a moral inventory for every impure thought I ever had. My moral inventories about John Stamos alone would fill a storage locker.

Every day we had to write a moral inventory and read it aloud to the group. I understood, from a Christian standpoint, why this was a critical part of the program. There could be past events that confused us sexually or opened our eyes to sinful natures and manipulations. Often, we had not yet dealt with these events, so putting them out there in the open had the potential to be therapeutic.

I wrote and openly discussed most every sexual encounter I took part in during our Moral Inventory sharing time. I confessed every session with Darren. I candidly talked about how I sexually preyed on Stitch. I spoke about my emotional dependencies on John, Nathan, and Travis. Every sexual and emotional sin that I committed was on display for the whole group to hear. We were not allowed to react to each other's moral inventories and had to stay silent while our group members shared. Since confession was a tool for healing, I did not mind exposing my secrets even though confessing had not healed me in the past, but I hoped taking another go at it would prove to God I was serious about the program and becoming fully straight.

Chapter Thirteen

PRAY AWAY

What once was an addiction to sex became an addiction to my Bible. Seriously, I've never memorized more scriptures in my life. I did my homework and was quite the overachiever when it came to the special projects and assignments. The Love in Action bubble was my happy place. I believed that healing was right around the corner.

To assure that nothing would distract me from my future as a heterosexual man, I *threw* myself into the Love in Action program. My relationship with Jesus grew spiritually stronger day by day. I wanted to be a prized pupil and model client, *not* for recognition, but so I could become heterosexual faster.

The spiritual aspect of becoming closer to God was the easy part. The homosexual attractions were another story. LIA staff would offer suggestions and activities to help guide us clients away from homosexual tendencies. They encouraged the guys to play football and encouraged a butch female client to wear a skirt once a week to get into the habit of becoming more feminine. I believed the program was doing precisely what it should be doing—affirming us in our manhood and womanhood just as God created us. It didn't help our case too much when we learned Bea Arthur passed away on April 25th of that year. When a real-life Golden Girl dies, and the news is spread within the company of gays; regardless of whether we're attempting to become straight, there will be mourning. RIP Bea.

Most of us were not in the program by force, although some clients were highly encouraged to be there based on their personal circumstances. We had the freedom to walk out the door anytime we wanted. Of course, there were consequences for those actions, but we were not handcuffed to our beds (though some of us may have liked that depending on who we were sharing a room with). While I was there, only one eighteen-year-old guy attended because his parents forced him, but he did not last long because he lacked participation and drive. If I had to guess, that poor kid did everything possible to get kicked out on purpose. He did not speak in group counseling, didn't engage socially, skipped on the assignments, and barely even went through the motions. I had pity that he was not "working the program." His parents eventually came to pick him up because his behavior was potentially destructive to other clients' progress.

Living closely and intimately with these people, making friends was not a choice but came with the territory. A guy named Justin became my best friend who entered the program roughly a month after I did, along with an older woman named Annette. When the staff told the current clients that new clients were moving in the upcoming Monday, our chatter amongst the guys revolved around how we hoped a cute guy would be moving in. When the van arrived at the house, we all peeked through the blinds and watched what people exited the vehicle.

"Nope, that's a girl. UGH! We have another lesbian," Nolan said in annoyance.

"Oh, but wait, who's the skinny boy with the Justin Bieber hair cut? He's kind of cute," I whispered to Nolan so Rosa wouldn't hear my acknowledgement.

That cute boy was Justin which was fitting name since he really did have the Justin Bieber mop of hair that he popularized during his breakout in 2009. Justin and I bonded quickly within the first week of his arrival.

As much as I got along with everyone, it was as easy to become annoyed with these people, living and being around them 24/7. At times it did feel like incarceration because we were never allowed to go anywhere, not even outside for a walk and fresh air. One evening I snapped and started an argument with Rosa for various reasons and had a complete emotional breakdown. As angry as I was, Rosa was not the problem. The LIA bubble was draining, and my hypersensitivity to the environment made me take out my frustrations on her. After my blow up at Rosa, I went to my bedroom and sat in the large closet (insert joke here), my go-to decompression space, to write in my journal and to cool off. You think *Real Housewives of New York* is drama? Try *"Real Clients of Love in Action."* It would have made for some great television!

After 45 minutes or so had passed, Steve walked into the closet looking for me. *Fuck!!! This is all I need right now! Go away, Steve!!!* I knew I had to play nice, though, do what was asked, and apologize to Rosa so we could all move on.

I developed a small attraction to Justin. He came into the program with a chip on his shoulder, and his issues ran much deeper than SSA. Narcotics and alcohol played a huge role in his life, and even though I loved my new friend, he probably would have benefitted from a real addiction program and not a place that was attempting to change his sexuality.

Justin had a rebellious side to him that influenced me, and the more I hung out with him, the more his rebellion permeated my behavior. After a month of no change in my sexual attractions, I became bitter, so I emulated Justin's bad attitude from everything he did and did not do.

We were joined at the hip, and he made living in the program much more tolerable. And boy, was there major sexual tension! How could there not be? One evening a conversation that Justin and I were having turned somewhat sexual. There was a large storage closet tucked away off the kitchen. I had always wondered if the closet was the prime secret hookup spot for all clients of the past. I mentioned the storage closet nonchalantly to Justin, and he jokingly said we should go in there, but not joking at the same time. We never closed the deal. The risk of getting caught was too great. Even though it seemed I had a change of attitude when Justin came into the program, he was not to blame for my downward spiral. It was inevitable that I would discover the program would not change my innate sexuality.

The staff noticed how close Justin and I became, and this was a major red flag. I was forced to move into another bedroom so we would not sleep in the same room, and to top it off, he and I were put on probation and not allowed to speak to one another because our relationship appeared far too intimate. The absurdity was laughable. Despite my feelings for him, we never did anything outwardly that would make anyone suspect we were having an inappropriate relationship. We were two guys who were close friends. However, in the LIA world, this was a recipe for disaster. No close friends allowed! We played along with their rules in the presence of staff, but when they were not around, we continued to speak to each other freely. After a couple of days, we had to meet with Counselor George and get approval to talk to each other again.

Not all was gloom and doom. Being trapped in LIA did offer numerous moments of hilarity in their attempt to heal us from homosexuality. Some of my favorite memories occurred when we would go on "trigger trips." For these trips, Steve would drive us to a public place, whether it was a shopping mall or Target, and we would write down everything we saw that would trigger our homosexuality. Yeah, I'm not kidding. This was as good as it gets!

We would walk through the mall or Target, pens and pads in hand. No talking would be allowed during the exercise as this was a private moment between us, God, and the shirtless Fruit of the Loom models on the Target underwear packages. Yup, I had to write that one down. The triggers were not exclusive to a physical person. It could be the scent from a bottle of cologne or a piece of clothing on the J.Crew mannequin, anything that reminded us of our sinful, homosexual past. If walking by the Adidas store reminded someone of an ex-boyfriend who looked good in those blue soccer shorts, we had to write it down. It was a trigger.

The trigger trips were mainly a "guard your thoughts" exercise. If we could pinpoint what triggered our homosexual feelings, we could prepare for those triggers and be prayed up in hopes we didn't stumble on those thoughts. We wouldn't want to create a domino effect into lust or action now, would we?!

If anything, this activity did the opposite of its purpose, giving us an *invitation* to stare and be reminded of our pasts. After my first trigger trip, I felt incredibly defeated.

How could I possibly be in this program for two months and still be attracted to guys? The Hot-Dog-On-A-Stick guy was really cute. I'm not "supposed" to have these feelings. They should be decreasing by now.

I was not satisfied with dormant or suppressed homosexuality that could rear its ugly head at any time. No, I wanted to be one hundred percent, sports loving, bro talking, get aroused by boobs, "Hey man, what's up dude" straight alpha male. That was the goal. I believed I had to get more serious working the program, read the Bible more, and be more fervent in prayer. God will heal me. There was still time. I had four months to go.

"You know what I want right now? Wendy's!" Annette said.

"Yes, I would kill for a Junior Bacon Cheeseburger right now," I quickly proclaimed.

"French fries to dip in my Frosty!" Justin screeched.

Living in such a closed-off environment, we missed the simple pleasures of the outside world, and our mouths were salivating for something other than gay camp food. Naturally, we were not allowed to stop anywhere between campus and the residence, and on days that Steve could not drive, I had enough seniority to be the van driver. It was never tempting to divert on our own during weeknights because we convinced ourselves that they would time us from when we left campus and arrived at the residence house which was fifteen minutes, give or take.

"We have to get permission from George," I said optimistically. "Not Linda! She'll think Wendy's is the devil!"

Annette and I walked into George's office. "George, we must talk about something. This has been weighing on our hearts, and it's important we confess this to you," I said, pulling out my best soap opera winning performance.

I looked over at Annette, and the natural actor within her motioned me to continue.

"I got your back," she spoke softly.

George's face shifted to concern, and I knew I didn't have it in me to keep the joke going, so I broke the charade by blurting out, "George, we need Wendy's! Cheeseburgers, French fries, *Frostys*!"

He let out the biggest laugh, relieved that the worrisome path we were leading him down was a ruse to simply get some familiar tasty food. He gave us permission with the stipulation that we had to get the food to go and not eat in the restaurant. After our pickup from the braided freckled girl, we poured into the house with our greasy bags and cold Frostys in hand, only to be greeted with hostility from Steve and his never-ending power trip.

"Did you have permission to go to Wendy's??" he asked condescendingly.

I could only muster, "Yes, George gave us permission," showing as much annoyance and passive aggression to his dumb question.

What I *wanted* to say was, *"Yes, fuck face! Do you think we would go to Wendy's without getting permission?? We know how things work around here, so go up to your room and continuing jerking off to your gay porn and leave us alone, you dumbass."* But I was too Christian for that kind of language.

Even though the staff hovered over us obsessively, there were plenty of moments when I would be able to get away with breaking the rules. It was almost a game to see how far I could push the limits. Whether it was buying a soda from Target that was not previously approved or going to the bathroom by myself without being "in-phase," I honestly felt empowered. However, the longer someone was in the program, the more freedom they were given, although that "freedom" had many conditions wrapped within itself.

One example was when I had permission to jog around the neighborhood. Usually, we were never allowed to leave the house without supervision, but with my seniority, I would be able to jog in the dead-end cul-de-sac near the house. I could only listen to approved Christian music on my CD player. What they did not know is that I smuggled in a Britney Spears CD (remember?), and she, not Hillsong, was who I was jamming to on my runs. Yep, another rule broke. *Oops, I did it again.*

Friday was an anticipated day of the week for us. Friday was shopping day. To my disbelief, the clients were allowed to go into town and run errands at Target and the supermarket to buy groceries and toiletries without any staff supervision. We had to write down everything we planned to purchase, get approval, and then bring back the receipt. None of us could quite fathom why we were allowed to go on this excursion alone every Friday without the gay therapy police babysitting us. I had the fortunate task of driving our big sixteen-passenger white van.

Annette hated that van. She would mention it every single day. "You know you are in a program when you are in a white van," she'd say.

Although left alone, we did not do anything illegal—at least within real life standards. By LIA standards, we would have been booked, fingerprinted, and charged. We took our time roaming around Target, the grocery store, and the chain of stores in the area to stall our trek back to the residential house. We all bought things we were not allowed to, including magazines, clothes, and unapproved snacks and hid them so staff wouldn't notice. These shopping trips were the only time we felt like normal, functioning human beings.

We had honest and raw conversations on those van rides, vented to each other our frustrations about the program, and my favorite thing to do, made fun of Steve. It was incredibly liberating. The bond we had as clients grew deep. Justin, Annette, and I even talked about moving to Florida to work on staff together at Exodus International Headquarters in Orlando. Despite our frustrations, collectively, we still hoped for healing and wanted to be freed from our sexual sin. Working on staff at the same organization responsible for Love in Action seemed to be a smart choice to continue our progress. It may have been a psyched-up conversation at that moment, and I couldn't speak for them if they had seriously considered the option, but I know I did and even considered applying for a staff position after leaving LIA. Truth be told, though; I could never live in Florida. Because Florida.

Toward the end of my third month of the program, I still felt defeated. I was frustrated that the effort I put into the program did not alleviate my sexual attraction to men. I was doing everything right. I paid attention during the counseling sessions. I took notes, wrote in my journal daily, did the homework, prayed, read the Bible, and did *everything* I was supposed to be doing. For the most part, I should have been healed by now. *This is ridiculous!*

Besides meeting with George and Linda for counseling sessions, I also met with Kenny, the LIA director. I eagerly looked forward to my sessions with Kenny, mainly because of my infatuation with him. He resembled a poor man's version of actor Jeremy Renner yet was still quite a handsome man. My counseling sessions with Kenny existed, I believe, for my personal enjoyment. I sat there across from him zoned out to his babble but listened enough to hear his sexy Matthew McConaughey accent. I gazed into his oceanic blue eyes and daydreamed about kissing his soft lips surrounded by a perfectly structured masculine jawline.

He had a nicely toned body that showed off his firm round chest and arm muscles through his slim fitted button-up shirts, and it took an effort to keep my eyes from looking down at his crotch because man, oh man, he knew how to wear slacks *just* the right way. As he spouted off advice and encouragement to keep fighting my homosexual attractions, I daydreamed about undressing him, so our meetings didn't do much except give me another moral inventory to write about.

How am I still attracted to men when I've been here for nearly three months?

One aspect of the program that never made much sense to me was that the counselors, George, Linda, and Kenny, were heterosexual. *None* of them had homosexual struggles, as far as we knew, and were all married to people of the opposite gender. I found it strange the program did not have actual ex-gay professional therapists working in the program, people we could be inspired from and instill a little bit of hope into our homosexual freedom. There were many flaws with LIA, besides the program existing at all, but to have no leadership claiming they were healed and free from homosexuality should have been a major concern from the beginning.

By the end of my third month at Love in Action, my frustration with homosexual tendencies unchanged, I wanted to leave the program early and get out of Tennessee. I committed to six months total, but I could not fathom staying another three months—this program was not working. I had no idea what my plans were though after I were to leave LIA. *Do I still move to Jersey? Will Chris even want me there?* My desire to move to Jersey decreased over the past three months, and even though I still considered it, I really didn't care about the church plant or becoming obsessed with Travis again.

One afternoon while checking my email, I saw a headline on an entertainment news website that read *Deal or No Deal* was returning in syndication, and production was moving to Connecticut. *Well, that's interesting!* Financially broke with depleted savings and unsure of what my next move should be, I stepped out of obscurity and called Neal about a job in Connecticut, and he offered me my old job back on the spot. I met with Linda who graciously granted my request allowing me to graduate from the program early so I could make my move to live in southern Connecticut.

LIA graduation was a simple ceremony that included staff, clients, and anyone I wanted to invite outside of the program. When I stood up, in front of all those people who had a significant impact on my life those last three months, whether good or bad, I became emotional.

I spoke to each person and how they impacted my life and gave them words of encouragement. The speech I remember the most is the one I directed toward Kevin, another client I befriended. Kevin was a sweet soul from Arkansas who struggled a lot with self-esteem, self-loathing, and insecurity. I saw myself in Kevin. I related to him and told him that he was loved and valued while also reminding myself of those same truths as I spoke those words aloud.

We all came from different walks of life, and as much as I loved experiencing those three months with these wonderful people, it is sad that we thought we had to be there at all, attempting to fix what was *not* broken. Katherine also showed up at my graduation, which blessed me tremendously. I don't think I could have left Memphis without one of her amazing, life-changing hugs. Even as much as I despised Steve, I left him a note on my last day, thanking him for all he did for me. As unorthodox as this program was, I clung to the good.

As I reflect on my time in Love in Action, I can't say that the entire experience was as horrible as one would think when they hear about a camp attempting to turn homosexuals into heterosexuals.

Thank God I did not experience the violence and hatred Garrard Conley was exposed to, but there was a different leadership in place during my time there. I met beautiful humans in Tennessee; some I keep in touch with to this day. Throughout my several months in LIA, I met about ten other clients who came to receive healing from their homosexuality. I have lost touch with some of them, but those I communicate with currently live their lives as gay people, and all have same-sex partners.

Counselor George said at the very beginning of my program that the program's goal was not to make me straight but to bring me closer to Jesus. In theory, that sounded like a very cute Christian way to say, "We can't promise you anything." I never felt closer to Jesus leading up to the program, and even in the first month, I was spiritually on fire and madly in love with Jesus. I went to LIA to become straight. The goal, and what I believed was promised to me by God for taking this leap, was that I would be attracted to women. Besides the relationships that enriched my life, I left Memphis spiritually worse than how I came in, suffering more in my relationship with Jesus and feeling more distant from him—the complete opposite of what Counselor George projected. I left with my heart in my hand, and it was breaking. I was devastated.

Chapter Fourteen

AWAKENINGS

OUT OF ALL THE people that I could have crashed with post-conversion therapy graduation, I ended up staying with the last people I wanted to stay with—my parents.

Staying with them before the move to Connecticut felt a bit awkward, at least for me. I assumed my mom wanted to talk about the last three months in LIA, but I sure didn't. How can I disappoint her and say it didn't work—that I am still attracted to men? Not only was I worried about letting my mom down, but everyone who supported me and hoped the same—that I would leave the Tennessee border as a heterosexual male. I wanted to talk to someone who could relate with me, so I contacted Nicholas.

A couple of weeks before I left LIA, Counselor George introduced me to Nicholas—a client who was in LIA for the one-week intensive program to be "de-gayed." The one-week clients did not live with us in the residential house and kept to themselves during lunch hour. Coincidentally, Nicholas lived in Queens—not too far from me. He was not a bad looking ginger of a man. Nicholas stood well over six-feet tall and possessed an out-of-practice football build, hair full of red curly ringlets, pale freckled skin, and an intense masculine presence. When he spoke, his Boston-bred "pahk the cah in the Hahvahd Yahd" accent made me weak in the knees. Counselor George thought it would be a good idea for us to get to know one another and be a good support system for each other back east. Oddly enough, Counselor George left us alone and closed the door behind him. I didn't get it; was he setting us up on a date? Nicholas and I had some uninteresting small talk for a little while but exchanged phone numbers and agreed to hang out when we were both back in New York.

I contacted Nicholas only a week after I returned home from LIA, and we made plans to meet at a Dunkin Donuts in his neighborhood. We talked for nearly an hour, chatting about life, work, and LIA. As the conversation died down, it was time to figure out the best way to call it a night. Somehow, we managed to avoid any awkward silence. As I was about to attempt to gracefully part ways, he said, "Hey, let's get out of here"

He directed me to get into his car with tinted windows, and we continued to chat. Everything changed for me once we left the comfort of the public seating in Dunkin' Donuts for the privacy of his car. My palms started to sweat, my heart raced, and I was unable to concentrate on conversation, very intimidated by him. I wanted to kiss him but making the first move has never been my strong suit. Sexual tension thickly filled the car, and before I knew it, he had placed my hand over his crotch. As I felt his erection growing through his jeans, he started the car and said he had a place that we could go. As we drove off, leaving my car in the random Dunkin Donut's parking lot, I suddenly feared that I would be the subject of a future *Dateline* episode. We drove into a seedy, run-down motel somewhere in the middle of Queens.

This is it. I'm going to be murdered.

He drove into the parking lot, opened his door, and said, "I'll be right back."

I looked around to see how I could make my escape until I saw him returning with a hotel key. I knew what was going to happen at this point—sex or decapitation.

Once inside the motel room, we laid on the bed and turned on the TV, but not much television watching occurred. We left the room about an hour later, and he took me back to my car. The next day we chatted, but he told me that he enjoyed our time together but not to contact him anymore because he was going back to being straight and having sex with women. He said he was only with me because he needed one more homosexual romp to get out of his system. Yes, he *really* said that. *Ok, Nicky. Let me know how that works out for you.* I never heard from him again.

I thought I would feel more guilty hooking up with Nicholas, especially graduating from conversion therapy camp one week before. Honestly, my heart was so numb to the disappointment and hopelessness of not getting healed, I didn't have regrets from that evening. I came to a breaking point and gave up on becoming straight. To say that I was "over it" was an understatement. I wanted to meet guys, freely date, and have a boyfriend—no more secret-keeping and no more hiding. No more pretending. I did not care what my parents, my Christian friends, *or* God thought.

This is it. I'm gay!

Connecticut was not really known for its wild gay scene, but I guessed it was better to start getting my homosexual feet wet in a smaller city. A big issue I would face in "coming out" was that my Christianity still stared me in the face. I still believed the Bible as truth, so in choosing to live the "gay lifestyle," I was actively living in disobedience to God. However, I lost the will to care. Pretending I did not like guys was not something I could fake anymore, nor wanted to.

The time came that I dreaded: telling my *Deal or No Deal* coworkers that I lied to them about where I had been the last three months. I told them the whole story, that I made up a lie about interning at a church in Memphis but really had attended a gay conversion camp to make me straight. *Would they be mad at me? Will this affect our friendship and working relationship?*

Neal, Luke, and Kristin were the coworkers from the original *DOND* casting team who came out to Connecticut. Telling them the truth was not a huge deal I thought it would be. Neal even said he knew that's where I was the whole time. Whether that was true or not, it relieved me to have their support considering I lied to them. Understanding my conflict with Christianity vs. sexuality, they offered me their sympathy, not their anger or resentment. Curiously, they asked me about my state of mind when it came to my sexuality, and I told them, in not so many words, that the program did not work as planned and, "I'm gay!"

It was the first time I said those words aloud, and it disgusted and liberated me at the same time. To say they were ecstatic for me was putting it mildly, and I reveled in a different sense of freedom that I had never felt before—yet still feeling a smidgeon of guilt.

I rented a large house with two of the male producers in New London, Connecticut. Our residence became party central with plenty of alcohol, co-workers hanging out, and girls in and out of the guy's bedrooms. I had the entire basement floor to myself. I never invited guys over, but I went to their place, and when my roommates caught me walking in the door at 2:00 AM and asked where I had been, I was not embarrassed or ashamed to tell them that I had been out hooking up with a guy. The freedom to voice my truth felt amazing, although with a small degree of insecurity. Deep down, I believed I was corrupting myself, indulging blatantly and recklessly in homosexual sin. My coworkers never condemned me, which I had to get used to because this was the first time that I allowed people to encourage and enable me *toward* homosexuality and not away from it.

On weekends I had off, I took turns visiting Long Island and New Jersey, still attempting to be involved with the church plant as much as possible. I assumed Jeff would not want me to be a part of the church if I accepted being gay, but we all know what happens when you assume. I sent Jeff an email explaining what had been happening in my life, and I was not spiritually fit to help lead a church. I requested to be removed from church staff emails as I was not living a life that pleased God. I didn't want to be that guy to lead someone astray at his church. I mean, it was quite melodramatic if I say so myself. However, Jeff emailed me with one word:

Denied!!

What I have always loved about Pastor Jeff is that he understood and embraced the messiness of humanity within the Christian worldview. He recognized that no one was perfect enough, admittedly himself, to plant a church. Imperfect people run churches, so why should that disqualify me? Pastor Jeff accepted me as I was despite my flaws and inconsistencies. If I may be so bold as to say, Jeff was the most human representation of the biblical Jesus I learned about in my 30 years of following

Christianity. I know Jeff would scoff at such a statement because he abounds in humility and modesty.

His world would fall apart years later as he suffered through a failed marriage, which ultimately cost him his position as pastor of his church, a church that he worked so hard to build literally from the ground up. But even amid chaos, Jeff remained strong and resilient, from what I could see outside the closed doors. He walked through that fire with grace, maturity, forgiveness, and, most importantly, the recognition of his weaknesses and shortcomings. Without a doubt, I guarantee he had his moments of frustration and anger, questioning the Lord's direction and wondering if the trust he placed in God was in vain. But he survived and is thriving.

My promiscuous lifestyle returned with a vengeance as I became comfortable with my surroundings in Connecticut. I fell into a hole of self-sabotaging behavior as the weeks progressed. Experiencing this freedom with my sexuality did have its fleeting moments of confidence. I was so upset with God for not healing me, so I did whatever and whoever I wanted. It was easier to place the blame on God instead of having to accept I was not doing enough to become straight. Placing the blame on God allowed me to make unwise decisions and indulged in erratic behavior. I could not take responsibility for my actions because if I did, I would have to face more pain, hurt, and confusion, and I was mentally unprepared to do that.

Once *Deal or No Deal* started production, I met Jeffrey, a producer. Jeffrey, a larger-than-life personality, extremely flamboyant, and obnoxiously loud, became somewhat of my gay mentor. Jeffrey took me to the first gay bar since Greg took me to that one in Miami years earlier. This sorry excuse for a bar may have been the only gay establishment in all southern Connecticut. It was by no comparison an evening in West Hollywood's The Abbey, which is packed with hot guys, go-go dancers, sexy shirtless bartenders, and inebriated gays. In this Connecticut gay bar, there were maybe ten other customers, watered-down drinks, and average-looking bartenders mixing cocktails with their shirts *on,* but Jeffrey and I made the most of it.

Scanning the scene, I was not happy that my new "out of the closet" revamp of life was exclusive to only those people in Connecticut. I wanted everyone to know that I was gay and proud, even though on the inside I was still overwhelmed with guilt and shame. I still very much believed being gay was wrong, but I was pissed off LIA didn't work and wanted everyone to know.

Facebook became my outlet to post statuses that reflected an acceptance of homosexuality, acknowledging hot guys, and referencing my "new life." Fortunately, my parents were not on social media, so they didn't see any of these postings. These public postings started after Neal and Luke took me shopping to update my wardrobe, buying attire that I normally would not wear, but "gay Aaron" needed to make an entrance. These posts confused many of my Facebook friends as many of them knew I recently went to Love in Action in the earlier three months and financially supported my attendance. A close conservative friend emailed me and expressed their disappointment in my posts, especially since they donated money for me to attend the program.

"Do you want your money back?" I asked sarcastically.

I sent an email to several of my closer friends, including Chris, Travis, and Megan, stating that I was gay and no longer seeking "treatment" for my sexuality. None of them responded to my email. I assumed they were disappointed and didn't know how to respond at the time. Their silence only amplified my defeat; however, I was much more upset with God than anyone.

God broke his promise, and I was at a complete loss. My prayers were not answered. How much longer can I fight this? I wanted to serve Jesus, but I also wanted a boyfriend. A collision of my passions had wrecked me something awful, and God's insurance had nothing left to pay out.

My Connecticut summer came and went, and it was time to figure out what was next on the agenda. Ultimately, and predictably, I decided to make that move to Jersey. Irrespective of my gay proclamation, Jeff and Chris opened the door to allow me to assist with the church plant and be part of the team.

The time in Connecticut was a summer I will never forget as I experienced a lot of triumphs, heartaches, awakenings, and a sense of freedom I'd been waiting for. As much as I esteemed the freedom Connecticut gave me, I continually wrestled with the fact that deep down in my heart, I believed my choice to live as a homosexual man defied the word of God. Coming up with a plan to venture into a mindset where homosexuality and Christianity *could* co-exist would be my priority.

Can God still love me if I accepted being gay? Will I still go to hell if I have a boyfriend but still passionately love Jesus?

These were some of the questions I hoped to find answers to in the coming months.

Chapter Fifteen

TITANIC

Normally having the beach practically outside your door would be a luxury, but I moved in October, during a cold northeast autumn, which could explain the dirt-cheap rent. I loved my furnished and affordable guest house on 2nd Avenue in Manasquan, New Jersey. It was reminiscent of the movie *Beaches,* and I was a glowing Bette Midler—just without the dying friend.

Once I settled in my chilly, yet cozy new home, my first order of business was to find a job that would allow me to have a flexible schedule so I could help Pastor Jeff and Chris with the church. Since I had experience with BJ's—waiting tables, that is—restaurants all over the Jersey shore would soon receive my application from Red Bank to Toms River.

This church now had a name: Relevant Church. The kickoff service happened a month before I moved from Connecticut, so the church was already underway and an initial success. I aided Pastor Jeff and Chris with whatever menial tasks they needed and was happy to do them. Our outreach ministry was strong, and I couldn't be more thrilled to be a part of it. Pastor Jeff and Chris had a vision for what the character of the church would stand for: "Come as you are."

They avoided coming off too "churchy" in their attempts to reach people for Jesus. Christians and "Jesus freaks" do not have the best of reputations, and we, as a church, did our best to convey that Relevant was accepting of all people: young and old, Christian and atheist, gay and straight. All were welcomed. We encouraged people to come with their hurts and hang-ups as this was a safe place for them to get refreshed and receive a new outlook on life.

The church launch team flourished. I met and befriended many people in the community, and I became part of Jeff's, Chris's, and Travis's families. The team had several get-togethers a week, from BBQs to car washes to worship nights. Both Chris and Travis were seriously dating their new girlfriends around this time, and both would propose in the coming weeks. I thought for sure I would be jealous and dependent on Travis again, but surprisingly, I was pretty chill—for now.

Since my "coming out" months earlier in Connecticut, Travis and Chris accepted my homosexuality so much, in fact, that they would often ask me about my dating life as if I had their blessing. Initially, this new aspect of our friendships was strange and even made me feel a bit uneasy because my relationship with them always revolved around the healing of my homosexuality, not the enabling of it. Chris expressed he was more concerned about my relationship with God, believing the sexuality "issue" was secondary. Secondary or not, being gay was still an issue in the church that did not go unnoticed. With all that aside, everything was pretty good as I navigated this phase of life in New Jersey.

I had some cash saved up from the summer, but my bank account gradually drained when the paychecks stopped. I was unsuccessful in my attempts to secure a job waiting tables in a restaurant. I honestly believed landing a serving job would have been a piece of cake, but I should had known that beach city autumns would not be peak hiring season.

As the weeks went by, things started to go a bit downhill. Once the church got off the ground, there wasn't much administrative stuff for me to do so I found myself home and bored a lot. Chris and Travis were my only social circle, but their time was consumed with family and girlfriends. I did not hang out with them as much as we all did when single and living in Los Angeles. Hours and days would go by, and I would sit in my tiny Manasquan apartment all day, every day, staring at the TV for hours. Sitting on my couch, remote in one hand, a bowl of spaghetti in the other, became a daily activity. The more days passed, the more depressed I became. I would stare at my phone, constantly checking to see if the volume was working, hoping for any restaurant to call me and offer me a job, or at least an interview! But the phone remained silent.

The plans I had to change the world and transform all homosexuals for Jesus were defeated in my weakness because I accepted my own homosexuality. I now accepted that God couldn't change my desires, but I still adhered to the way I interpreted the Bible. Homosexuality was sinful. So, I essentially believed that God created me gay, loved me, *but* simultaneously condemned me and would send me to eternity in hell if I continued to accept the way he created me. What a fucked-up catch-22.

To make matters worse, I woke up one morning to find my cute little beach apartment completely flooded with two to three inches of water. Perplexed, I called my landlord, who conveniently forgot to mention when I first rented the place that "the area is subject to flooding because of the high tides in the winter." Luckily, I read the fine print of my lease that gave me an out if the apartment became unlivable—which it was. By the time the landlord was on his fifth apology, all my clothes were packed, soaked with cold and dirty Atlantic seawater. I threw my drenched luggage in my waterlogged Honda Fit, took a moment of reflection in the driver seat, then burst into hysterical laughter. I was too angry to cry, and then soon realized, *I'm homeless!*

Travis offered up his vacant Point Pleasant house rent free. He had been trying to fix it up and put it on the market but stalled so that I could stay there temporarily. The house was mostly emptied out besides a couple of beds in the bedrooms and one sofa chair in the living area. The refrigerator, laundry, gas, and electricity still functioned, which turned out to be a good deal. I was living on the rent and security deposit returned to me from my landlord and the little savings I had left in my account.

I entered the bleak house with my wet suitcases and stumbled to the laundry room to do a several loads of laundry. Sitting on the brick step of the fireplace in the ghostly empty living room, not a sound could be heard but the sprinkling of running water from the washing machine. Paralyzed and devoid of all emotion, I stared at the wall in a contemplative state, trying to understand the present. The washing machine made a clicking sound as it turned to the wash cycle.

Swish. Swish. Swish.

Physically I washed out to shore, but emotionally I was sinking, and my soul was drowning. In that moment, I had my first raw emotional breakdown pent up from the events of the past two days and beyond. Unlike that day in the BJ's parking lot when I was upset God was not making me straight, this time I broke down, not only because I had been displaced, but because I was feeling convicted for accepting my homosexuality. As I realized I was in a no-win situation, I let out a good cry. Every tear that dripped down my face had a name. Homelessness, non-purpose, sadness, and confusion, to name a few, fell from my eyes into my folded hands, desperate for peace and comfort.

If this is a test, God, I am failing.

Nothing but silence. The house remained dark except for the few ceiling lights that scattered throughout. I was also suddenly painfully aware that I did not have cable to watch *General Hospital.*

Man, could this get any worse?

Moving to New Jersey was not a good decision, and I knew it, but I forced the situation not considering other alternatives. I got too comfortable staying rent free in Travis's house, including installation of cable and internet, and it was not too long before I gave in to some very familiar temptations and started browsing the gay websites to meet up with guys.

I stopped looking for work altogether and barely left the house. My relationship with God was nonexistent, and I was in a complete state of apathy. The only time I found solace from the pain was when I would fall asleep at night, hoping I would never wake up. I was numb to God's presence. He did not make himself known to me. I was lost and alone and hated myself for having sex with other guys. I knew I was sinning, and I didn't care.

As the weeks went on, even the anonymous hookups became boring. I attempted actual dates with some guys, but nothing worked out. A depression that I never experienced before made its home in my heart; I felt an ominous dark cloud hovering over my head. My life had no purpose, and I felt so ashamed giving into homosexuality. It didn't matter that I publicly accepted it; internally, I felt dirty and vile.

One evening I came to a breaking point. I paced the floor in a panic because Travis did not text me back promptly, but also because I was restless, emotionally exhausted, and aching for a little bit of internal peace. I hated my life, filled with so much self-hatred for still having homosexual attractions and non-purpose.

My life is worthless. How can I stop the pain?

I walked into the kitchen, with bloodshot, tear-stained eyes, and grabbed a kitchen knife, placed it on top of my left forearm, and started cutting myself. As much as it hurt, it felt good. The arm pain surpassed the torment in my heart, and that was the goal. I cut again, and again, and again. The welts I created up and down my arm ached for relief—just as my heart did. I dropped the knife, as reality set in on what I had just done. The slices on my arms became itchy and swollen. I reached out to Travis angrily calling him out for not being a good friend when, in actuality, he was just not living up to the expectations I set for him. He and his girlfriend came over, but I didn't want to talk once he was there since playing mind games was my specialty. I showed them my arm and confessed to everything that was going on in my life the past month. Travis was kind, sympathetic, and compassionate, which was undeserved considering I did not have an ounce of respect for our friendship.

I never resolved to cutting before or after this isolated moment; however, my capability to slice my arm scared me beyond belief. Something needed to change.

That evening instigated a lot of soul searching, and it did not take long to conclude that my life in New Jersey needed to end. My world was dominated by not only the shame I felt accepting homosexuality but the renewed codependence on Travis and feeling as if I let Jeff and Chris down. I decided to leave New Jersey and head back to California, extremely despondent and ambivalent about the future.

Chapter Sixteen

THE TRUTH ABOUT CHARLIE

French fashion designer Coco Chanel said, "Don't spend time beating on a wall, hoping to transform it to a door." A woman who built an empire should surely know failure and heartbreak during a journey. New Jersey was a wall that never became a door.

The long drive back to Los Angeles from the East Coast that December of 2009 filled me with immense sadness as I reflected on what a failure the past year had been. However, I knew I was making the right decision to leave, especially because of how quickly doors opened for my Los Angeles return. Brea had an extra room in her condo that I would be able to stay in until I found my own place. After a call to BJ's, they said they would hire me back. I had a warm and dry place to crash and a job, which was more than I had in Jersey.

Returning to Oasis was my priority. Going to church there would be different without Pastor Jeff, Chris, and Travis, but I needed a fresh start without depending on them; plus, it would be good to reconnect with other friends. The guilt for accepting my attraction to men weighed on me tremendously. I felt foolish for "coming out" the past summer and knew I was disobeying God and the church. However, I did not know what else I could possibly do or any other means to eradicate my homosexual feelings. I needed to get back into church before I made more bad life decisions.

Once I settled in Brea's spare bedroom and became accustomed again to pizza sauce soiled uniforms and balancing Cherry Pepsis on a tray, a familiar but productive routine kept me in high spirits. The first person I knew to contact from Oasis Church was Caleb. Caleb was close with Pastor Jeff and Chris, but I never connected with him much prior to Tennessee. Describing Caleb with words does this man no justice. Experiencing him in person is the only way to fully understand what a gift he is.

He's loud, extroverted, funny, and quick-witted. Caleb is a true man of integrity, honesty, authenticity, and love. A one in a million treasure of a human whose only flaw is how excruciatingly tight he wraps his arms around you when giving one of his monstrous hugs. We all have that person: your first phone call if you need to be bailed out of jail. Caleb is my person. My love and respect for him has no bounds because he has proven himself repeatedly that he is a man of quality that I could depend on, no matter what. One can only be so lucky to have a person in their life that changes the fabric of your core being and brings you to tears simply because you are so overwhelmed by their character and who they are. Yep, that's Caleb.

When first connecting with Caleb, I instantly found him to be that safe person to confide in and break down my emotional walls. His "tough love" approach with advice and guidance was crucial to reinstate my walk with Jesus. With Caleb there is no sugar-coating, coddling, or insincerity. He was not afraid to get emotionally ugly, call me out on my bullshit, all while embracing the humanity within and never reducing words into cliché "Christianese" rhetoric.

I also reconnected with the worship leader Danielle, self-labeled as my "California big sister," who also became one of my biggest cheerleaders welcoming me back to Los Angeles and Oasis Church. I adored Danielle. She was a bright ray of sunshine and spread so much warmth and joy wherever she went; it was contagious. As much as I could be candid and open with Caleb, there was something special about my connection with Danielle. I could easily go that extra mile, most probably because of how much easier it was for me to be more open with females than males.

Luke from *Deal or No Deal* reached out to me upon hearing the news I was back in town and offered me a job on a new NBC primetime game show, *Minute to Win It*. I would also be working again with Kristin, my "work wife" from *DOND*. Suddenly within only a few short weeks my life became exhaustively busy with two jobs and as a fully active church member—a complete 180 from life in Jersey where I sat in a dark house all day, every day. I also moved out of Brea's Playa Del Rey condo and moved into a one-bedroom apartment in North Hollywood. Finally, adulting again!

Something stirred within me as I returned to my Oasis Church stomping grounds. I recognized that accepting my homosexuality would be continued disobedience to God. Life in Connecticut led me astray of what I truly believed deep down in my heart: being gay is a sin. I no longer could continue living in a fantasy world where God would approve of me dating other men and still claim to be a Christian.

Not one person—not Caleb, not Danielle, no one—told me this.

It was an epiphany that came to me, and me alone. Granted, Oasis Church encouraged me to continue these steps to homosexual healing, but that is only because I wanted them to and asked for the help. With that said, I reversed and denounced my "coming out." I did not view this backpedaling as a return to the closet but as obedience to God. I had to pick up the bat and attempt another hit at the heterosexual ball, no matter how many times I struck out. (Yes, a baseball analogy. I'm so bro.)

Initially, I did not take specific steps to find a new gay reparative therapy avenue. I was wary of doing another program or therapy considering I surpassed my capacity for hurt, so I could not face another failed healing scheme. God had to heal me from homosexuality in his own time, and I did not want to rush his timing. However, Danielle mentioned that Celebrate Recovery was coming to Oasis and encouraged me to check it out.

Celebrate Recovery (also known as CR) is a widely known Christian recovery program founded by Pastor John Baker from Saddleback Church in Lake Forest, California. The website states, "Celebrate Recovery is a Christ-centered, 12 step recovery program for anyone struggling with hurt, pain, or addiction of any kind. Celebrate Recovery is a safe place to find community and freedom from the issues that are controlling our life."

About 35,000 churches around the world participate in the CR program, and it has been moving outside the church and into universities and prisons. Caleb was the staff leader in charge of overseeing Celebrate Recovery at Oasis Church.

I rejected Danielle's suggestion immediately. CR sounded familiarly like Love in Action, as it was a twelve-step Christian recovery program. The only difference was that Celebrate Recovery did not solely focus on issues of sexuality. They also focused on drug and alcohol addiction, codependency, sexual/physical abuse, gambling addiction, and eating disorders. The thought of attending the program overwhelmed me, so for the time, I settled on only attending and volunteering at the church.

Minute to Win It became a massive undertaking and kept me working nearly 60-70 hours a week, not including my weekend hours at the restaurant. As the months passed, work became my whole life. Soon enough, without much Christian community and low church attendance, I started finding guys online to hook up with. I even met a guy who worked in an office on the same studio lot and would hook up with him during lunch breaks in a small storage closet. That dark cloud of shame resurfaced, and I had to reach out to Danielle and Caleb for accountability. They kept pushing CR, and since I didn't have any other options to aid in my healing, I relented and said I would go.

CR's evening structure started with everyone gathered for announcements and worship before breaking out into same-gender small groups of their chosen issue. I had not yet decided which small group I would attend. My options were limited since I did not have an eating disorder or a chemical dependency. Oasis's CR had yet to create an SSA (Same Sex Attraction) healing group, but I was somewhat thankful for that. The men's sexual addiction issue was the only group that made sense, so I made my way to that room and saw only one person sitting in there—Dustin.

Dustin! No, not Dustin!

Dustin, a well-known attendee of the church and a CR leader, was candid about his past addiction to pornography and how his relationship with Christ set him free, so it made sense he was the group leader. I always had a deep lust for Dustin since the first day I ran into him at Oasis. A long wavy-haired, tanned New Zealander with the sexiest Kiwi accent. A surfing enthusiast, he often posted shirtless pictures on social media that made me wish I was his surfboard he climbed on top of every morning. I often reminisced about the time I saw him bare-chested at a men's paintball church event a couple of years prior. The Los Angeles summer heat drenched his hard chest and rippling abs with glistening sweat. I stared at him, wishing to play with his paintball gun.

Initially, I was thrilled to be in the room with him, but the reality that his presence would exacerbate my problem more than alleviate it slowly set in. *How can I not have homosexual thoughts if he is leading the group?* I entertained the thought of Dustin becoming my new confidant and taking me under his wing—a.k.a. a new emotionally dependent victim.

I sat across from him. However, he never looked up from his phone to acknowledge my entrance. I waited for other guys to walk in to cut the tension as the silence between Dustin and me was deafening. *Hello, earth to Dustin!* He continued to ignore me, and no other guy came into the room. I was too intimidated, shy, and overwhelmed to initiate the greeting.

Despite my lust toward him, I became too apprehensive to stay. *What if I had to confess all my gay sins to hot Dustin?* After what seemed like an eternity but was probably no more than four or five minutes, I walked out of the room, through the church's front door, and headed to my car, hopeless, upset, and sad—the opposite of what behind the church doors should bring.

Dustin reached out to me the next day offering to buy me lunch for not engaging and welcoming me into the group. *A date with Dustin? Sign me up!* Unfortunately, our lunch date did not provide any long-term friendship, which was probably better for the both of us. I did not want to become emotionally dependent on yet another guy falling into that debilitating trap again. I did not return to CR for quite some time.

On August 4, 2010, a federal judge ruled that Proposition 8 was unconstitutional under the U.S. Constitution and barred its enforcement.[1] To recall, Proposition 8 eliminated the right for same-sex couples to marry, a measure that I voted *yes* on due to my insistence that homosexuality was against God's plan for marriage and humanity in general. In 2008, the measure was approved, prohibiting gays and lesbians from legally marrying and taking away marital rights that heterosexual couples already possessed. When I read the news that Prop 8 was overturned, my heart sank, fearing the nation was headed down a very dangerous road. Not only did I believe in homosexual healing for myself, but also for the thousands of gay citizens that were living in sin who accepted their sexuality. Acknowledging disgrace for this turn of events made me feel powerful as if I could be the one person God would raise up to help free the homosexuals from their broken hearts and demonic lifestyle.

When I was in YWAM, I often compared my life to Esther's story from the Bible. Esther, a closeted Jewish woman, was chosen to be the queen after the king banished his wife and replaced her. When instructed, a man named Mordecai, Esther's cousin, refused to bow down to the king's counselor Haman. In an act of revenge against Mordecai, Haman requested to the king that all Jews in the Persian Empire be killed. This put Esther in a predicament as the Queen and a Jew herself, which nobody knew. She was now at a crossroads. Should she keep silent and witness the death of her family and Jewish people or tell her secret to the king facing the potential of her own mortality. Mordecai encourages Esther in the well-known verse Esther 4:14, *"For such a time as this."* In a riveting and suspenseful end, Esther exposed Haman for the jackass he was, came clean about her ethnicity, and found favor with the king.

I was Esther. My task was to save my people (homosexual strugglers) from impending hell. The only way I could execute such a plan was to be exactly like Esther. I was convinced that I had to speak up and tell my story to rescue my fellow gays and lesbian strugglers from a fate worse than death and introduce them to Jesus, who can cleanse their sins and turn them straight—ironically, something that had not yet happened to me. I still was very much attracted to men. My anger for the overturning of Proposition 8 inspired me to address my thoughts in an email that I sent to some friends:

Dear friends and family,

Today Proposition 8 was overturned in California. For those who do not know, Proposition 8 is the act that provides that only marriage between a man and a woman is valid or recognized in the state of California. Those in favor of Proposition 8 had a victory because it was previously passed, but today it was overturned, and a federal judge declared Prop 8 unconstitutional and now allows marriage for homosexual men and women

I have to say I was a little bit disheartened at first, feeling that we may have lost a huge battle as Christians. Then what really got to me was certain friends on Facebook who do not know Jesus and were happy that Prop 8 was overruled. Most of those same people I know live very promiscuous lives yet are celebrating a ruling for a monogamous union. HUH? It's pretty ironic. Then I was just flooded with despair and just asked Jesus, "What do we do as your people??"

The Lord gave me this verse from 2 Chronicles 7:14. "if my people, who are called by my name, will humble themselves and pray and seek my face and turn from their wicked ways, then will I hear from heaven and will forgive their sin and will heal their land." Inspired from hearing from God, I looked up the chapter and read in context what was going on when God said this to Solomon. Solomon was dedicating the Temple of the Lord. Let's read what verse 13 says: "At times I might shut up the heavens so that no rain falls, or command grasshoppers to devour your crops, or send plagues among you." I believe the Lord is saying the same to us in this situation, or ANY situation that God is going to test us as a church, as a body, and He will intentionally throw mountains in front of us. But in the same breath, he already tells Solomon the answer to those mountains. PRAY PRAY PRAY!!! And he will listen! It's not just about us praying, but it's about humility and purifying ourselves in the process. Didn't God give Joshua those same instructions to the Israelites?? "Purify yourselves, for tomorrow the Lord will do great things among you" (Joshua 3:5).

God continues to say in 2 Chronicles 2, in verse 15, "My eyes will be open and my ears attentive to every prayer made in this place. Let's not get depressed; let's not have resentment and hate stir in our hearts. God is building a church, a body whose mission is LOVE to enter in the darkness."

I write this email, not as a perfect man. Not as someone who has 100 percent victory in overcoming my own homosexual struggle YET. But I write this is a man who loves Jesus and is still pressing on to relentless pursuit of freedom and the Will of my Father in heaven. Join me as I pray for the homosexual community. Join me as I worship in spirit and in truth. Join me as we crumble down the kingdom of darkness together. Join me in this journey of falling in love with Jesus.

Love you all,

Aaron

Man, that must have been some tasty cherry Kool-Aid!

I had zero control over my own sexuality, yet I wanted to control everyone else's. A huge motivation in writing that email was to express that I was still a man on a mission, to ultimately be healed of homosexuality and help the world of the same problem. However, hypocrisy flowed like the blood in my veins. As I fought for the homosexual healing for others, I wanted to love and be with a man, every single day.

The verse 2 Corinthians 12:7–9 reads, *"To keep me from becoming conceited because of these surpassingly great revelations, there was given me a thorn in my flesh, a messenger of Satan, to torment me. Three times I pleaded with the Lord to take it away from me. But he said to me, 'My grace is sufficient for you, for my power is made perfect in weakness.' Therefore, I will boast all the more gladly about my weaknesses, so that Christ's power may rest on me."*

However, the apostle Paul made no mention of exactly what his "thorn" was. In context for the secular, the word "thorn" here describes some kind of ailment, whether emotional, physical, or mental, that Paul dealt with. There are many theories speculating what Paul could have been struggling with: physical sickness, persecution from his enemies, or sexual temptation. Like Paul, I prayed for God to take away my thorn of homosexuality, and God said, *"Aaron, my grace is sufficient for you, for my power is made perfect in weakness."* Paul prayed that prayer only three times, but I prayed that prayer 3,000 times. I had to accept homosexuality as my thorn but planned to obey Christ despite it and resist.

The beginning of 2011 started on a high note. I felt strengthened in my Christian faith, gained control of my emotions, and denounced homosexuality—a very different outlook from what I had in the summer of 2009, only a year and a half earlier, when I came out of the closet and said I was gay. I began to pursue counseling and therapy again to dig deep into why I still had this gay sickness. Because I'd accepted that my attraction to men was natural did not mean I easily could affirm it in spiritual conscience. Discovering the root cause of my attraction would ultimately help me heal, which was touched upon in Love in Action, but I hadn't yet discovered my root. It must be *really* deep! I believed a person could not be born gay, so I had to figure out what caused my homosexuality and its origin. The concept of "root issue" stemmed from the belief that emotions and trauma run deep, like that of a tree. We could cut off the leaves, branches, and even the tree itself, but if the root is still present, parts of the tree will inevitably grow back. I treated my struggle with homosexuality as a tree. I may be able to control the behavior and suppress the attractions by "cutting them off," but if the root is still intact, the attractions will be sustained. I had to find the root to cut out once and for all.

Removing the root looks different for various people. However, the encompassing practice of removal is usually prayer and coming to terms, confronting, and dealing with relational, sexual, or physical trauma endured in the past. Some typical roots gay men have that supposedly cause their homosexuality are having an over-bearing mother, emotionally passive or non-existent father, lack of connection to other males in adolescence, and sexual abuse, to name a few. I dove headfirst, reading every book on the topic and researching any counselor in my area that could help me discover why my attraction to men existed.

I started one-on-one gay conversion therapy with Joe Dallas, author of the book *Desires in Conflict*, a prominent personality in the ex-gay movement and former Director of Exodus International, the leading organization for gay conversion therapy. I looked forward to the sessions, hoping to finally unbox what had caused my same-sex attraction. I listened to his every word and devoured his book, highlighting and underlining anything pertaining to my problem. He sat and listened, with a notepad and paper in hand, jotting down everything I said as if he was taking dictation.

Not surprisingly, after a handful of therapy sessions, I stopped seeing Joe. I blamed quitting the sessions on the inability to pay his fee, but the truth was that nothing about our sessions helped me become less attracted to guys. I still acquired other resources to help me, such as the books *You Don't Have to Be Gay*, written by Jeff Konrad, and *101 Frequently Asked Questions About Homosexuality*, written by "ex-gay" Mike Haley. My most helpful resource was Sy Rogers, the man responsible for my stay in Love in Action. There was not one of his books or taped sermons that I didn't read or watch. When Sy came to Oasis Church as a guest speaker, I never missed one sermon, even staying for multiple services to hear the same message, again and again, hoping something he said would stick. Yet, no matter how much time, money, and hope I invested in Joe Dallas, Mike Haley, or Sy Rogers, at the end of the day, nothing worked. There's a definition for this—doing the same thing over and over again expecting a different result…that's insanity.

I decided that a specific person or resource wouldn't be the saving grace for my sin, so I relinquished help from humans and pursued more of Jesus and the Bible. I held steadfast that one day the faith, trust, and hope I had put in God all these years would not be in vain. I would succeed. My testimony would be astounding, and all glory would be God's. I proclaimed I would meet my wife and desire having sex with her. I still believed for eventual healing.

Oasis became a valued priority as I threw my energy and availability into the church. The incredible community and friends that I developed were incomparable. The Oasis staff were a safe haven. On any given day, I could walk into the church office and be surrounded by loving, kind, and generous people. I was at the top of my spiritual game. I believed I was only weeks away from total healing, thriving in my relationship with Jesus. Unfortunately, my quest for God and heterosexuality would unleash a moral superiority I believed I earned. I became spiritually arrogant, judgmental, and self-righteous—which brings me to a story about Charlie Brown.

Growing up, my favorite comic strip was *Peanuts*, featuring Charlie Brown, Linus, Lucy, Snoopy, and the rest of the gang. During trips to the Brentwood Public Library as a kid, I checked out a different Charles M. Schulz book every week. Even in SCS elementary school, students were required to attend library class once a week. I don't recall much of what we did in that class besides learning the Dewey Decimal System. However, we had to check out a book. I exhausted the entire *Peanuts* catalog that was in stock (and eventually became obsessed with *The Babysitters' Club* series, but that's another story).

Every holiday came with its own television airing of a *Peanuts* special including "You're in Love, Charlie Brown," "It's the Great Pumpkin Charlie Brown," "A Charlie Brown Thanksgiving," and "A Charlie Brown Christmas." I always had full ownership of the TV on those evenings to watch my Charlie Brown movies. Every Sunday, when my dad would come home with bagels and Sunday's Newsday, I would instantly rip into the paper, searching for the comics to find out what antics Snoopy and Woodstock were up to that day. I read the comics every day, but Sundays were different. Not only were the comics longer in content but they were also in color!

I related most to Linus. He had Lucy, his bossy older sister, and Rerun, a pain in the butt younger sibling, both of which I had. (I love you Rebecca and Sarah!) What I also had in common with Linus was that we both had a security object we could not live without. Linus had his blanket, but I had a stuffed animal, a white and pink lamb named Patricia (just another piece of the puzzle).

Even in adulthood, I have sustained great affection for the comic strip and the *Peanuts* gang. I am not ashamed to admit I bought cutouts of the characters to hang on my bedroom wall in my late 30s and currently own stuffed Snoopy and Charlie Brown dolls that are propped up on my shelf for all visitors to see. Nothing else in my past brings me back to my childhood like the *Peanuts* gang. With that said, I did not take it lightly when I felt somebody was polluting something that I held extremely sacred.

An actor couple that I befriended through Oasis, Ned and Krissy, invited me to see them in a play based on the *Peanuts* brand called *Dog Sees God: Confessions of a Teenage Blockhead*. I did not know anything about the plot of the play before the viewing except that it reimagined the *Peanuts* characters as high school kids.

Not only did I think that it would be enjoyable to see two friends perform, but better yet, they would be portraying characters I had adored my entire life. Ned would be in the role of Charlie Brown. Krissy informed me that while she usually played Peppermint Patty, she'd be playing a different role that evening. If I wanted to, I could come another night and see it again when she had more of a prominent role. I had agreed to that invitation before I saw it the first time.

I sat myself down in a creaky seat of a small theater house in North Hollywood, enthusiastically waiting to see what the *Peanuts* gang could be up to as high schoolers. Unfortunately, what started as something thrilling and riveting turned out to be heartbreaking and confusing. It turned out that both Charlie Brown and Schroeder were both gay, and not only that, but the entire play also seemed to be one big production of accepting and embracing homosexuality. In my skewed perception of morality, I was extraordinarily disappointed and appalled that Ned had kissing scenes with another male. Also, and more infuriating, how could Charlie Brown be gay?!? It's well documented he's in love with the Little Red-Haired Girl! A valid homosexual argument could be made for Peppermint Patty, and I'll even give you Schroeder, but *not* Charlie Brown.

Clearly, I had many issues with this play. First and foremost, Ned and Krissy's involvement concerned me. Not only did I question their participation based on how I think a Christian actor should conduct themselves and have discernment over the roles they choose to take, but why would they invite me to this play knowing my past with homosexuality?

To my knowledge, both Ned and Krissy were aware of my story and pursuit of healing. I was the self-proclaimed poster boy for homosexual healing of Oasis Church, and I counted on my Christian friends to steer me in the right direction, toward resistance, when it came to my struggle. *Did they even consider my feelings and how this would affect me?* They were friends I worshipped and prayed with, and now I wondered if we were even serving the same God, a God who denounced same-sex relationships.

I cordially gave an obligatory "good job" and "you were great" at the end of the evening. Yet, my arrogant and self-righteous sense of virtue shot silent daggers of anger into their eyes of hypocrisy. I drove home that evening, slightly depressed that two of my "Christian" friends subjected me to a performance that accepted homosexuality as normal and something that should be affirmed. I also believed part of my innocent childhood was now tainted having watched Charlie Brown and Schroeder display gay feelings toward each other, which impacted me way more than it should have. Most of all, Ned is straight! How could he engage in a romantic kiss with another male—and Krissy was OK with that? My sensitivity to the whole evening proved how excessively dramatic my restraint to homosexuality had become. The sad part of this equation is that my anger's deep-rooted issue was not with Ned and Krissy or the message of the play in and of itself.

It was jealousy.

Jealous that I could not have a love or a romance with whom I choose because of my faith in God and belief in the Bible.

Jealous that I was not allowed to consent to the liberal mantra to simply "be me."

Jealous because *I* wanted to be kissing Schroeder that night.

The jealousy proved I was nowhere near "healed." To deviate from the sexual cravings I wanted, lashing out on Ned and Krissy seemed to be a soothing outlet. I had no choice but to place blame on them because accusing someone or something else as responsible for my homosexual attraction diminished the secular belief that romantic desire and attraction are innate and natural.

As soon as I got home, I sent Krissy and Ned an email telling them I would not be attending their play again to see Krissy play Peppermint Patty. I expressed disappointment in them for inviting me to a play that encouraged and glamorized homosexuality. I also condemned them for choosing to act in a play that promoted a sinful lifestyle. Oh, and I made sure I told them they hurt my feelings.

My Kool-Aid pitcher had free refills.

I had a severely distorted sense of gratification, sticking up for myself and calling them out on how they "wronged" me. I experienced an elated moment of counterfeited spiritual bliss which became a twisted sense of entitlement to God, proving that I loved him more, obeyed him better, and took the Bible more seriously. Surely my crown in heaven will have more jewels than Ned and Krissy's.

Ned wrote me back with a maturity and respect that I lacked, responding with a tender grace to my email that was accusatory, condemnatory, and disrespectful to their craft and personal convictions. It was not until years later that I realized I owed them an apology. Christianity, as I knew it, was supposed to be about love, acceptance, and kindness. Yet, somehow, those attributes were lost in my response to Krissy and Ned, as I portrayed nothing but judgment, arrogance, and criticism. I was very wrong and ignorant that my version of Christianity was more detrimental to my character than beneficial.

No matter how much I defended the Bible and God's ultimate healing over my sexuality, I continued to be attracted to men despite consistent daily prayer, reading the Bible faithfully, attending church, and having spiritual accountability. *Seriously, God, what else do I have to do?* The legitimacy of the belief that my homosexual attractions would come to an eventual end faded day by day.

I confided in a friend from church, who told me to reach out to a guy named Eric for advice, giving me his contact info. Eric was a former staff member of Oasis who was gay and lived with his husband. I had no intention to be swayed into accepting homosexuality but wanted to hear Eric's experience to understand how someone who worked for the evangelical church at one point turned away from God and embraced his sinful lifestyle. Eric wrote back enthusiastically and agreed to meet, but we could not get our schedules to work out, especially with him living out in Long Beach and me on the road with my new television gig, NBC's *The Biggest Loser*. We agreed to meet in the future. I did not know it at the time, but Eric would be the reason everything in my life would soon turn upside down.

The Biggest Loser casting tour took me all over the U.S., with a memorable stop in Dallas, TX. In Dallas, the hotel that my company put me up in was smack in the middle of the city's gay community, Oak Lawn. I found this to be problematic to my sexual sobriety. It was as if I was an alcoholic, and the neighborhood was a big fat bottle of tequila. Of course, my distaste for the area did not stop me from taking nightly strolls down the street. It's not sinful for me to peruse, *right?* Walking past gay nightclubs, porn shops, and restaurants with rainbow flags in the windows showing off their pride made me queasy. Even the male Subway employee with pink hair and feminine mannerisms made me lose my appetite, which was unfortunate since his friendliness and kindness while making my sandwich portrayed that he was much more comfortable in his skin than I was in mine.

This Sodom and Gomorrah neighborhood made me uncomfortable enough to resort to my hotel room and watch HGTV the rest of the evening. My ongoing crush on *Property Brothers* Drew Scott proved it to be a welcomed alternative than walking those streets. Obedience to God was more important than this liberal mantra of "be true to yourself," and I held on to the faith that God would someday reward me with heterosexual attraction.

I'm waiting, God. Still waiting.

Chapter Seventeen

THE PURSUIT OF HAPPYNESS

Time to quit.
    Working in the entertainment industry would be a disservice to my healing. I was surrounded by people who accepted the gay lifestyle and it created fear I would give in again at some point. Subjecting myself to people who encouraged and enabled my homosexual struggle had to stop, even if I considered them friends.
    After *The Biggest Loser* job ended, I applied for an internship program that Oasis Church offered. Officially quitting as a television producer and working in the church was the best option for me to live a pure and holy life for God. So yes, my spiritually brilliant plan to live off my savings and not work would be my next attempted step to heterosexuality. I didn't even have the BJ's job anymore since I had to quit during *The Biggest Loser* gig. BJ's wanted more shifts from me, but I couldn't oblige working as a full time TV producer during the week. But who needs an income when God will provide if you are doing his will?
    I was placed to intern with the Creative Arts Department under my favorite person in the church, Danielle. This area had a huge function in the flow of Sunday services, responsible for all things creative, including the worship team, the band, the dance team, and the technical team, including lighting, audio, and graphics. My responsibilities were straightforward: assist the department in any way they needed.
    My job was mainly administrative, from organizing the worship music lists, taking attendance on Creative Arts nights, helping new church members get involved in Creative Arts, and acting as the liaison between the band, choir director, and Danielle for whatever they needed for Sunday services. More than anything, I enjoyed working in the church office nearly every day, surrounded by people who loved Jesus and did

not condemn me for pursuing heterosexuality, something I could not expect working with my TV colleagues.

The four months during the internship kept me spiritually grounded. I proudly conducted myself as a "heterosexual" man of God, "sober" from homosexual sin. But four months goes by fast when you are having fun and suppressing your sexuality; so, what's next, God? I asked Danielle about a staff position at the church, but nothing was available. I needed a paycheck but didn't want to go back to the entertainment industry—my sexuality depended on it!

I had no choice. I put out feelers to my colleagues and I immediately booked a gig working on the Animal Planet show *My Cat from Hell*. Let me tell you, one has not made it in Hollywood until the job requires interviewing aggressive cats for two months. As a proud card-carrying cat person, this show, by far, was one of my favorite projects I ever worked on.

In keeping with the church's culture, Oasis took advantage of any opportunity to allow congregants to tell their transformation story and how God restored an aspect of their life. Cardboard testimonies were making a reappearance for Easter 2012. When the request came for me to participate the second time, I initially wanted to sit it out, but this boy who constantly craved affirmation and validation could not easily take a step out of the homosexual poster-boy spotlight. If God was truly healing me from homosexuality, a "disease" that liberals, scientists, and secular therapists are convinced there is no cure for, then it's my responsibility to accept my calling as God's chosen one to contradict their theories. God *will* heal me of homosexuality—for such a time as this! I believed that with every fiber of my being.

The last nine months of celibacy had to count for some progress, despite my laptop screensaver having numerous shirtless photos of Ryan Reynolds bouncing across the screen. My impressive sobriety and willingness to believe that God could change my attractions had me convinced that was all I needed to make people think I could be healed. I told Danielle I wanted to change the verbiage from my 2008 cardboard because I was uncomfortable with the prior statement claiming that God changed my desires, which was untrue. This time around, the front and back of my cardboard would state:

Front: "*Lost and lonely in a homosexual sex addiction.*"

Back: "*Now found and alive in God's grace & truth. Nine months purity. Praying for a wife!*"

I swapped out a lie for a lie. God did not change my desires last time, nor was I praying for a wife this time. A standing ovation erupted when I turned my sign around to show the church how God healed me, and at that moment, I disregarded that little fib with ease. The accolades, applause, and praise that followed as I proudly held my sign up high from the pulpit surpassed the reaction from the previous time. Claiming nine months of "purity" may be subjective. Sure, I was not physically having gay sex, but could I proclaim homosexual purity when Enrique Iglesias was serenading me in my daydreams wearing nothing but Calvin Klein briefs? The more I deceived people, the more I became increasingly proficient in cultivating a fraudulent broken spirit, a spirit that had already been slowly disintegrating for years. Out of pure ignorance, I continually picked up the chisel and further chipped away at my soul, which was already in a completely shattered mess.

All for the glory of God, right?

As I stood on stage with my cardboard lie receiving those accolades and praises from the crowd, I recall seeing Hollywood power couple Brian Austin Green and Megan Fox in the back row, witnessing my alleged transformation. Brian played David Silver on *Beverly Hills, 90210*, while Megan is well-known as *Transformers* movie royalty. I felt empowered. Because of my bravery, God's truth would be unveiled to them so they could proclaim to all of Hollywood, on my behalf, that homosexuality could be cured. Yea, I really believed Brian Austin Green had nothing better to do than to tell all his Hollywood friends about my cardboard testimony. Also, when did geeky David Silver become a hot grown ass man? Ok, daddy Brian, I see you.

After the 6:00 PM service, a church friend had a get-together at her house, and a bunch of us went over to celebrate the magnificent day of God's healing power. I sat down next to one of my church friends, Samantha, enjoying a Sprite with some cheese and crackers, sharing our thoughts about the day, expressing how happy and free I felt in the moment, relishing in the power and sovereignty of God. Then the conversation took a turn. I was not prepared for what happened next. As she opened her mouth, she spewed out something that not only caught me off guard but rendered me entirely speechless.

"I don't think there is anything wrong with being gay," she said casually.

I wished I heard her wrong but knew I hadn't. My arms became shaky. I was filled with confusion. All I could get out of my mouth was, "Huh?"

"My brother is gay, and I don't think there is anything wrong with it," she said firmly.

Instantly all the joy and happiness that overflowed my spiritual cup from the day evaporated as I sat there in shock, not knowing what to say. I came close to questioning her remarks and why she disrespected my testimony but held in my anger, not wanting to start a debate with her.

The harrowing questions that circulated my brain at once jumped to the offense: *How could she say that to me? Did she not see my cardboard sign? Had she not witnessed the praise and applause I received when I showed the entire church that God healed me? Does she not read her Bible? She's in the church choir. How can she say such a horrendous and hypocritical thing? She can't be a real Christian!*

My austerity on the topic of homosexuality and how it broke the heart of God blinded my humanity so much I could not even see how much Samantha *loved* her brother. Few people want to believe in something that would result in their loved one going to hell, yet I believed in that very thing; but the person that would be sent to hell was not a loved one, it was me. I felt pity on Samantha, and I prayed for her brother that night—for God's perfect love to descend upon him and that he would be set free.

The events of that day propelled me to make some changes. I assessed my life and decided to purge things that would encourage or enable homosexuality. I set up a block on specific websites, tossed out my iPhone and bought a Google Smartphone because Grindr and similar gay apps were incompatible with those phones at the time, removed *Will & Grace* reruns from my DVR recordings, and gave away my *Golden Girls* DVD set.

Yes, I did not sell the DVD set; I gave it away for *free*! I spent $150.00 on those DVDs and *gave* them away! The reason behind this transaction was self-explanatory, at least to me. *The Golden Girls* had a huge gay fan base and was the most popular TV show among most gay men. I was embarrassed to admit, at the time, that I fell into that category.

Still, I did not want to admit it because I believed I was sinning, embracing something that the homosexual community held in high regard. I felt God tell me to dispose of the DVDs for cleansing and recovery. The perverse idea of the manhood and masculinity I wanted to uphold and portray became intoxicating. I posted a Facebook status offering to give the first person who responded the entire seven-season set at absolutely no cost. In quite the hysterical irony, the first person to respond was Samantha. The same girl who rubbed her homosexual affirming salt in my hopeful heterosexual wound wanted my DVDs! I was not thrilled she won my little contest, but I kept my word. The following Sunday, I brought my box set to church and begrudgingly gave them to her, never relaying the reason why I was handing them over. I wondered if, I had told her why, she would have rejected them and told me that it's OK to watch the *Golden Girls*—and be gay. If such words came out of her mouth, I would have rebuked her in the name of Jesus! Not today, Satan.

I could not be any more ignorant of the personal hell I put myself through. Not one person from the church told me I could not watch *The Golden Girls*. My relationship with God, what I read in the Bible, and what I *diagnosed* as godly and ungodly influenced my decision to part ways with the DVDs and every other decision in my life—it was borderline cultish.

The spiritual high of giving cardboard testimonies led me to have another conversation with Caleb about Celebrate Recovery (CR), and I decided to make another go of it. Stubbornness kept me away from pursuing another healing program, but since CR at Oasis did not have a specific Same Sex Attraction (SSA) group, it couldn't hurt to receive healing in other areas of my life. Even though I had been celibate for nearly a year, I returned to the men's sexual addiction small group anyway.

Participating in Celebrate Recovery became more of a social and spiritual avenue for me, and not so much a healing prospect. Attending the sex addiction group wasn't bad this time around, even though hottie Dustin was still the group leader. There were roughly twenty guys in the group, sitting around in a circle, who expressed their struggles with sex, porn, and masturbation, among other less amorous subjects such as insecurity, isolation, abuse, and depression. I scoped out the circle weekly, quietly targeting which of these straight guys could be my new "healthy male friendship" that I could bond with and help me walk the straight and narrow—literally. I tried and failed miserably in the past with Nathan and Travis, but I'll always find a reason to befriend a hot guy if they'll help me become straight—makes sense, right?

Unfortunately, attending the men's sexual addiction group ignited my craving to hook up with guys. Like my experience in *The River* healing program I attended in college, I would sit in the group and listen to these guys, many of whom I was attracted to, divulge their struggles with porn and masturbation. This group's intent may have helped these guys relate to each other and introduce a level of accountability, but for me, it was ammunition for my gay lust. When the hot guy in the circle confessed sorrowfully to watching porn, the sympathy and encouragement for his purity that I should have toward him was lost within my lustful play by play of his shame. *How was this supposed to help me?* This group disrupted my purity more than sustained it.

One Sunday evening at church, Caleb talked to me about a new CR small group that formed, the SSA group for men. He mentioned that two guys from church, Josiah and Parker, would lead the group. I knew Josiah, becoming friends with him long before Celebrate Recovery, and knew he struggled with homosexuality as well. Parker was an acquaintance at most. He worked on Oasis staff as their office manager, which was a fancy and more masculine title for "secretary." Parker and I met during my church internship but never communicated much. However, when Caleb told me that Parker was going to co-lead the SSA group alongside Josiah, I was puzzled why a straight guy would lead a group for a bunch of gay strugglers. Initially, the SSA group for CR didn't interest me. I didn't want to subject myself to another homosexual healing group that was reminiscent of gay conversion therapy.

In a separate conversation later, Caleb confirmed that Parker did, in fact, struggle with homosexuality, which floored me. I hid my shock convincingly, trying not to let on that Caleb "outed" him. It has been said that stereotypes exist because they are true. However, Parker embodied the complete opposite of a gay male, coming off as a seemingly typical straight guy. Curious, I started a conversation with Parker at the next Celebrate Recovery meeting to get the 411 on his life. We drove to a nearby Wendy's after the meeting and talked for hours, getting to know each other, and establishing a new friendship. Having someone to relate with, especially about this struggle, was unparalleled. No one understands what it's like to be a Christian person who has unwanted attractions to the same gender unless you have walked in those shoes.

Parker and I came from similar backgrounds, growing up in Christian homes, raised in the evangelical church, attended Christian universities receiving theology degrees, and believed accepting homosexuality will be an afterlife of torture, so, we "got" each other. Unlike me, though, Parker had increasing doubts about the Christian faith and the Bible as a whole. As a church staff member and one of the main worship leaders, his questions about Christianity were disconcerting.

To keep my celibacy and purity on track, I wanted to find Christian roommates who could offer consistent accountability. The luxury of living alone made it easy for me to invite guys to my place for sexual encounters, so having roommates would counteract those temptations. I moved in with two friends from the church in continued attempts to heal by expanding my spiritual community and surrounding myself with straight Christian guys. Granted, one of my roommates, Brody, was a fitness model who walked around the apartment all day without his shirt on, but I didn't stare—too much. The temptation to engage in anything immoral or lustful was at an all-time low for me, and I could not have been more secure in my relationship with Jesus and my potential homosexual healing.

One of my most favorite Christian recording artists, Amy Grant, wrote a song called "Never Give You Up," a song I sang to God during my private one-on-one prayer times. I declared a promise that I would never give up on him as Lord of my life as long as I lived. This song was my mantra. I was wholly and hopelessly, head-over-heels in love with Jesus. I vowed to never give up on Jesus, not in a million years. However, a most significant test was yet to come.

Chapter Eighteen

THE BLIND SIDE

I WOULD SOON FIND how much of my life related to the movie *The Truman Show* with Jim Carrey. No, I would not find myself in a world where a reality TV show about my life is filmed and aired without my knowledge. However, I would grasp the reality of portraying life as a fraud. Although an exaggerated version, this film highlights the chaos and turmoil a person faces when their entire existence and everything they thought was right and pure is false, dishonest, and filled with uncertainty.

Like Truman, I would soon come to a crossroads with an old life that I knew and a new life I was unfamiliar with. The trouble is that the life I grew accustomed to for thirty-plus years, though familiar, brought me so much heartbreak and confusion. Also, like Truman, signs proving my current life was a sham stared me in the face, which I regularly ignored because of a diluted promise from God that my sexual attraction would magically transform. Truman's story didn't unfold overnight, and neither would mine.

This story of mine now takes a turn. I would soon receive an email that changed the course of my life and threw a curveball so unexpected that it knocked me off my evangelical feet.

On Tuesday, May 29, 2012, I received an email from Eric, the former Oasis Staff member who lived with his husband, Russell, in Long Beach. We never got the chance to meet up because I wanted to avoid being around him and his husband who may persuade me into accepting my homosexuality. They claimed to be gay Christians—two labels I emphatically disagreed could not co-exist.

The email was an invitation to a seminar that upcoming Saturday at his church in Bellflower. As he stated, the seminar was to be presented as an honest discussion about what the Bible says about homosexuality. It would be divided into two sections: theology and testimony where gay Christians would share their story of faith and sexuality.

This is a bunch of bullshit, I said to myself. I quickly wrote Eric back, thanking him for his invite but declining due to a leadership meeting at Oasis that day.

More importantly, I already knew what the Bible said about homosexuality, so I did not need or want anyone telling me something that could contradict God's commands or twist Scripture as an excuse to live a filthy lifestyle.

Over the next several days, Eric's email would nag at me, and I would obsess over it constantly. *What's the big deal if I go and see what they have to say?* My rationale rested in that my faith was strong, and I believed I wouldn't be tainted. I took my internal debate to my two main people, Danielle and Caleb, who told me I shouldn't and should go respectively. Danielle thought I would be exposing myself to a world of deceit while Caleb gave me his blessing, thinking it could be beneficial to know their perspective.

Reluctantly, I decided to go but could not shake off the feeling I was rebelling against God. Later that evening, I texted Eric to let him know I was attending. I expressed to him I felt like I was doing something "bad" because I believed I was going to a seminar that would twist and turn the Bible into what they wanted it to say. Eric assured me that I would meet wonderful people and that there was nothing wrong with having more knowledge on the topic, no matter how I felt about the content.

On Saturday, June 2, 2012, I took the drive south toward Bellflower. I blasted my worship playlist, praying for the people of this church that they would see the true light of Jesus and asking God to prepare me for the spiritual battle I was about to face. *How are these people convinced that God condones homosexuality?*

The seminar was sponsored by Glory Tabernacle Christian Center in Long Beach, pastored by Sandra Turnbull, whom I found out soon enough, was a lesbian. *A lesbian pastor?* Blasphemy! Pastor Turnbull wrote a book called *God's Gay Agenda: Gays and Lesbians in the Bible, Church and Marriage,* which was prominently featured in the small sanctuary we gathered in. I skimmed the room, scanning as to where I might want to sit. I saw a cute guy around my age sitting alone, so naturally, I sat next to him. The irony of intentionally sitting next to the cute guy, hoping he would talk to me, while preparing to reject the evening's pro-gay message did not go unnoticed by me.

I sat down near him, leaving a chair in between us, hoping he would start a conversation with me, which he did. Anthony introduced himself, and we chatted briefly until the seminar began. *This guy is cute! Marry me!* My prayers against the topic of the seminar were suspended as Anthony's smile turned me into a puddle.

Pastor Sandra snapped me out of my daydream—a hot make out session with Anthony—as she began the seminar in prayer. I was highly perplexed as to how a gay person was praying so fervently and passionately to God—just as those who prayed at Oasis and any other church I attended. My unenlightened and ignorantly brainwashed worldview didn't allow me to accept that a Christian church could have a lesbian pastor praying to the same God I did.

She spoke of her own story and how it led to her marrying a woman and becoming a pastor. Nothing she said up to that point even came close to convince me of anything different than what God's word says about the sinfulness of homosexuality. Even after she shared, I remained unyielding in my viewpoint that she was compromised in her thinking and living disobediently against God's Word.

As she finished her testimony, she segued into the meat and potatoes of the seminar—the theology behind why she, and her congregants, were convinced that God approves of a homosexual lifestyle. I braced myself.

Here we go!

Pastor Sandra immediately went into detail and described the "clobber passages." They are called the clobber passages because these verses are exhaustively quoted or clobbered over a gay person's head (metaphorically). This whole concept of clobber verses was brand new to me. The clobber passages refer to the six verses religious conservatives use to condemn homosexuality as a sin. Pastor Sandra explained why these verses don't mean what we as non-affirming Christians think they mean.

Well, this should be interesting.

Pastor Sandra dug deep into the scriptures, picking apart these verses one by one. She was forthright and direct in her explanation of why the verses, in their proper contexts and translations, didn't condemn a loving and monogamous homosexual relationship between two people. She even went as far as to say that even though God rejoiced over a homosexual union, sex and purity before marriage was still something that should be obeyed and adhered to. Baffled, I sat there in a trance, hearing every word that came out of her mouth. The guard I had on my heart began to crack, and the veil on my eyes gently pulled back.

She talked about the many translations of the Bible that had been published over time, understanding the culture of that era, the importance of context, and translating the text back to the original Greek and Hebrew, the original languages of the Bible, as I sat there for almost two hours, barely moving, understanding the logic and interpretation of these specific Bible verses through her. I also heard the stories of other people in the same state of mind I was in, believing their sexuality was a sin, but found their truth and happily lived with their same-sex partner while maintaining a personal relationship with Jesus Christ. I started to experience a mental shift, and for the first time in my thirty-three years of living as a born-again Christian, I began to have something that is undeniably the most extremely dangerous thing someone in the conservative Christian church could have regarding the Bible and their faith: *questions.*

And I had lots and lots of them.

From the beginning, the intent of this book was to tell my story and not attempt to persuade anyone in one direction or another with theology and how I interpret the Bible.

There are dozens of resources I would recommend looking into that go into great depth on this topic of clobber verses. Two that I recommend are Pastor Sandra's book *God's Gay Agenda* and *Unclobbered*, written by Colby Martin, a straight megachurch pastor who was fired for affirming homosexuality.

The CliffsNotes version from what I gained that day was the importance of context, translation, and the relevance of the cultural practices during that time in history. The word "homosexual" was never in the original manuscripts of the Bible; in fact, the first time that the word "homosexual" was written in the Bible was when it was incorrectly translated in the Revised Standard Version published in 1946. Many subsequent versions used the RSV's mistranslation of the word ever since.

After Pastor Sandra concluded the seminar, I sat dumbstruck, contemplating if everything I believed about homosexuality was a lie. I talked with Anthony some more, telling him my story, and he shared his with me. He introduced me to his parents, who were not accepting of his homosexuality at first until they were awakened to the same information of the clobber passages. He even invited me to his weekly Bible study—a meeting of people who loved Jesus, were passionate for the Word, and welcomed inclusion of the homosexual orientation. I accepted and attended his Bible study several times in the future. Anthony became a dear friend, then one of my biggest allies in navigating my sexuality.

I took an opportunity to talk to Pastor Sandra after the meeting, sharing with her my sexuality journey and how I did not accept it, attempting countless methods over the years to become healed of this bondage. She would then say something that stuck with me in months to come,

"Aaron, these attempts all these years to be healed from homosexuality was the *real* bondage," she gracefully said.

I looked at her mystified, fighting away tears. I had always believed the exact opposite: that living as a homosexual was the actual bondage. At that moment, a tiny part of my heart created permission for her to be right, contrary to the chaotic clinking and clanking that racketed in my head, and more so, in my soul.

Pastor Sandra prayed with me, hoping that I would accept God's love for me the way I was and someday realize that having a boyfriend or husband will not send me to hell. God would ultimately bless my relationship and marriage, regardless. That was difficult to hear, and I still doubted what she preached.

But *what if* she's right? I could finally step off this exhausting emotional rollercoaster that kept me twisting and twirling, fearing hell would be my only future if I allowed myself to accept these attractions toward men.

On my way back to Los Angeles to the Oasis leadership meeting that afternoon, completely overwhelmed, confusion plagued my spirit. Pastor Sandra's explanation of the clobber passages posed critical questions—the question surrounding homosexuality and if it is something God truly frowned upon, and even more pressing, the question I had about the Bible and its claim to have no errors (inerrancy), and its claim that what it says about faith and Christian practice is reliable and trustworthy (infallibility).

I took a seat in the back of the Wilshire theater as the Oasis leadership meeting was underway and almost over. I was stone-faced, oblivious to my surroundings, rehashing teachings of the seminar. I snapped out of my sedation once I heard the worship band close the meeting with songs, but I was unable to engage, something not common to me as I was usually the one dancing for Jesus at the front of the stage. I tried convincing myself that I was allowing Satan to deceive me. *Aaron, you know better, homosexuality is wrong, just get over it.*

Did I think it would be easier to continue living in perpetual disarray and keep traveling this rocky road of transforming my sexual orientation?

This mentality was indicative of the powerful grip that Christianity had over my life. My loyalty to God and the Bible were drastically more important than my happiness and mental health. So long as I remained religiously obedient and adhered to God's rules for sexual living, the depression, loneliness, confusion, and heartache were secondary and trivialized.

I took a seat next to Caleb after the meeting, who happened to be chatting with Josiah and Parker. All three of them listened to me explain what I had just learned the past two hours. They heard me out and related to having doubts and questions. Still, nothing they said would instantly comfort me or result in Pastor Sandra's voice inside my head instantaneously vanishing.

That evening, my bedroom became a personal church service. I prayed and worshipped for hours to find some peace and comfort, despite the nagging in my stomach that wouldn't go away. I reached out to Eric since his invitation to attend the seminar got me in this unfamiliar mental space.

Hey, Eric, I don't know if I want to thank you or punch you in the face, I started our text chat that evening. I explained how I wrestled with Pastor Sandra's message and the uncertainty that now plagued me.

He encouraged me in my doubts, texting, *Ultimately, no one can tell you what God has for you (though many will try). We each have to find God's truth for us or at least try the best we can. Not always easy!*

I wrestled all night long, unable to sleep due to the questions that cycled through my mind. Eventually, I fell asleep in the wee hours of the morning, only to wake up the same way I fell asleep: tormented by this seminar. I spent the following day online, searching websites and gaining more insight and knowledge about the clobber passages, only to find the same information written by different people. I even read articles from pastors and theologians who argued against the clobber passages' translations only to find their arguments did not hold too much weight. I wanted to find anything that would discredit these heretics claiming homosexuality was accepted by God, but no such evidence existed.

I reached out to Parker, remembering he recently expressed the doubts he had about Christianity, so I figured he might be a good sounding board. Talking to him helped a little, and we lamented together, sharing our questions and doubts. Parker urged me to leave the men's sexual addiction group at CR and join the SSA (Same Sex Attraction) group. I had avoided the SSA group but maybe that move was what I needed to move on from the seminar rhetoric.

The SSA group for Celebrate Recovery was an eclectic mix of guys from all ages and belief systems. Every week I sat in that circle, listened to stories and confessions from men who did not want to be gay, and like myself, strived to find healing, peace, and normalcy.

The echoes of Pastor Sandra's seminar started to ignite a wave of anger within me that could not be hindered. Why were the homosexuals at Pastor Sandra's church okay with being gay, and we served the same God? And here I am, in another damn conversion therapy group to be set free from these homosexual attractions—*again!* How many homosexual healing groups do I need to go to before I realize nothing will ever work?

I was more confused than I ever had been before, not because of progressive impatience but because there were born again, Jesus-filled, worship loving, Bible-believing Christians in a church thirty-five minutes away not struggling to affirm their sexuality. I was not ok with this, and I needed fucking answers.

When I was not at work, church, or watching *General Hospital*, I researched anything and everything I could get my hands on that would hopefully give me some answers, or at least some contentment. My Google and YouTube search history pummeled with every which way I could formulate what I was looking for:

"Homosexuality and the church"
"Homosexuality and the Bible"
"Can I be gay and Christian?"
"Does God care if I'm gay"
"Clobber passages"
"Jake Gyllenhaal shirtless"
"Gay and Christian"
"Going to hell if gay"
"Gay churches in North Hollywood"

I made a list of gay affirming churches to visit. My first one was Christ Chapel of the Valley in North Hollywood pastored by Jerrell Walls. I went one Sunday morning, but it was odd to me that the sermon did not sound very gay. I'm not sure what I expected. A crucifix with Cher instead of Jesus? Rainbow and glitter hymnal covers? Drag queen ushers?

Christ Chapel was a beautiful church with amazing worship. People of all sexualities praised, danced, and sang out to God—some holding hands *with* their same-sex partners and worshipping Jesus. How could an all-loving God send these people to hell because they were gay? It appeared obvious they loved Jesus and accepted him as their Savior. Isn't that what Christianity was all about? I scheduled a one-on-one meeting with Pastor Jerrell, but I was hesitant to follow through. I feared he would say something that would genuinely confirm that being gay was OK, yet I was optimistic for the very same reason.

Pastor Jerrell, a gentle, mature soul, shared with me his story, and I told him mine. He did not attempt to push any agenda, as he knew that this was a personal journey. Knowing the hardships of this controversial issue, I know he wanted me to come to peace with my sexuality and be gay and still love Jesus, serving him as I always had been. He made it sound so easy, but I didn't think I could ever find peace with that.

He told me a story of a woman that would grant God permission every day to make her straight, and yet he never did. Well, I related to that immensely. Of all the prayers I had prayed, that's the one God never answered. When I asked God for strength to make it through the day, I came out stronger in the evening. When I asked God to take away my pride, he humbled me. When I asked God to protect me while driving on the road, I arrived at my destination safely. When I asked God to provide financially, I gained stability in my career. When I asked God to ease my anxiety, a peaceful presence descended upon me. When I asked God to make me straight—nothing but silence.

I left Pastor Jerrell's office somberly. I initially sought him out to gain clarity, but I left with more questions than answers. I emailed him later, thanked him for his time, and told him how beneficial it was chatting with him. He wrote me back. Here is part of that email that resonated with me the most:

> I'll keep praying that God gives you peace and assurance as you work through figuring out what God wants for your life. That it is what God wants and not what others think it should be. One lady told me she spent half her life being the co-star in the movie about herself. Meaning she lived her life to others' expectations. She found such freedom when she started living as God intended for her. Then she found her purpose.

Bullseye! When I read that statement, I knew how abundantly true it was that I, too, lived my life for other people's expectations, including God. My entire life was about honoring the invisible God, pleasing the church, obeying the Bible, and making fellow evangelicals proud of me, all while unaware of the complicity I had in my own downfall. I was a grown man letting circumstances and other people make decisions for me. Although unintentional, I was an active accomplice to my unhappiness. The truth was there all along, but I couldn't see it.

My quest to find answers became obsessive but only bred more questions as I dug deeper into the Bible's history and origins. I had believed so heavily in the Bible that I never considered it could be flawed. Without hesitation or curious thought, but by pure faith, this divinely inspired Word of God had me so convinced of its dependability and reliability that I never stopped to wonder if this book could be capable of having errors. I always envisioned the great book's pages magically coming together, without a hand to a pen and pen to a paper.

I researched and studied, looking for anything that could make sense of my uncertainty. My online research sent me into an overwhelming number of articles from atheists and theologians explaining that the Bible is not a perfect book, filled with numerous contradictions and errors. At first, I did not entertain those articles. My focus was strictly on the homosexuality issue. I had to convince myself that what I knew of the Bible, the inerrant and infallible Word of God, stood flawless as it was. I had to solely concentrate on the context of the clobber passages so if I did accept being gay, it would be a decision I could stand behind confidently.

I finally met up with Eric and his husband Russell to hear their story. As baffling as it was to hear the heart of a Christian couple who faced no biblical shame being gay, I desired their life of a guilt-free homosexual relationship while still able to love Jesus. Deep down, I knew one conversation with a Christian gay couple wouldn't fully allow me to embrace my truth, but their story inspired me to keep researching and asking questions.

Amid all this, I was about to receive my one year "sobriety" chip from Celebrate Recovery. At that time, I had gone 15 months without a sexual encounter but never received a chip. When a CR member had a significant growth and abstention period, they received a sobriety chip to celebrate how many months successfully sober, similar to AA.

For those 15 months, I had not hooked up with another guy. Prior to the seminar, this chip receiving ceremony would have meant so much more, but now I didn't care. My doubts and questions about God's acceptance and affirmation of homosexuality clouded my excitement of receiving this accolade. But had I really avoided homosexuality for 15 months? Nope. The conflict was not with the physical act of sex but the battle of the mind. Attraction to males and indulging in steam room fantasies with Orlando Bloom continued regularly.

Exploring, researching, and discovering answers to all my questions thankfully was not something I had to do on my own. Parker was now deep in the throes of his own personal journey of faith and homosexuality. We helped each other maneuver through our doubts, emailing each other articles, videos, book suggestions, and anything and everything that could trigger a conversation about God, the Bible, and homosexuality. Parker and I also visited gay churches and gay Bible studies, meeting so many different Christian people with diverse backgrounds, and most importantly, various convictions. We would get together to watch documentaries and movies about atheism, gay marriage, and pretty much anything that would be classified as anti-biblical, which inspired and provoked even more questions and more doubts about Christianity. It was a never-ending cycle.

As the doubts and questions continued to pile up, my mind and heart remained intricately fragile in the process of discovering answers and peace of mind. How did I get to this point? Why did I allow some random lesbian pastor at one random seminar potentially uproot my entire belief system, or better yet, why did God allow it?

My life continued as normal going to church, attending Celebrate Recovery, avoiding physical homosexual behavior, worshipping God, and reading my Bible yet simultaneously and earnestly looking for clarity on why I was doing all those things in the first place. Questions invaded me day and night: *Does God care if I'm gay? Do I need to translate and search for context on every single verse in my Bible?*

My brain hurt.

Inevitably within my search for the truth about the sexuality issue, I gradually started to doubt Christianity as a whole. My Google searches progressed from "Can I be a gay Christian" to "Why does God allow evil to happen" and "pre-destination vs. free will."

Now I was questioning God's character, something I never considered to be anything but loving, merciful, sovereign, and perfect. As I continued my exploration, those words that I used to describe my Savior God and Lord Jesus Christ began to lose their meaning, little by little and piece by piece. Three of those words were omnipotence, omnipresence, and omniscience.

Omnipotence means God is all-powerful and is the only supreme being. He can do what he wants and not be subject to any kind of limitations. *Omnipresence* is the belief that God is present everywhere at the same time. Lastly, *omniscience* means that God is all-knowing, that he has full knowledge of the past, present, and future and knows everything about everything, and nothing surprises him. I struggled the most with God's omniscience even beyond my situation. God's acceptance or unacceptance of me as a gay person seemed trivial compared to why he allowed evil and atrocious things to happen. Growing up in the church, the cop-out response to "Why does a good God allow bad things to happen?" was usually by quoting, *"All things God works for the good of those who love him"* (Romans 8:28) or *"My thoughts are not your thoughts, neither are your ways my ways"* (Isaiah 55:8) or cliche responses like "He is sovereign" and "God is in control," statements I accepted without hesitation but are now troublesome to grasp.

How did this "good" God watch and allow six million Jews to be slaughtered by Nazi Germany? The God I adored as kind and loving allows one in five girls and one in twenty boys, statistically, to be sexually abused by grown adults.[1] Since he's omnipresent, is he sitting in that room watching this abuse take place? Since he's omnipotent, why isn't he intervening and stopping the abuse? Since he's omniscient, doesn't he know the psychological trauma that will await those children as they grow older?

Where was God on September 11, 2001, when he allegedly watched and allowed four commercial airlines to be hijacked by terrorists, ultimately leading to the deaths of nearly three thousand people? Where was he? As all over the world, we watched in horror as the Twin Towers collapsed. I could go on mentioning so many unfortunate and horrible things that happen in this world, including rape, natural disasters, mass shootings, car accidents, cancer—the list is never-ending.

My heart and my head were at odds with each other, and I had no clue how to come to terms with both. My head was leaning to believe that there was no God, at least not one who personally invested in the lives of people or had control over day-to-day events, but my heart still couldn't quite let go of the Father God I had cherished all my life.

Chapter Nineteen

RELIGULOUS

Living with two different identities takes a toll on a person. Bruce Banner had to keep buying new clothes every time he turned into The Incredible Hulk—that gets expensive! I'm sure Bruce Wayne screamed obscenities many times seeing the bat signal in the sky calling for his Batman alter ego at 3:00 in the morning to fight crime. Ok, I'm no superhero but my point is the same. I was living as two different Aaron's, and it was taking a toll. There was the Aaron that still believed in God, the Bible, and everything I knew of Christianity. The other Aaron doubted God's existence and questioned the Bible's validity. I was not fighting crime but fighting for my long-held beliefs and logic—two things that contradicted each other. I was strongly concerned that my Christian faith was in jeopardy.

Starting to accept my homosexuality came more easily in comparison to figuring out the Bible and everything I knew about faith and Jesus. Don't get me wrong, it was a gradual process after Pastor Sandra's seminar. Giving myself the freedom to believe the backstory of the clobber verses and their interpretation helped ease my way to accepting my sexuality as it was—once and for all. This was vastly different from when I came out of the closet in Connecticut several years back. At that time, I still believed wholly in the Bible, but I chose to disobey God and be gay, yet still had guilt and shame...which is why I went back to attempt healing the following year. This time around, I didn't have any guilt or shame because the perspective had changed when viewing the Bible in a more historical light, and the doubts of its complete accuracy added to my newfound acceptance. It still wasn't easy. To believe something was wrong your entire life and then accept it as right takes some time getting used to, to say the least.

I continued my quest into Christianity as a whole, drowning in articles, documentaries, movies, TED Talks, books, and any other media paraphernalia I could find to further answer my questions. However, it only perpetuated my belief that

Christianity was simply another religion like Islam or Mormonism and the Bible was just another spiritual book like the Qur'an or Book of Mormon.

One documentary that really slapped me across the face was *Religulous*. Bill Maher is a popular television host most notable for his HBO political talk show *Real Time with Bill Maher*. He is known for his blunt and critical views on religion and speaks exactly what he thinks about the topic with humor, candor, and logic. In 2008, he wrote and starred in a documentary named *Religulous*, which examines and challenges religion and its beliefs. The film's title fuses together the two words, religion and ridiculous, seemingly to prove that the two words are synonymous with each other. Parker came upon the documentary and asked me to watch it with him. As someone who was way too deep and over my head in discovering the truth, I became magnetized to any resource that made me question my belief in Christianity. We ordered pizza and some Cokes, not expecting the effect the film would ultimately have on my already dissipating beliefs.

I pretty much knew from the beginning of the film, when Maher scoffed at the legitimacy of a talking snake, that my Christianity would be challenged. Almost immediately, my doubts hit the ground running. After many segments destroying all logic, which is non-existent in Christianity, my faith in the Bible weakened minute by minute. Maher touched on contradictions of the Bible, God's omniscience, science vs. scripture, and the church's hypocrisy. I am sure there were theological minds who could debate my assessment of Bill's opinions and would assume my faith was not strong enough in the first place to fall victim to his doubt. Maybe so. My faith was already quite shaky going into the film, but I knew that before my doubts, I loved God relentlessly. I passionately upheld the cross of Jesus as my saving grace. However, looking back, I recognized how religion caused me harm. I spent years believing my sexuality was broken and needed to be fixed. I dedicated my life to confusion, emotional turmoil, and spiritual pain.

Bill Maher's film proved to have a profound impact on my faith. However, although pivotal to my fated religious deconversion, watching his documentary was not the final nail in the coffin. It did not break me. No, that honor went to an actor named Scott Clifton.

Scott Clifton was an actor from my adored soap opera, *General Hospital*. Several years before my biblical doubt and in the height of my Christianity and anti-gay stance, I stumbled on a YouTube video and saw Scott Clifton's face on the thumbnail, with a channel named *Theoretical Bullshit*. Like I did with all *General Hospital* related YouTube content, I clicked on the video to watch its contents. In utter disappointment, I listened to this actor spew filth about atheism, discrediting Christianity, and the Bible. In pure disgust, I continued clicking through some of his other videos, but my stomach couldn't handle his passion for godlessness, biblical sarcasm, and rejection of faith. I prayed for his salvation and stopped watching his videos.

Sometime shortly after watching *Religulous*, I stumbled on Scott's channel again after searching theological YouTube videos at midnight one evening, you know, as a de-convert would do. *Theoretical Bullshit* popped up and I was instantly intrigued, exactly the opposite response from years earlier when his videos appalled me. I must have watched every single one of his videos in the upcoming weeks. Some nights I would find myself up until dawn, watching Scott's anti-God rants, despite having to be up for work in a few hours.

As an atheist, Scott's intellect and knowledge of Christianity and the Bible far surpassed any evangelical preacher, scholar, or theologian I ever heard. Video after video, I listened to him talk on assorted topics such as the origin of evil, morality, God's love, heaven and hell, faith vs. evidence, and Christians and biblical context, to name a few. With colossal intelligence, coupled with humor and a touch of smugness, Scott brilliantly dissected these topics to understand and rationalize the concepts of Christianity, an apparently flawed religion in his opinion. Many of Scott's videos were responses to Christians who challenged him to theological duels and debates. Not once did Scott sweat, wince, or was unable to give a retort that was not saturated with logic and reasoning.

I may have put Scott on a pedestal as my go-to guy for truth. However, everything he said disentangled some of my confusion and contributed to my forsaken beliefs in Christianity and the Bible. The tremendous analysis I invested in Scott's opinions and views transcended any biblical "truths" I valued my whole life because I found someone who put a logical stamp on my passport of doubt. Scott's valid arguments and justifications gradually stripped me of my faith. It was scary, I admit. I did not know how life could exist without prayer, worship, reading the Scriptures, and suppressing homosexuality.

One specific video of Scott's officially closed the deal. It took only one video to completely abandon my faith, relinquish my worship, and surrender my Bible to the storage closet. The video was titled *God's Checklist 2.0*. Throughout the video, Scott lists God's plan for the world in a facetious but subtle tirade, exposing Christianity's nonsense and ludicrous nature. He set the tone sarcastically from the beginning explaining God's ridiculousness in creating Lucifer (Satan), knowing that Satan would betray him and cause an infinite amount of suffering. Scott continued for nearly ten minutes touching on the insanity of hell, the creation account, Noah's three sons populating the entire world through incest, the virgin birth, Jesus's death on the cross, and the lack of God's ability to preserve evidence of his miracles among other irrational and illogical Christian doctrines and beliefs.[1]

I stared paralyzed at my laptop after the video ended.

After months upon months of researching God, faith, Christianity, and homosexuality, my journey had brought me to this moment of disbelief. A nine-minute and forty-seven-second video completely made me lose my faith.

I had to gain control, fearing I could be overreacting. *But was I?* An atheist would say no, telling me to get a grip and enjoy the freedom of that nonsensical belief in a God and salvation. However, a Christian would say that I was allowing the devil to deceive me and must pray to Jesus for clarity and reassurance. Neither of these hypothetical pieces of advice would be helpful. Believing in Christian salvation was not nonsense to me. It was what my entire existence was based on.

Not to sound dramatic, but it was traumatizing to have my Christian faith ripped out from underneath me. I accepted Jesus as my Savior when I was four or five years old, launching a 30-year relationship with God. He was the one I depended on, ran toward, cried to, and screamed at when things were rough. I lived and breathed Jesus. Hardships came and went, but God's love prevailed, and I beat the odds to stay faithful. I remained loyal and devoted to only him and put no other Gods before him. God was my Father, my beating heart, my everything.

Now, it was all gone. Talk about a bad breakup.

In retrospect, this relationship was one-sided. I never saw God. I never heard him speak to me. He never answered my prayers, and if prayer was allegedly answered, I could chalk up those "answered prayers" to human interaction or coincidence. But how can I just throw this all away? I believed God had great love for me (Ephesians 2:4), my name engraved in the palm of his hand (Isaiah 49:16), he created my inmost being (Psalm 139:13) and called me his child (1 John 3:1).

If you are there, God? Why the silence?

I positioned God as an extension of myself, equating him to oxygen but now barely breathing. My inability to cope without this God would be substantial, heartbreaking, and devastating. I didn't know there were two words for what I was going through, deconstruction and deconversion. Former Evangelical blogger Sara Martin explained these two terms simply.[2] Deconstruction is the process of reevaluating what you believe and why when it comes to your religious faith. Deconversion is the process of no longer identifying as belonging to your faith. The deconstruction process was already taking place in my life the last several months, however, after Scott's video, deconversion more aligned how I defined my path from that day on, although I still had plenty of deconstructing still to do.

I grieved the loss of my faith. It was not easy. My search for answers began as I learned how to navigate life without Christianity, and my beef with the Bible was about to get very real. Motivation to dig deeper and educate myself on its alleged infallibility was in overdrive. In only a few short months, my born-again Christian beliefs flirted with heresy, which ultimately led me down a mind-fuckery path to atheistic enlightenment.

Throughout my life as an evangelical, there was no escaping that the Bible was superior to all other books. The Bible's characteristics compared to no other human or surpassed any other religious text. The scriptures are claimed to be completely perfect, infallible, and inerrant. *Biblical infallibility* means that what the Bible says regarding faith and Christian practice is reliable and trustworthy. *Biblical inerrancy* is the belief that the Bible is without error or fault in all its teaching. Another claim on the Bible that it is "God-breathed," meaning that despite the many authors who allegedly wrote the 66 books of the Bible, God himself inspired all the writings.

This Bible is also said to be life-giving, powerful, impactful, and relevant, transcending history, language, and time—but what I discovered was a book filled with many inconsistencies, contradictions, and errors. My story will not go into a Bible hating rant, as I do believe there are life lessons that can be found and applied. I encourage anyone to do their own research, but I could no longer be convinced that this Bible came together magically by a spiritual being when it was written by humans and copied by humans hundreds of times over in many different translations and languages throughout many years.

It was supposed to be one little seminar. I took that drive to Bellflower to dispute what I would be told and maintain my stance that homosexuality was indeed sinful and that I must continue to pray the gay away. Now there I was, only several months later, browsing gay dating apps guiltlessly while watching YouTube religious debates, and allowing a soap opera actor to completely obliterate my faith.

Man, did *that* take a turn or what?

Chapter Twenty

A GOOD YEAR

I STRUGGLED TO SAY the word "gay," and still to this day. It's a word that's difficult for me to verbalize.

I can write it down on paper or type it into a book but to speak the label is troublesome. It is not because I'm embarrassed or have lingering feelings of sinfulness to say that I am, but the word "gay" had such a negative connotation on my life. I cannot translate it into something positive. It's still very much a process.

The extremely nerve-wracking time came to tell my mom that I would no longer be seeking treatment from homosexuality. At 33 years old, I was finally taking ownership of my life and no longer feeling spiritually bullied into denying something within me that was innate and real. During my visit home back east during Christmas 2012, I waited until after New Year's to chat with my mom. I didn't include my dad in this conversation because we never talked about my sexuality. I already had the support of my sisters from the beginning, and I knew I would eventually have to tell my brother.

Part of me did not want to stay home much longer after the talk with my mom, fearing the atmosphere in the apartment would be awkward or tense. When we found time to be alone, I told her I wanted to chat. We sat at the dining room table, her loving eyes upon me, waiting for me to speak. I caught her up in my personal life, talking about all the steps I had taken to become straight. I mentioned all the conversion therapy and counseling I endured, ultimately explaining that nothing had worked, and nothing will work. For that reason, I was no longer going to attempt any avenues to become straight. I explained that I was attracted to men. "Mom, this is who I am," I told her, "And I'm done trying to 'fix' it. I'm done."

She seemed a bit shocked, not so much of the acceptance of my homosexuality but to the great lengths I went through to rid myself of the attractions. In her defense, I had not told her all the effort and years I put into therapy and counseling. She seemed off-kilter and confused but still expressed her love for me. The conversation ended, and I was relieved. I can't say for sure there was any closure for my mom, as I knew it would be something she had to work through personally.

My mom did not hesitate to say how much she loved me regardless, something I already knew. I did not anticipate she would disown or treat me differently because her character and nature are that of pure love, and I expected nothing less. I am saddened hearing stories of people coming out to their Christian parents and wound up abandoned and unloved. I do not take for granted the unconditional love and kindness my mom displayed despite her questions and uncertainty.

The year of 2013 would be key for two reasons. It was my first year in over a decade that I did not seek out some sort of conversion healing program or "pray the gay away" shenanigan. Secondly, it was also the first time I fully embraced my sexuality, not embarrassed or ashamed if I casually mentioned to a friend if a guy was cute or if someone called me gay. In years past, if someone either said or assumed I was gay, I would internally retreat, becoming uncomfortable, quiet, and awkward.

The freedom was exhilarating! Pretending I was attracted to girls was a thing of the past. I no longer experienced guilt or shame when watching *Golden Girls* and *Will & Grace*. I could now unashamedly voice the desire to have a boyfriend or husband someday—Aaron Gyllenhaal has a nice ring to it, right? (Jake Gyllenhaal, if you happen to be reading this book, I swear I'm not creepy.)

The year 2013 was big for another reason. After 37 years of promoting homosexual healing, Exodus International, the leading ex-gay conversion therapy organization, closed its doors. Then-president Alan Chambers made a statement saying, "I am sorry for the pain and hurt many of you have experienced. I am sorry that some of you spent years working through the shame and guilt you felt when your attractions didn't change. I am sorry we promoted sexual orientation change efforts and reparative theories about sexual orientation that stigmatized parents."[1]

This was a huge win in sending the message that not only does conversion therapy not work, but it is damaging to a person's mental health. There are statistics that state conversion therapy has caused depression, anxiety, drug use, homelessness, and suicide. What I have unfortunately witnessed from my own experience is that there are conservative religious people, churches, and organizations who care more about legalistic religious rules and less about humanity and loving thy neighbor. The Jesus I knew embraced sinners, engaging in relationship with them.

When Jesus was asked why he hung out with "bad people," his response was *"'I desire mercy, and not sacrifice.' For I came not to call the righteous, but sinners."* (Matthew 9:13). What about the woman who was to be stoned for being caught in adultery? Jesus defended her saying, *"Let any one of you who is without sin be the first to throw a stone at her"* (John 8:7). This is not a man who would throw someone out of his house for being gay, yet many anti-gay religious leaders somehow believe this same Jesus would do just that, and it's truly mind boggling. Nah, dude.

The Jesus I read about is not a homophobic bigot—so why are there so many of them behind the church doors?

As I started to deconstruct and eventually deconvert from Christianity, I allowed several emotions to emerge, especially anger. After so many years of conversion therapy and never allowing myself to experience true romantic love, I became angry that I wasted away so many opportunities. Angry at myself for believing in convoluted rules of religion. Angry at people who claimed my relationship with God never *really* existed, therefore, resulting in how easily I "walked away from him." However, nothing angered me more as when anyone suggested that I didn't do enough, fight hard enough, pray enough, or love Jesus enough to receive true healing of my homosexuality, especially from someone who had no understanding or experience of having unwanted same-sex attraction. I *always* chose my faith first. My faith and sexuality were constantly at war with each other, and in full submission and reverence to God, I chose faith—every time—and never received the healing I devoted my entire life to.

I struggled most to find contentment in the concept of *hope*. For years, *hope* is what kept me alive. I held on to hope so tightly because it brought me joy and peace throughout some undeniably challenging times. Hope eased the hatred I had for myself. Hope helped me to believe that one day everything would be fixed. God promised me that I would be heterosexual and have the life everyone else dreamed of for me. The Christian influences in my life enabled me to cling on to hope, and I was the sucker who believed it would all come to fruition.

"Aaron, God will heal your homosexuality."

"Aaron, you will have a wife someday."

"Aaron, the cross of Jesus will impart freedom to your sexuality."

Yes, with bated breath, *hope* would reign victorious. I believed it. Hope was disguised as warm, inviting, and good, but it secretly built up into something vile, burning a slow death into my soul for 13 long years. Proverbs 13:12 even states, *"Hope deferred makes the heart sick, but a longing fulfilled is a tree of life."*

My heart could not bear another loss on an unfulfilled longing. I had done everything asked of me to become a whole heterosexual person, spiritually seduced by a heavenly promise that my homosexual attractions would disappear, and I would be someone God could be proud of. I became so intoxicated by this ideal of heterosexual normalcy I didn't even realize how much damage I was imparting on my soul and mental health. The more I attempted to fix myself, the more broken I became. I no longer even felt like a person anymore because I was dehumanized into an issue. The "SSA" acronym labeled my existence, so much in fact, that I did not know myself without the consistent efforts to change my orientation. My relationship with God was wrapped up in my sexual identity, and I know full well that orientation is not, and should not be, the core aspect of Christianity.

My sexuality became the main character of my faith, and the failed persistent attempts to get rid these gay attractions allowed me to only see failure in the mirror for over 13 years. Hope brought me to a place of unrest, and all this spiritual devotion to repress my homosexuality slapped me in the face, which left me feeling betrayed and developing a hardened heart. When I think of hope, I equate it to defeat, pain, and hurt. Hope had to be redefined in my vocabulary as I no longer saw it as something positive but inherently negative.

I often reflect on this burden I carried—the symbolic weight of trying repeatedly to become a straight person, or how I described it: a "normal" person. Matthew 11:28-30 was a key life verse. *"Come to me, all of you who are weary and carry heavy burdens, and I will give you rest. Take my yoke upon you. Let me teach you, because I am humble and gentle at heart, and you will find rest for your souls. For my yoke is easy to bear, and the burden I give you is light."* It's heart-wrenching to realize that the burden, unbeknownst to me at the time, was believing I had a burden in the first place. But I feared hell.

Let me take a second and break down that last train of thought about fearing hell. Evangelical Christians believe that you must accept Jesus Christ in your heart to achieve salvation and eternity in heaven. There is no more quoted Bible verse than John 3:16, stating this promise. *For God so loved the world that he gave his one and only Son, that whoever believes in him shall not perish but have eternal life.* But I did that, I believed in Jesus. I loved Jesus. Why wasn't that enough? Why was my salvation solely dependent on my sexuality and not *just* believing in Jesus as we are biblically commanded to do so? How did this verse translate to God's promise being conditional? Where is the Bible version that reads that only heterosexual people who believe in him will not perish but have eternal life? All I had were questions and no fucking answers.

Despite the doubts and disbelief, I continued going to church because it was a place of community and thriving friendships. When previously I would run up to the altar during worship to praise and dance to Jesus, now I stood still and quiet in front of my chair. Listening to the sermons used to inspire hope, renewal, and revitalization of my spirit, but now they had me unrecognizably cynical, attempting to reason why the speaker could believe such a ridiculous thing about God or the far-fetched stories in the Bible they passionately preached about.

The spiritual overhaul that was taking place within me allowed me to be open to so many other religions and cultures. All my life I believed anyone who was not a born-again Christian was going straight to hell. However, now I believe there can be peace, love, and acceptance in whomever or whatever you choose to worship without fearing an afterlife of torture. Most religions, at the core, are foundational for good values and living a positive authentic life—whether Hindu, Catholic, Islam, Mormon, Buddhist or Christian. Unfortunately, I am aware there are a few religions in existence that manipulate, cheat, and abuse their congregants and members, and there are some that incite violence, but I would personally not classify those organizations as religions but cults. A vast difference. For some, religion is not part of their worldview at all. An atheist could have just as good character, moral compass, and peace of mind as anyone worshipping a supreme being. The deconstruction of my Christianity allowed me to be more tolerant, keep an open mind, and most importantly, love people more no matter what religious building they walked or didn't walk into.

Chapter Twenty-One

ISN'T IT ROMANTIC

At 34, I was single and free to mingle. Feeling like a teen who had *finally* been granted permission to date *and* a later curfew, I couldn't wait to hit up the dating apps. Also, like a teenager, I was clueless and very hormonal. I had been celibate for nearly two years by this point!

All my experiences with guys were mostly sexual, without depth or potential for a relationship because "I was not allowed to." I found the dating world to be daunting, especially the world of gay Hollywood. Whether I put the high demands of gay dating on myself or if they were true, trying to date in Los Angeles proved difficult when lacking six-pack abs. I did not fit into the mold of what the ideal gay person should be in a city that emphasizes outward appearance. The job that paid my bills centered around talking to strangers daily, getting to know all about their lives, and analyzing their personality to see if they fit into a particular TV show. However, my experience with talking to strangers did not translate well into my dating life. I was insecure, shy, and feared rejection. The gay apps promoted hookups and one-night stands, something that I was no longer interested in but, at the same time, was open to it with my new guilt-free freedom to date other guys.

Nonetheless, I was beyond ready to put myself out there. Now that I was without the constraints of organized religion, which had dictated my choices of whom I slept with, the two-year cherry popped, and I did meet up with a guy I met online. For the first time, I did not feel guilty for having sex with another male. I found it interesting that once I accepted my homosexuality, I no longer fell into a pattern of sexual addiction nor desired it as much as when I was fighting against it. Also, the allure of the hookup app depreciated my moral bank account and could not be relied upon as an adequate avenue to find a potential significant other, so I closed those accounts for the time being. Subconsciously, I was quite uncomfortable of even the thought of having a boyfriend despite finally accepting my homosexuality. To believe something was sinful my whole life and then do a complete turnaround made it hard to just flip off the switch and pursue a relationship, regardless of how curious I was to be in one.

I would come face to face with maneuvering in the dating world in the most likely of places: on the job. Considering I boycotted the apps and never wanted to go out to meet guys in person, a good ole fashioned work romance threw me right into the fire.

I took a gig for a Burbank production company, casting personal trainers and fitness freaks for a TV pilot. Within a short time of my employment there, I would frequently pass a certain male staff member in the hallway who looked at me differently with a sort of a lingering stare. I could not put my finger on it at the time, but there was something unique about the way he gazed at me that went beyond mere friendliness. From first glance, I recognized his shimmery light eyes, broad frame, dull blonde hair creeping on the edge of silver fox, but not quite, and a devilish smile that oozed flirtatiousness.

Ricky eventually introduced himself to me. He worked in a different department of the company, a full-time staff member while I was a freelancer, working there for only a couple of months.

To say I did not know how to handle this crush on Ricky was an understatement. By the time most guys are into their mid-thirties, they are fully experienced and capable of maturely approaching a situation like this because of nearly two decades of dating experience. I hid behind secret anonymous encounters via phone apps, but Ricky introduced me to a real human interaction.

Ricky made purposeful attempts to chat with me, and his deliberate exchanges did not go unnoticed. I had no desire to ignore them. What I did not know was how to take these interactions to the next level, which at that point would be anything beyond the friendly "hello" and "how are you" in the hallway. I took my queries about Ricky to my two female co-workers, Gina and Sabrina. To protect his identity from nosy cubicle neighbors, we renamed him "Frank" so that we could talk about him freely.

Gina and Sabrina were knowledgeable of my past with gay conversion therapy and newly accepting my homosexuality, so they knew the whole dating thing was brand new territory for me. They understood my nerves, fear, and inexperience in pursuing a guy, so having them to lean on for advice was significant. Eventually, Ricky would make frequent visits to my cubicle and engage in small talk, confirming that maybe he was interested in some way, but I did not want to read too much into it. At times, he would suddenly rub my shoulder or give a quick tap on my back when whisking behind my chair but did my best to keep my expectations and excitement contained. I convinced myself, sparing potential humiliation, that he was just a super nice guy, albeit a bit handsy, and I should not think anything more of it. But Sabrina and Gina convinced me to make a move and let Ricky know I reciprocated whatever vibe he was giving off.

Sidenote to my boss Luke: I promise I was hard at work when not stalking Ricky. Promise.

Every Tuesday, the company provided bagels and cream cheese, understanding that free food builds employee morale. I don't touch bagels not made in New York, an unfortunate food snob trait when one grows up on Long Island, land of the best bagels in the world. (Same goes for pizza and Chinese food, FYI.) As I was filling up my water bottle in the staff kitchen one Tuesday morning, Ricky walked in, and per usual, we engaged in small talk. The usual crowd of staffers surrounded the bagels and cream cheese which didn't appeal to either of us. Ricky quipped that he didn't like bagels, but if it were donuts, all bets were off. As I headed back to my cubicle, I wondered if I could make use of his confessed affinity for the ring-shaped treat. I had an idea. Of course, I immediately took this information back to Sabrina and Gina, my very own flirtation coaches.

"Frank likes donuts!"

My crazy plan to win Ricky's adoration was not that elaborate. How I wish to tell you I stayed up all night baking donuts from scratch, forming them into letters that spelled out his name and then dusting them with edible glitter and serving them to him with a mimosa and a cloth napkin in the shape of a heart. (But let's keep that in the files.)

Simply and quite boringly, I planned to purchase a box of fresh donuts and place them in his office with a note. Both Sabrina and Gina gave me their stamp of approval, and so "Operation Donuts" was in motion.

I thought I would be terrified to put myself out there, considering this was the first time I pursued a real *human* guy and not a mystery person behind a gay phone app. Naturally, I did not know Ricky's intentions, but his overt flirting gave me the courage to make this move with the donuts, as corny as it was. In deep contemplation, I thought to myself that this must be the life of a teenager, the wonder and mystery of a first crush—the butterflies in the belly, the heart racing when they smile at you, the chills when they put their hand on your shoulder, and the anticipation of the first kiss. Regretfully, I did not have those opportunities.

When I first started developing sexual attraction, it was met with guilt, shame, condemnation, and confusion because my attraction was sinfully toward the same gender. In a sense, the whole situation with Ricky was my teenage story, twenty years too late. Ricky created my first real "puppy love" experience. With that said, I was excited to navigate the potential of whatever this was, and if donuts were going to get me there, donuts it was.

Operation Donuts had to be set in motion sooner than later; otherwise, I would lose my nerve. Ricky mentioned that he had a business trip to Denver and was leaving in two days, which meant I had to get myself to the donut shop early the next morning. I pulled into the donut shop's parking lot, surprisingly not at all nervous.

On the contrary, I was eager and confident to make this move, which was unexpected given my history of insecurity and low self-esteem. I figured, what's the worst that could happen? It's just donuts. With the pink box of donuts in hand, I walked into the office way before working hours, ensuring Ricky would not be there to ruin my surprise. I grabbed a sharpie and wrote a note to attach to the donut box:

Ricky, yesterday you mentioned you don't like bagels but prefer donuts. Well, here is some to get you through the day. ~Aaron. (I also drew an adorable smiley face.)

I left them on his desk, and now it was a waiting game. Ricky's office was entirely on the other side of our floor right before Sabrina's desk, so bumping into him was rare unless it was intentional. I frequently manufactured excuses to discuss work with Sabrina so that I could stroll past his office and peek to see if he was there. However, this time, I had to wait for him to initiate and acknowledge my pastry token of affection. At around 11:00 that morning, Ricky came by my cubicle to tell me he appreciated the donuts and the gesture. Unfortunately, Cupid's arrow did not pierce Ricky's loin. He did not unleash his uncontrollable desire onto me, nor did Kenny G and his saxophone suddenly appear playing a love medley. Ricky jokingly (or not) made a reference about me trying to get him fat, but I'm glad I listened to my intuition and Sabrina and Gina's advice. Operation Donut was a success.

The next morning, while he was out of the office on the way to Denver, I received a Facebook friend invite from Ricky. The teenager within me internally freaked out. I mean, a Facebook friend request? Imagine a prepubescent girl who received a notification that Justin Bieber was now following her on Instagram and multiply that by ten. That's how I felt about that invite. This was a relationship-defining moment. I had previously stalked his Facebook page (c'mon, we all do it) but had not taken the plunge to press that "Add Friend" button.

After gasping for air, I walked briskly, with an extra pep in my step and flushed cheeks, to tell Gina and Sabrina about my new Facebook friend—Frank! I messaged Ricky almost immediately, which started a full two days of non-stop conversation back and forth. Eventually, he gave me his phone number and we took our messages to text. Neither Ricky's work trip to Denver nor my requirement to diligently find personal trainers for my show seemed to deter us from getting to know each other as much as possible within the next couple of days.

Sidenote to my boss Luke: I practically did not do any work these two days. Sorry.

We chatted about various topics from work, sports, growing up, and countries we wanted to visit. We exchanged small talk with an underlying flirtation that was received and given in equal measure. After Ricky returned from Denver, we planned to hang out. I made it clear that I was not looking for sex, and I told him upfront that nothing physical would occur. My love life, if you can even call it that, up to this point, had been one shallow, unfulfilling, sexual encounter after another, and I was sick of it. I had to find something, or at least attempt to find a relationship a bit more gratifying and meaningful than giving the dude down the street a five-minute blowjob.

Don't get me wrong. From the day I met Ricky, I wanted to rip his clothes off and have my way with him, but I wanted to take things slow for my sanity and newness to the pursuance of an actual relationship. Ricky and I never defined, nor was it necessary, what was taking place between us. I mean, we barely just met. In my delusional state of mind, Ricky was "the one," even though we did not yet have an actual face to face conversation besides those quickie chats at my cubicle. I doubted giving him donuts would be the gateway to his heart, but my fixation with him distorted my judgment.

Ricky returned from Denver, and we met at his apartment that evening. All we did was talk for two hours straight, getting to know each other deeply and intimately. At one point, he put his head on my lap, and we continued our conversation. I was falling for him so fast that even the speed of light could not catch me. Sitting there next to him and all alone, I regret telling him I wanted to refrain from doing anything physical. I wanted to kiss him. I wanted him to kiss me. I hoped he reciprocated those desires but only avoided it because he respected my decision to keep the evening platonic. I eventually left, and that was it. I drove home in a daze. Is this what love felt like? I know now how Sandy felt singing "Hopelessly Devoted to You" to Danny Zuko in *Grease*. I could not wait to hang out with Ricky again!

After that evening, things with Ricky took a strange turn. To put it bluntly, I felt that he lost interest, but I think I know why. The morning after our hang out, I texted and asked him where this was going between us. Were we dating? Were we boyfriends? I don't remember the exact words I used, but I jumped the gun, practically putting a ring on his finger. I didn't even know his favorite color, middle name, or how his lips felt pressed to mine. Ricky said what any rational person would have said and simply stated that we would have to "see how things go." However, after our first date, if you can even call it that, he did not respond to my text messages as quickly as he had before. When he did, his responses were unenthusiastic and one-worded, which was exasperating. Then I thought about it.

Aaron, you idiot. You scared him off!

Mesmerized by his beautiful eyes, engaging sex appeal, and adorable charm, I concocted an imaginary future with him, which was ridiculous given that we only had one evening together. I desperately wanted to have a real connection with someone so much that I came off way too strong, way too quickly. Although the subtle office flirting still came and went, I felt I had to work for his attention a bit more. I tried to make plans again to hang out again outside work, and although he said he wanted to, there was always an excuse he gave explaining why he was unable. For all I knew, Ricky only wanted something surface and casual, and maybe he took a step back so I would not become too attached. Too late for that.

To make matters worse, one month after I fell hard for him, my department moved to a different floor of the building, so seeing Ricky was not the daily occurrence it had been. Once I moved to the new office on the 5th floor, a whole four levels below Ricky, our text conversations went back to normal and became a lot more sexual. That overall intention of taking things slowly went out the window, and now I was on a mission to finally shove my tongue down this guy's throat and rip off his clothes. Even late at night after work, our text conversations became extremely erotic, but I enjoyed every minute of it. The "sexting" would continue into the offices the next day, our hormones at full capacity. The tension was building, and we were both about to explode. As our texts became more arousing, we toyed with the idea of finding a location in the building to have some "fun." Little did I know that Mr. Frank here was a bit of an exhibitionist.

Well, well, well.

During my last week at the office, our determination to be alone together somewhere in the building intensified. Ricky remembered that our company had a storage closet in the basement. What happened next suddenly turned into a game of *Mission Impossible*. Ricky had to swipe the key to the storage closet from the office assistant while I went down a hallway that I didn't even know existed to take the freight elevator down to the basement, where he would meet me. Nerves, excitement, and relief flooded my veins so fast I thought I would faint. After waiting over six weeks to be intimate with Ricky, it was about to culminate.

I waited for him in the cold basement, wondering if he was going to abandon me there alone and send me a text that he "punk'd" me. The elevator doors opened, and he walked out with that grin that drove me crazy, unlocked the closet door, and then it finally happened.

Fireworks!

Well, barely. More like sparklers, to be honest. The meeting was not what I imagined in terms of location and length, but it scratched an itch for both of us at that moment. Yet again, I lacked that very familiar emotion that usually would follow a tryst with another guy. I did not feel guilty. That moment with Ricky felt right, normal, and comfortable. I enjoyed the quickie, and based on Ricky's post-coital text message, he did, too. I would have liked to hang out again, but I sensed Ricky's intentions for our relationship were nothing more than friendship and physicality. I only wished he told me because I was smitten.

After I left the company, I continued to pursue Ricky, but with apparent disinterest, he lacked the effort to solidify a plan. I practically threw myself at him, but eventually, I suspended my advances to save any dignity I had left. Thus, my infatuation with Ricky ended—for the most part. I would see and work with him several more times over the next several years, but our relationship never went beyond what took place in the basement that day.

I'll never exactly understand why Ricky had such a dynamically vigorous effect on me. Ricky may not have been "the one," but through his actions and reactions, intentional or not, Ricky showed me that I had worth and that he saw me, which validated my existence as a homosexual man. I realized I had attachment issues to sort out and had to learn to reel in my emotions. Still, I needed that experience with Ricky as a teachable moment for future romantic interests, despite how convoluted and messy it may have been.

All my life, I was taught to hate myself and tolerate existing miserably, unworthy, and fractured simply because I was attracted to the same gender, never having the freedom to act on those feelings. Ricky was the first guy who came into my homosexual world and imparted truth to those lies and gave me a hint at something I swore I had put to death—*hope*. I felt special. Even if I was another guy in Ricky's bucket of conquests, he gets a pass from me because he gave me the confidence to keep moving forward to date, discover, and uncover curiosities in the context of other men, something that I had to suppress since my late teenage years. I am still a work in progress in this area, but he may never know the profound impact he had on my life, so if you read this, Ricky, thank you. And thanks to you, too, Frank!

Chapter Twenty-Two

50 SHADES OF GREY

Oasis Church never avoided talking about sexual issues that affected everyday people. As I previously mentioned, Sy Rogers came to speak often to tell his redemption story as a man who was gay until he had his spiritual awakening. Another woman, Harmony (Dust) Grillo, a long-time attendee of Oasis Church, had spoken publicly about her transformation story as a victim of sexual exploitation and about the organization she launched, Treasures, that helped women find a way out of the porn industry by not only providing them with a better option for life, but sending the message that they are loved, valued, and purposed. I highly recommend reading Harmony's life story in her memoir, *Scars and Stilettos*.[1]

Craig Gross, founder of XXXChurch, also became a staple guest speaker, sharing his views of how pornography is destructive and giving tools to men (and women) who struggled with porn addiction. Craig had a blog that I followed through Facebook, and only a couple of years after my deconversion, I read a blog from him that gave me pause and enough curiosity to reach out to him personally.

In 2014, a film adaptation of the biblical story of Noah was released, starring Russell Crowe and Jennifer Connelly. Craig Gross' actor son Nolan portrayed one of Noah's sons as a child. Naturally, as any proud father would do, he excitedly promoted the movie to his mostly large Christian audience. He posted an article he had written about the movie for Relevant Magazine, a Christian lifestyle publication exploring the intersection of faith and pop culture. Craig controversially spoke about how he, even as a Christian, did not live his life through the scope of black and white but through a grey lens.

This concept alone abhorrently contradicts how a standard Christian *should* believe, and it invited arguments, debates, and condemnation from some of God's most loyal followers. The movie, *Noah*, had hit on some of those grey areas, and the evangelicals were in an uproar, as the movie took liberties with the writing and story and strayed slightly in some scenes from the exact account of the Genesis story.

Craig's followers retaliated, accusing him of heresy, backsliding, and overall being a bad Christian. Filmmakers have been doing this for years, doing what they do best to create an appealing and gratifying piece of art, even if that means fiddling with the original novel, adding and deleting scenarios that will improve the movie. However, changing the Bible story even slightly was flagrantly sacrilegious.

Craig Gross positioned his viewpoint fairly, stating:

> None of us are going to be perfectly true to the Bible. But if we can live our lives, make films, and create music and art that attracts nonbelievers to Jesus, then we're fulfilling the Great Commission. A film like Noah is a great opportunity for Christians to introduce this **grey** world to the black-and-white Jesus.

I became stuck on this word "grey," relating it to the Jesus I once knew. What does it mean to believe in a grey Jesus? Life can be so complex, especially in the realm of sexuality, that the complexity is overshadowed by religious tyrants enforcing biblical rules and mostly from people who have no idea what it's like to be attracted to someone of the same gender against their will. Love, kindness, and acceptance somehow become displaced in the black-and-white Jesus point of view. How would my life be different if someone, if anyone, told me that in addition to God loving me unconditionally, I would not go to hell even if I accepted my attraction to men? *Where* was this grey Jesus years before I went to Pastor Sandra's seminar that led me down a road to agnosticism?

For clarity, if and when I'm asked about current positions on religious affiliation, I will say I'm agnostic or agnostic deist. In simple terms, agnosticism is not knowing if a god exists, however deism is the belief in a creator god, but not a supernatural presence that has an active investment in day-to-day life. So, I am more inclined to believe that a god created the world but has nothing to do with me personally.

I frequently pondered that if I had someone in my life that showed me this grey side of God that Craig spoke, I could still be walking with Jesus, a relationship I missed so terribly at times. I ached for the comfort and peace that breathed in my soul so long ago. I had to reach out to Craig to gain more clarity of this concept of a grey God and have someone to bounce thoughts off of. After a lengthy email telling Craig my story, from beginning to end, homosexuality to deconversion, I awaited a response. The funny thing is, even though I did not know Craig on a personal level nor had any insight into his personal Christian walk, I was confident my story would not shake or rattle him because I knew, without a doubt, that the grey God mentality would place the position of a Christian in a more accepting and empathetic state of mind.

I was right.

He expressed gratitude for my email, which stood out amid all the hate mail he received about the *Relevant* article. He suggested we grab lunch, and we did two days later at Granville in Pasadena. I did not know then how much this meeting would change my life.

I had a vague familiarization with Craig since he frequented Oasis Church, but this was the first time I would have a one-on-one conversation with him. As a person, he intrigued me visually from his skinny skater frame and a spectacle head of hair that was styled intentionally to look like it was not styled at all. His calm, cool, and collected demeanor was refreshing, like a chilled pool in the middle of a northeast humid August day. Craig's gentle voice soothed me with relaxation, and I felt comfortable sharing my life with this familiar stranger. I always admired his passion for helping men conquer their addiction and his mission to expose the dangers of pornography.

We talked over chicken sandwiches for about an hour and agreed to keep in touch. By the time I arrived home that day, I had an email from Craig telling me he had an idea for a new blog post that would include my story and asked permission to submit it. Without even giving it much thought, I granted him permission. Over the next few days, Craig sent me his writing, and after making some tweaks for accuracy, I gave him permission to post, which meant that my whole story, homosexuality and deconversion, would be public. Many of my friends and leadership from Oasis followed Craig's blog, and it would not be too difficult to figure out who this "Aaron" was he wrote about who struggled with homosexuality, praying the gay away his whole life.

Not only did I have to mentally prepare myself for the day Craig would post his blog, anticipating and fearing the backlash, but I also had to send my mom, among several other conservative Christians in my life, the blog before it went public. Here is that blog post:

> I recently wrote a piece for talking about how Christians need to follow a Grey God instead of a Black or White God.
>
> A couple of weeks later, I got an email from a guy named Aaron I met once before who read it and felt like he needed to reach out to me. Here is a piece of that email:
>
> *The reason I felt impelled to write you this note was not to discuss the movie, but more so declare my admiration for how you handled your accusers. It also made me wish that you were the type of person I had in my life when I was in the process of de-converting from Christianity.*
>
> *Yes, you read that correctly. De-converting. A quick backstory on myself. Born in a Christian home. I was the model of the perfect child*

of a Christian parent. I went to youth group, went on every mission trip, went to a Christian University. I loved Jesus. When I was 19, I became aware of my homosexual attractions, and I have spent the last 15 years in reparative therapy trying to reverse those attractions. I have finally now come to the conclusion that reversing my orientation is not possible. My journey of having my homosexuality "fixed" is long, complicated, heartbreaking, and exhaustive. Unfortunately, through all of this, my faith in God suffered. I started asking too many questions, I was suffering with too much doubt and all paths led me to where I am today: agnostic. I actually prefer to say "Agnostic Deist" because although I don't know for sure there is a God, I choose to believe there is a creator God. The concept of a personal God is completely lost on me, and I don't believe in the reliability, relevance, or inerrancy of the Bible like I once did. This is not something that came overnight or was an irrational decision based on me not getting my own way. The last two years of figuring out the ridiculousness of Christianity and detoxing from strong beliefs that I once thought helped me have been extremely intense. What I thought helped me actually hurt me.

I loved the part in your blog when you were talking about the grey areas and that "grey" represents your belief system. This is the part where I wish I had someone like you in my life years ago and I could have that same mentality. Unfortunately, I was raised, indoctrinated, and educated in a religion that only endorsed black and white thinking and if I made one step or had one thought in the opposite direction, I was going straight to hell. Living a black and white life is destructive and my relationship with Jesus suffered because of it. I think that the Jesus of the bible lived in a grey belief system. That's the Jesus I think I could love now if I ever had the faith again to believe his existence was true and worthwhile. I could fall in love with a grey Jesus. The Black and White Jesus failed me. The grey Jesus could have restored my hope in a personal God. Black and White Jesus only presented me with despair. I could fall in love with a Grey Jesus. I could. But I've been tainted. Faith in God represents hopelessness to me.

I read this email and knew I had to meet this guy in person. If you know me, you know I act pretty quickly on things, so I contacted Aaron and met him for lunch the next day. I sat and listened to Aaron's story for almost two hours, asking a lot of questions and discovering more reasons why I wish people who "issue statements" or "take a stand" would just listen a bit more.

I found it interesting that Aaron's church enlisted him to do a video testimony that played on Easter Sunday about his freedom from homosexuality—even though he was still gay. And then he did a "cardboard testimony" stating the same thing, and *then* some donors in his church (as well as the church itself) spent thousands of dollars to send him to "Straight Camp" so he definitely wouldn't be gay anymore.

The problem is it didn't work.

Nor did the nine months he spent at YWAM's discipleship training school.

Nor did any of the countless therapy sessions, psychologists, counselors, homosexual healing groups, books written by ex-gays, bondage-breaking intercessory prayer, or anything else he has tried for the last 15 years.

So, what has the church left him with? Unbelief. He can no longer believe in God because everything he has been told about God "curing" him and "fixing" him hasn't worked. All it's given him is a long list of questions about God and about himself.

I can sympathize. If I was told for years that what I was doing was wrong and the feelings I felt were wrong and that God would give me a way out, but still felt all that stuff after thousands of dollars and thousands of hours invested... yeah, I'd have trouble believing, too.

I shared Aaron's story with a friend today and she told me, "Come on, Craig. I get the idea of a 'grey God' but he has to be black and white on some things..." I wanted to mute her. She's got it all wrong.

Last month World Vision got it all wrong, first issuing a statement saying they would employ homosexuals who were either celibate or were in legal, church-sanctioned marriages. Countless vehemently angry phone calls and 10,000 cancelled child sponsorships later, they retracted the employment policy and reassured donors everyone working there would be straight.

Let me say this clearly, Christians: *we don't need more statements and stances.*

You know what we need? More people who are willing to see that this is not about morality or culture wars or doctrinal differences.

It's about *people*.

Think about the people who were welcomed to work at World Vision one day and unwelcome the next? How do they feel about Jesus now?

What about the 10,000 kids whose sponsorships were cancelled? What should we tell them about Jesus?

What about Aaron and a 15-year struggle that has left him on fragile terms with his family, as well as without a church family or God? How should he feel about Jesus?

I've said this before, but it needs to be said over and over: be quick to listen and slow to speak. Most people and companies issuing statements and talking about a definitive black and white God have never sat and listened to the people and lives on the other end of their statements. That takes a little work; you have to get out from behind your stance and sit down for a two-hour lunch with a confused kid who's been told he doesn't belong. You have to blow past the black-and-white rhetoric of the establishment and get down in the grey dirt with the outcasts.

You know. What Jesus did."[2]

Craig's words far surpassed anything I could formulate, and I was grateful for his voice to help my story go public. I felt it was time to set the record straight, so to speak, about where I stood in terms of my sexuality. I had many friends that still attended Oasis, and I did not want to offend anyone. The individual people were not the problem. However, the precepts and culture of the church as an institution is what troubled me. I have known and befriended the most beautiful, kind, and loving souls through those church doors, some I keep in touch with regardless of our disagreements. With the admittance that I am generalizing the faith, the fundamentalist

Christian religion is what I considered to be the problem. Too much black-and-white thinking and not allowing for grey.

Before the blog went public, I emailed it to my mom. I did not hear from her for three days. Three days of heightened anguish took over my soul, but I knew this would be something she would have to process. Mom raised her kids to love Jesus, and she did a great job fostering that within us all, and I assumed she would be devastated when I told her that I no longer considered myself a Christian and was now a gay agnostic. I no longer believed what my mom raised me to believe, and I struggled with breaking her heart because she revolved her life on a passionate love for Jesus Christ. I was not embarrassed or ashamed of where I now stood with my sexuality or my evaporating Christian belief system, but I wanted to protect her feelings.

When that third day arrived after receiving my email, my phone rang, and as I glanced at the screen, looking at my mom's picture flash up on the phone, nerves consumed me. Honestly, I do not remember much from that conversation—I must have blacked out from the anxiety after we hung up. I do, however, remember she was generally more concerned about my relationship with God than my homosexuality. I was confident her love would surpass any belief system I stood behind. I also talked to my brother that week after sending him the blog and he had the same sentiments as my mom that my faith was vitally more important than my sexuality.

On April 21, 2014, I was in Chicago on business when Craig Gross's blog went public. I sat at my computer, looking out the skyscraper's window, at the buildings running down Magnificent Mile. My fingertips trembled as I reposted the blog to my Facebook page, officially going public about my sexuality and my deconversion in a more unorthodox avenue, letting Craig do the work for me with his words.

I worked most of the day, saving myself from the torture of staring at my Facebook page waiting for the notification counter to activate, hoping for comments of affirmation but fearing words of hate and disappointment. I have lived a diverse life obtaining many friends and acquaintances from different seasons of my journey, including all walks of faith, religious views, and political affiliations. I expected the blog's response to be a smorgasbord of accolades, pity, misunderstanding, excitement, anger, and division. Overall, the response was positive, as most of my circles by that time leaned toward liberal and non-religious. The private messages I received from people who opposed my choices were not hateful but concerned about my salvation and potential destructiveness of engaging in same-sex relationships. I didn't even have a boyfriend yet and was already receiving shame for a relationship that did not exist.

The only backlash I cared to remedy was from Caleb and Danielle, who I found out were deeply upset and hurt by the blog but not because of my personal epiphanies regarding sexuality and religion, but because of how the blog was written, implying that Oasis Church was an accomplice in forcing me to participate in testimonial videos about my healing from homosexuality. To make it abundantly clear, *nobody* from Oasis Church coerced or manipulated me to do anything I did not want to do. Any opportunity I had to share my testimony of homosexual healing, regardless of how untrue it was, were my own choice and completely voluntary.

Regarding the Love in Action conversion therapy program, I attended that program on my own accord. Although Oasis Church did help financially and provided spiritual encouragement, they never required or forced me to go.

With all that said, the truth remained. I publicly stated that I was homosexual and agnostic. Making a claim was only the beginning. How do I even begin to do this thing called life in a totally different mindset than the one I was brought up in? In some ways, I found it very easy, but in other ways, it was the biggest challenge I would ever face.

Chapter Twenty-Three

THE SPECTACULAR NOW

So, this is that part where I'm supposed to write about how I have permanently thrown religion under the rug, married the man of my dreams, and that we are together with our three cats and our rainbow-colored, picket fence. Although I do not (yet) have a fairytale ending to the tragic tale of my attempts to "de-homosexualize" and leave Christianity in my rear-view mirror, I don't necessarily have a bad ending. I actually don't have an ending at all, considering I'm still alive as I write this chapter.

After Craig Gross's blog went public, I fielded numerous questions and comments from various people while defending and explaining my doubts and concerns with Christianity. A common question I faced mostly was why I couldn't just be a "gay Christian." Why couldn't I accept my sexuality and still love Jesus? Believe me, I often wish my journey led me down that path so I could experience life with Jesus without the dark cloud of guilt and shame of believing my same-sex attraction was sinful. The concepts of unconditional love from a spiritual father and relentless grace are what kept me in the faith as long as it did despite all the agony and grief of submitting my sexuality to this higher power.

Yet, the discoveries of biblical origin that were brought to light in my investigation of the clobber passages took me down an agnostic road I didn't see coming. Referring to the Bible as a perfect book, in my opinion, was just not possible. I also really struggled with the dissolution of the personal one-on-one relationship I thought I had with God/Jesus. Having God as my right-hand man all my life gave me such a sense of security and having that vanish was extremely difficult. Bert without his Ernie. Lucy without her Ethel. Batman without his Robin. Aaron without his Jesus. It did not feel right.

I often reminisce back to that eight-year-old little boy in Faith Tabernacle Church, dancing and singing to Jesus graced with so much admiration and wonderment of a loving God. Even as I am pushing 40, it's still somewhat difficult to recognize my life without the comfort of a heavenly father or the peace that would descend upon me during a time of worship. I'm free from the rules that constrained me but hollow from a lost religion that gave me solace, delight, and a joy that could only be found in believing in something so out of this world because the promise and hope for a better life after death kept me alive and thriving. It's not easy to simply go on with life after something so incredibly radical disappears in exchange for nothingness and uncertainty. Contrary to some beliefs, I did not choose to simply deconvert as a Christian and reject God. The facts that logically made sense were in front of me, and I could not disregard this newfound knowledge.

Why didn't God intervene that Saturday of June 2, 2012, if he knew my life would turn away and not toward him? This God and Jesus of the Bible I thought I knew no longer had a place in my heart, which devastated me. I missed the feeling that a God was for me, endlessly protecting me from the dangers of the world. In a sense, I developed sort of a Stockholm Syndrome with the God who kidnapped my heart and hurt me something fierce. I missed his presence along with the fabricated unconditional love and immeasurable comfort I fooled myself into believing he imparted. This manufactured presence I commanded into existence only occurred when I believed it to be true.

There are many aspects of Christianity that I do miss, and some I do not. I miss the dependence on God, this higher power I trusted and relied on so faithfully and effortlessly every single day of my life. The loss was painful and unbearable at times. I had lost my first love. My whole world, everything I ever knew about myself, creation, the universe, my past, present, and future, now ended with question marks where exclamation marks and periods had once stood firm. I don't miss wasting time trying to change my sexual attractions—this indescribable freedom outweighed the loss my spirit endured when the Christian faith was no longer part of me.

As I continue to live my life without the necessity of religion, the Christian faith constantly surrounds me almost daily. Along with various family members, I have many friends who are still active in the church, and Christianity remains an integral part of their life as it once was mine. Sometimes I still even listen to Christian worship music on occasion for pure nostalgia. Yep, the classics like Hillsong, Chris Tomlin, and the very sexy Jeremy Camp. Listening to worship music always had a tranquil, calming effect on me. Although I no longer believe the theology, I can be reminded of how I felt when I would hear a specific song and how it once resonated within my heart.

I no longer view God as an interactive personal supreme being. God still exists in my life but in a very different way. Who says God is even a "he?" Maybe she's a "she." Or dare I say, maybe God is non-binary. I believe that God is whoever I allow or want them to be. The motion of the wind, the guide of my consciousness, the energy around me, and of course, Betty White, God incarnate. Also, my entire life I viewed myself as a broken person who clung to this idea of Jesus, the son of God dying on the cross for my sins. However, now that I no longer see myself broken coupled with my doubts on this biblical Jesus, I don't rely on this necessity of a divine savior.

Living as a Christian for so long and then deconverting from that faith has given me the advantage of seeing both perspectives of two very different viewpoints to many topics and situations. With that said, I had to assess my own ethical, social, and political standards. Without having the Bible for direction and instruction, I had to figure out how to conduct my life and the boundaries I needed to set for myself. Although I believe it to be fiction, the Bible has some incredible principles on how one could and should live. When it came to action, word, and deed, I did not want to skimp on my standards of integrity. If I could have one quality, one aspect of my character that would be carved into my headstone someday is that I displayed kindness, endlessly and unequivocally.

In and of itself, the word "kindness" is soft and subtle but holds power and strength that could demolish discrimination, hatred, bigotry, racial injustice, and homophobia. I do not think there could be a better characteristic to possess because kindness is all-encompassing. To have kindness, one must have love, acceptance, grace, peace, and goodness.

I read a news article where I believe kindness and even the grey Jesus mentality that Craig Gross spoke of could have made an impact. In January 2013, a lesbian couple, Rachel and Laurel, were happily planning their wedding after being together for ten years. When at the Portland Bridal Show, they met Melissa Klein, owner of Sweet Cakes by Melissa in Gresham, Oregon, and Melissa invited them to come into her bakery for a cake tasting. When Rachel and her mother went into the cake shop to discuss with Aaron (Melissa's husband and co-owner) the specifics of the cake, they were refused service saying their bakery does not make cakes for same-sex weddings, and Aaron allegedly quoted Leviticus verbally calling the brides an abomination. Laurel filed a complaint with the Oregon Department of Justice. Within a few short weeks, this Christian-owned bakery's refusal of not making a cake for the lesbian couple made national headlines. Whether the Kleins knew it or not, Oregon's state law banned business owners from turning people away because of their sexual orientation.[1]

After years of legal battles and courtroom antics, the judge ordered the Kleins to pay a fine of $135,000 and they shut down their bakery. As of writing this, Laurel and Rachel still have not received the ordered fine because the case still must go through the Supreme Court. The lesbian couple faced extreme backlash from the anti-gay community becoming targets of verbal abuse and death threats. Their world was turned upside down, because of a cake.

This could be an example of a situation avoided if kindness and the grey Jesus came into the kitchen. I believe, from the depths of my soul, that the biblical Jesus, *regardless* of if he thought homosexuality was sinful, would not have only blessed the hands that made the cake for Rachel and Laurel but would have thrown on an apron, whipped up some frosting, and made the cake for them himself.

A crucial command of Christianity is sharing the love of Jesus with those who are not believers. It's a mystery to me how this Christian couple disregarded kindness and acceptance and did not seize the opportunity to show this lesbian couple the compassion and grace that Jesus showed them by which they became saved. The simple act of doing business with the brides would have opened that door for Aaron Klein to display Jesus. However, what allegedly came out of his mouth was a death sentence, not an opportunity to communicate eternity. Yes, the purpose of making the cake may have violated their beliefs, but can a soul be reached if they are driven away in disapproval and rejection? Is that an effective Christian witness? Also, it's just a fucking cake! The Kleins chose legalism over humanity, and that's not Jesus or kindness.

Popstar Lady Gaga understands kindness. Ironically enough, back in the days of fighting my sexuality, I openly voiced dislike for Lady Gaga for representing herself as a "gay icon." In my mind, disliking Lady Gaga, or anything that had a stereotypically gay male following (i.e., *The Golden Girls*, Broadway Shows, pedicures), were the right steps in the heterosexual direction. Now I can boast I'm a proud member of the Little Monsters. I stumbled on a YouTube video of Lady Gaga during a recorded event at the U.S. Conference of Mayors in Indianapolis on June 26, 2016. She grabbed my attention immediately. She was poised, and classy. She presented a view on kindness that is so eloquently and terribly accurate that I had to transcribe it:

> The really fantastic thing about kindness is that it's free. And it can't hurt you or anybody else. It is the thing that brings us all together. In times of chaos and crisis, what we all tend to do is start pointing fingers at where we think the bad guys are, where the evil is. We all start arguing. Everybody has different opinions about that. Please do not forget: Hatred or evil, whatever you want to call it, it's intelligent. It's smart. And it's invisible.
>
> It doesn't have a color, it doesn't have a race, it doesn't have a religion, it has no politics. It's an invisible snake that while it is planning to make its attack it is thinking to itself, 'I am going to divide my enemy into smaller, less strong groups. And then I'm going to make them hate each other so that it's easier to take them down'. And as we're all yelling at each other, trying to figure out which group it is that's causing the problem, evil's winning all around us. We need to shift the perspective. The solution is that we need to build a kinder and braver world. Get rid of those labels. These different factions: gay,

straight, rich, poor, mentally ill, not mentally ill, gun owner, not gun owner. None of this can matter anymore. We are unified in our humanity and the only thing that we all know, we all appreciate in one another, is kindness. So, this has to come before all things, and you must operate relentlessly this way with everything you have.[2]

Yes, kindness. An action so small but in all its energy could derail hatred, stop violence, halt racism, terminate gay-bashing, and bring a world that is desperately divided into a place that can be brought together in unity. I admit, at times, I have failed to be kind. Maybe I was having a bad day, or someone was unkind to me, so I retaliated in a manner that is opposite of what I attempt to promote. Regardless of my failures, today and tomorrow are more opportunities to show kindness. To the man behind the counter at 7-Eleven when buying a lottery ticket, to the homeless lady who begs for money while I stroll down Venice boardwalk, to the young waiter who's having a rough shift and has yet to give me my free refill, or to the woman who is too self-involved and doesn't hold the door open while I'm right behind her walking into the store, I will show kindness as much and as best as I can. Another great thing about kindness, and something I have proven to myself in years after leaving Christianity, is that believing in a religion is not necessary to display kindness. Kindness is not wrapped up in a set of rules and regulations that one must abide by. Kindness is personal, and we, as humans, choose whether to use it or abuse it. An atheist can show kindness as much as a Muslim or a Christian or even a Scientologist. Kindness is a choice that comes from within, and I vow to continue practicing kindness for the rest of my life.

One other characteristic that I intend to hold up in my life, despite a loss in biblical faith, is gratitude. One of my all-time favorite quotes speaks on gratitude:

> Gratitude is not simply a form of "positive thinking" or a technique of "happy-ology," but rather a deep and abiding recognition and acknowledgment that goodness exists under even the worst that life offers.[3]

I had many reasons to remain angry, resentful, and resort to a victim mentality because of the brainwashing religion caused me. The psychological effects of gay conversion therapy have severely damaged many people who have endured it. Few come out unscathed, suffering from the troubling aftermath of depression, personality disorders, psychotic breaks, and suicide. Luckily, I escaped nearly untouched in comparison, and if nothing else, I owed it to myself to be grateful that I endured such trauma without lasting adverse effects. Gratitude extends way beyond and much deeper than simply being thankful. I'm thankful that I'm alive today, but I'm grateful that I'm not locked in a five-by-five white padded cell, drugged up as a result from almost 15 years of gay conversion therapy. *So grateful*. My story is never-ending until I take my final breath, and maybe someday I will have the happily ever after when it comes to romance, financial stability, career satisfaction, and those three cats. I am certain that my life turned out spectacularly despite the tribulations and heartaches, primarily because I embraced gratitude. My life is rich in love, from family and friends. No matter whether they agree or not with the direction my life has taken, I have peace.

I will always wonder how my life would have turned out if I did not go to the seminar on that June day in 2012. I think of the movie, *Sliding Doors*, starring Gwyneth Paltrow. Paltrow's character, Helen, misses a train. From that one seemingly insignificant incident, the movie details the very different paths her life would have taken if she had and had not missed the train. *What if I didn't go to the seminar? Would I still be fighting homosexual attractions? Would I still be a Christian? Or would I still have come to the same conclusions as I have now?* Helen's journey and ending turned out very different in both scenarios. I can't help but think that if I didn't go to the seminar, I would still be fighting off my attractions and seeking more therapy. Maybe it's better that I will never know.

If you are reading this book and struggle with this hardship of navigating sexuality while it conflicts with your religion, please hear me when I say I know what you are going through, and I know it's not easy.

But I hear you, and I see you.

I spent my entire life believing I was a broken human that needed to be fixed, and I lost out on so much life that I could have experienced. I would never want someone else to go through that torture. My advice is biased, seeing how I have come out on the side of self-acceptance, but what worked for me may not necessarily work for you. I know many gay Christians who love Jesus and still profess the Bible as the inherent Word of God, yet still accept their homosexuality. There is no "one size fits all" solution here. It's a journey you will have to walk yourself but not *by* yourself. However, only find people you trust and do not condemn you. It makes all the difference in the world.

Thank you, readers, for going on this journey with me. Thank you for listening to my story. I know some readers will be happy and excited for where this path of self-discovery led me to while others will be sad, praying that I will believe in Jesus again someday. The theme of my earlier Christians years was unceasingly to "let go and let God." Yet in later years, *letting go* of letting God brought me to a life of peace I didn't know could exist. I do not know what tomorrow holds. Life is unpredictable, and I will remain open to all it has to offer even if it contradicts every discovery that I uncovered in my journey that inspired this book.

I always think back to that little boy who praised Jesus in his living room but played with Barbie dolls and wore his mom's high heels. He had no idea of the life of insecurity and shame that awaited him because he preferred *The Babysitters Club* over *The Hardy Boys*, Rainbow Brite dolls over G.I. Joe action figures, or fantasized kissing Zack Morris over Kelly Kapowski.

He was innocent in the present but ignorant of a future with years of emotional torture, spiritual confusion, and psychological torment that could have been avoided had someone told him at 19 years old that Jesus loved him exactly how he was, despite his natural desires to date boys instead of girls. Although he was taught about the love of God at an early age, he was not displayed that message within his circumstances, and it caused him to believe he was broken, shamed, and damaged. Beyond my realm of understanding, somehow, he turned out perfectly fine and is living life, thriving day by day, always bettering and improving himself to be happier than the day before.

Recently I watched the 2021 movie *Palmer*, starring Justin Timberlake. It tells the story of Palmer, an ex-convict who unintentionally becomes the unofficial guardian of Sam, the young boy next door, due to Sam's mother abandoning him. Sam's appeal for the feminine things in life disturbs Palmer and what he believes to be inappropriate for a young boy. Sam enjoys makeup, princess dresses, and tiaras leaving Palmer in a place of unrest, not wanting anything to do with Sam. In a poignant scene, Sam is watching his favorite cartoon, Princess Penelope, and asks Palmer to help him write a letter so he can earn a certificate to be part of the Princess Penelope fan club. The brief scenes' last sentence of dialogue sent chills up and down my entire body:

Palmer: *Look, there's things in this world you can be and things you can't. Ok? How many boys do you see on that show?*

Sam: *None.*

Palmer: *What does that tell you?*

Sam: *I can be the first!*

What I truly loved about this scene is Sam's self-acceptance and pride that he possessed without any shame or embarrassment for something that truly brought him joy. With five simple words— "I can be the first!"—Sam proclaims he could be the person to break down stereotypes and disrupt gender "rules."

I grew up in a tainted religious worldview where complexities within sexuality were not allowed to exist and that a "black and white" mentality of social norms were heavily applauded, and if not adhered to, were deemed as inexcusable behavior. No grey allowed. I lived many years addicted to a religion that dictated rules of how I should live despite the inhumane hatred it caused in how I viewed myself and others who didn't live according to God's supposed ideals for romantic relationships.

I will always admit that something was missing in my heart when agnosticism replaced Christianity, but I can live fully because I'm freed from the duress and spiritual coercion that consumed my soul. I now cherish living a life where I value humanity *over* religion, love *over* politics, and kindness *over* precepts. My future only looks bright. I expect to witness more walls of bigotry, homophobia, and hate to crumble in the coming years. I hope I can use my story to amplify the wreckage. And, if I come across a wall that has not yet been torn down, well, I can be the first!

Somewhere, it's 2:00 PM, and I'm off to watch *General Hospital* so it's time to put this book to bed. Thank you again for reading my story.

ACKNOWLEDGMENTS

I didn't know how much of a team effort it would be to write a book. I'm just the author, a mere fragment of the whole part that is involved in this massive undertaking. Doing this alone was not possible, and I had the most amazing individuals who helped me with the process.

To Matt Distefano and Keith Giles. I know you came into this project when it was already underway but thank you for making the transition flawless and comfortable. Your expertise in book publishing put me at immense ease and I appreciate every step you took with me along this journey. Your professionalism is outstanding and I'm proud to be a Quoir author under your leadership.

To Meg Calvin, Peter Muhr, Lia Ottaviano, Josh Roggie, and Anna Rhea. This book went through many versions and rewrites over the years, and I thank each one of you for your editing expertise, whether it was developmental or grammatical, your eyes on my words were monumental in making this the best manuscript it could be. Your advice, suggestions, and corrections only made me a better writer, and I appreciate the work you put into this passion project of mine.

To Lauren Elkerson, Megan Gordon, Parker Jones, Milena Kazarian-Keers, Kristin Malley, and Brea Simpson. It was an honor that you wanted to read my book in its infancy stages, giving me the most incredible feedback, even if some of it was hard to hear—I appreciate your guidance and recommendations you offered to elevate my story into something extraordinary. I love you guys so much.

Last, but certainly not least, Ralph Polendo. This book would not be possible without you. You knew I had a story to share, and you gave me the opportunity and platform to do so. I am forever in debt to your generosity. You took a chance on me, and I hope more than anyone, I made you proud.

Writing a book this personal would not be possible without the emotional support and encouragement of a few people in my life:

To my sisters, Rebecca and Sarah, who have been my cheerleaders since the beginning—thank you and I love you.

To Ruth Krais and Serena Liguori—you are my anchors and I cherish every moment we have and will ever spend together. You both are my lifelines, and I cannot imagine this life without you. Thank you for consistently showing me that my life has value simply by being my friend.

To Michele Darcy, Robyn Stone, and Craig Muller. My 2nd family. Making me a part of your family has truly been an indescribable joy and precious gift—I am one lucky guy to be an honorary "Muller." Your love, support, and acceptance have been an invaluable treasure to my heart. You are my sisters and my brother—I would do anything for you. Anything.

To Rita Koutsoulis—You have known me through so much of my journey and have seen me fighting against something that was slowly killing my soul. I know how ecstatic you are that I have finally found the strength and commitment to be true to myself. Your gracious support and unrelenting kindness never went unnoticed. Thank you for rooting me on—I felt it every step of the way.

Lastly, I want to thank Megan Gordon. You have unwaveringly been by my side, throughout all my dramatic freakouts, unnecessary worries, and irrational processes of thought while writing this book. I have no words to properly express my gratitude to you for being there when I needed you the most. You reassured me when I was unsure, you guided me when I was confused, and encouraged me when I had doubts. How did you put up with me? Megan—If you only knew how insanely proud I am to call you friend and confidant. Your life has graced mine with something so pure and magical, I could never define it, because it surpasses any kind of earthly definition. I love you forever.

END NOTES

Chapter 1

1. See https://worldpopulationreview.com/regions/long-island-population.

Chapter 5

1. Youth With a Mission, "Who we Are."

Chapter 6

1. Psychology Today, "Dependent Personality Disorder."
2. Paul, "Is it Love or Is it Emotional Dependency? How to Tell."

Chapter 7

1. Biola University, "Academic and Behavioral Standards."
2. Biola University, "Sexuality & Relationships Policy."
3. Desert Storm, "Who We Are."
4. Ibid.

Chapter 10

1. Zanzonico and Sorrentino, "Sex Addiction."
2. Farley Center, "Watch Online."
3. Romans 12:2.

Chapter 11

1. You can visit their website at https://createchange.me.

Chapter 16

1. Judicial Council of California. "Background." (Retrieved June 15, 2021). https://www.courts.ca.gov/6465.htm.

Chapter 18

1. See https://victimsofcrime.org/child-sexual-abuse-statistics/.

Chapter 19

1. Clifton, "God's Checklist."
2. Martin, "Religious Deconstruction is Not the Same as De-Conversion."

Chapter 20

1. See https://www.glaad.org/blog/closing-time-ex-gay-group-realizes-theyre-wrong.

Chapter 22

1. Also check out www.iamatreasure.com.
2. Gross, "Grey God."

Chapter 23

1. Avakian, *Sweetcakes*.
2. Gaga, "84th Annual Meeting – United States Conference of Mayors."
3. Emmons, *Thanks!*

REFERENCES

Avakian, B. Melissa and Aaron Klein dba *Sweetcakes* by Melissa. (2015).

Biola University. "Academic and Behavioral Standards." *Biola University*. (Retrieved July 21, 2021). https://catalog.biola.edu/general-information/academic-behavioral-standards/.

———. "Sexuality and Relationships Policy." *Biola University*. (Retrieved January 6, 2022). https://studenthub.biola.edu/undergraduate-student-handbook-sexuality-relationships.

Chambers, Alan. "Sorry, We're Closed." *Glaad.org*. (June 19, 2013). https//www.glaad.org/blog/closing-time-ex-gay-group-realizes-theyre-wrong.

Clifton, Scott. "God's Checklist 2.0." *YouTube*. (August 25, 2009). https//www.youtube.com/watch?v=DvRPbsXBVBo.

Deseret Stream. "Who We Are." *Desert Stream Living Waters*. (Retrieved August 10, 2021). https://www.desertstream.org/who-we-are.

Emmons, Robert. *Thanks! How the New Science of Gratitude Can Make You Happier*. Boston: Houghton Mifflin Harcourt, 2007.

Farley Center. "Watch Online: Sex Addiction: Diagnosis and Treatment. *Farley Center*. (June 13, 2019). https://farleycenter.com/Sex-Addiction-Diagnosis-and-Treatment.

Finkelhor, David. "Child Sexual Abuse Statistics." *National Center for Victims of Crime*. https://victimsofcrime.org/child-sexual-abuse-statistics/.

Gross, Craig. "Grey God." (2014). https://craiggross.tumblr.com/post/83074210107/grey-god.

Judicial Council of California. "Background." (Retrieved June 15, 2021). https://www.courts.ca.gov/6465.htm.

Lady Gaga. "84th Annual Meeting – United States Conference of Mayors." *YouTube*. (March 8, 2017). https://www.usmayors.org/meetings/84th-annual-meeting/.

Martin, Sara. "Religious Deconstruction is Not the Same as De-Conversion." *Medium.com*. (February 5, 2019). https://medium.com/@sarasmiles2493/religious-deconstruction-is-not-the-same-as-de-conversion-12035f836100.

Paul, Margaret. "Is it Love or Is it Emotional Dependency? How to Tell." *Mindbodygreen.com*. (February 21, 2020). https://www.mindbodygreen.com/0-14987/are-you-in-love-or-are-you-emotionally-dependent.html.

Psychology Today. "Dependent Personality Disorder." *Psychology Today*. (February 17, 2019). https://www.psychologytoday.com/us/conditions/dependent-personality-disorder.

World Population Review. (2002). https://worldpopulationreview.com/regions/long-island-population.

Youth with a Mission. "Who We Are." *Ywam.org*. (Retrieved July 8, 2021). https://ywam.org/about-us/.

Zanzonico, MD, R., and Sorrentino, MD, R.M. "Sex Addiction: Playing Now in Theaters." *Pyschiatrictimes.com*. (2018). https://www.psychiatrictimes.com/viewsex-addiction/playing-now-theaters.

For more information about Aaron Simnowitz,
or to contact him for speaking engagements,
please visit him on Twitter and Instagram @AaronRulz19.

Many Voices. One Message

For more information, please visit
www.quoir.com

CPSIA information can be obtained
at www.ICGtesting.com
Printed in the USA
LVHW082124250323
742599LV00015B/1540